Daytrips

PENNSYLVANIA DUTCH COUNTRY & PHILADELPHIA

D1111166

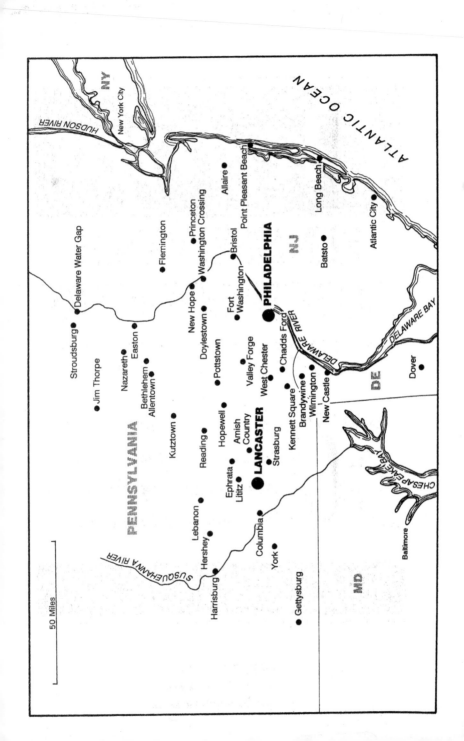

Daytrips

PENNSYLVANIA DUTCH COUNTRY & PHILADELPHIA

50 *one day adventures from the Philadelphia and Lancaster areas—including forays into New Jersey and Delaware*

EARL STEINBICKER

HASTINGS HOUSE
Book Publishers
Norwalk, Connecticut

Printed in the United States of America

10 9 8 7 6 5 4 3 2 1

Comments? Ideas?

We'd love to hear from you. Ideas from our readers have resulted in many improvements in the past, and will continue to do so. And, if your suggestions are used, we'll gladly send you a complimentary copy of any book in the series. Please send your thoughts to Hastings House, Book Publishers, 9 Mott St., Norwalk CT 06850, or fax us at (203) 838-4084, or e-mail to info@upub.com.

Contents

Introduction

Southeastern Pennsylvania, southern New Jersey, and northern Delaware form a region so compact that all of its varied attractions lie within easy daytrip range of either Philadelphia or the Pennsylvania Dutch Country's unofficial capital, Lancaster. A drive of just 50 miles takes you to some of America's most intriguing destinations, while extending that to 100 miles encompasses much of what the region is famous for.

For both residents and visitors alike, daytrips are the ideal way to probe this treasure-filled corner of the nation. And, if you have a weekend or more at your disposal, why not combine several daytrips into a mini vacation?

Philadelphia is, of course, a fabulous destination in itself. To help you enjoy its wonders, this book opens with five one-day walking tours and three one-day driving tours that explore the most interesting corners of town, ranging from the history-strewn Old City to the vibrant neighborhoods of Chestnut Hill and Manayunk, from world-class cultural centers to the colorful outdoor food markets of South Philadelphia. You won't need a car for most of these short excursions, as they can easily be reached by bus, subway, cab, or even on foot.

Southeastern Pennsylvania is next, with 17 daytrip destinations ranging from nearby Chadds Ford and Valley Forge to as far away as Delaware Water Gap and the lower Pocono Mountains. Most of these are within 50 miles of Philadelphia, and a few can even be reached by public transportation.

New Jersey lies just across the Delaware River, with a number of daytrip possibilities less than 100 miles away. These include nearby Princeton, the Pine Barrens, the Jersey Shore, and Atlantic City. Delaware—the state, not the river—is also close at hand, offering magnificent estates and gardens, one of the oldest towns in America, and a variety of cultural and historic sites.

The Pennsylvania Dutch Country is a whole world in itself, with an intriguing culture that differs markedly from that of mainstream America. While it is best explored from a base in or around Lancaster, all of the 14 daytrips in that colorful region can be made from Philadelphia as well, as only three of them are more than 100 miles away—and then only by a few miles, and easily reached via the turnpike.

Whenever practical, the daytrips have been arranged as walking tours following a carefully-tested route on the accompanying map. This works well in the larger towns and cities, and sometimes even in historic villages. In other cases, however, the attractions are just too far apart to see on foot, so their descriptions are arranged in a driving sequence from which you can pick and choose, matching site numbers with those on the trip's road map. A few of the daytrips, such as that to the heart of the Amish countryside, are designed for the sheer pleasure of driving, with just a few attractions that you might want to see along the way.

Dining well is a vital element in any travel experience. For this reason, a selection of particularly enjoyable restaurants has been included for each of the daytrips. These are price-keyed, with an emphasis on the medium-to-low range, regional cooking, and local atmosphere. Their concise location descriptions makes them easy to find.

Time and weather considerations are important, and they've been included under the "Practicalities" section of each trip. These let you know, among other things, on which days the sights are closed, when some special events occur, and which places to avoid in bad weather. The location, telephone number, and Web Site (if applicable) of the local tourist information office is also given in case you have questions.

Please remember that places have a way of changing without warning, and that errors do creep into print. If your heart is absolutely set on a particular sight, you should check first to make sure that it's open, and that the times are still valid. Phone numbers for this purpose are given for each of the attractions, or you could contact the local tourist office.

One last thought: It isn't really necessary to see everything at any given destination. Be selective. Your one-day adventures in southeastern Pennsylvania, southern New Jersey, Delaware, and the Pennsylvania Dutch Country should be fun, not an endurance test. If they start becoming that, just find your way to the nearest antique shop, gallery, or historic inn and enjoy yourself while soaking up local atmosphere. There will always be another day.

Happy Daytripping!

Section I

DAYTRIP STRATEGIES

The word "Daytrip" may not have made it into dictionaries yet, but for experienced independent travelers it represents the easiest, most natural, and often the least expensive approach to exploring many of the world's most interesting areas. This strategy, in which you base yourself in a central city (or its suburbs) and probe the surrounding region on a series of one-day excursions, is especially effective in the case of a region as compact as the Pennsylvania Dutch Country, Philadelphia and its surroundings, nearby New Jersey, and Delaware.

ADVANTAGES:

While not the answer to every travel situation, daytrips have significant advantages over point-to-point touring following a set itinerary. Here are ten good reasons for considering the daytrip approach:

1. Freedom from the constraints of a fixed itinerary. You can go wherever you feel like going whenever the mood strikes you.
2. Freedom from the burden of luggage. Your bags remain in your hotel while you run around with only a guidebook and camera.
3. Freedom from the anxiety of reservation foul-ups. You don't have to worry each day about whether that night's lodging will actually materialize.
4. The flexibility of making last-minute changes to allow for unexpected weather, serendipitous discoveries, changing interests, new-found passions, and so on.
5. The flexibility to take breaks from sightseeing whenever you feel tired or bored, without upsetting a planned itinerary. Why not sleep late in your base city for a change?
6. The opportunity to sample different travel experiences without committing more than a day to them.
7. The opportunity to become a "temporary resident" of your base city. By staying there for a while you can get to know it in depth, becoming familiar with the local restaurants, shops, theaters, night life, and

other attractions—enjoying them as a native would.

8. The convenience of not having to pack and unpack your bags each day. Your clothes can hang in a closet where they belong, or even be sent out for cleaning.

9. The convenience (and security!) of having a fixed address in your base city, where friends, relatives, and business associates can reach you in an emergency.

10. The economy of staying at one hotel on a discounted longer-term basis, especially in conjunction with package plans. You can make advance reservations for your base city without sacrificing any flexibility at all.

And, of course, for those who actually live in the region, daytrips are the key to discovering one of America's most fascinating regions—one day at a time.

CHOOSING A BASE CITY

PHILADELPHIA AND ITS SUBURBS:

Centrally located and easily reached from just about anywhere, Philadelphia is the hub of major transportation routes radiating out across the entire region. Most of the area's attractions lie within easy daytrip range of Philadelphia and the Delaware Valley, making this the ideal base for all but the most remote of destinations. On top of that, Philadelphia is rapidly becoming one of the most attractive and fascinating cities on the East Coast, right up there in the same class as New York, Baltimore, and Washington DC. Its accommodations vary from ultra-luxurious downtown hotels to neighborhood B&Bs to inexpensive motels in the suburbs, so you're sure to find something that's both convenient and within your budget.

GETTING TO PHILADELPHIA:

By Air: Many of the nation's major airlines, along with several foreign and numerous small carriers, fly in and out of **Philadelphia International Airport** (PHL). Located just eight miles south of Center City, it is easily reached by car, taxi, or the convenient SEPTA Airport Rail Line. ☎ *215-937-6800, Internet: www.phl.org*. Other convenient airports include Newark International (great connections to Europe and beyond), and Lehigh Valley International near Allentown.

By Rail: Amtrak (☎ 1-800-USA-RAIL) provides fast, frequent service along the Northeast Corridor from points as far south as Florida and as far north as Boston or Montreal to Philadelphia's 30th Street Station, with connections at Richmond, Washington, Baltimore, New York, and New Haven for other services. They also offer service west to Pittsburgh.

By Bus: Practically all intercity buses serving Philadelphia wind up at the convenient downtown Greyhound Terminal, next to the Convention Center and close to many major hotels.

By Car: Philadelphia is well served by the Pennsylvania Turnpike, I-76, I-95, and the New Jersey Turnpike, making it exceptionally easy to reach. Driving in the city is not especially difficult, what with a logical grid layout of numbered streets, and parking is relatively simple. Try to avoid driving inbound on weekdays from 6:30–9 a.m. and outbound from 4–6:30 p.m. You'll certainly need a car for most of the out-of-town daytrips, but in the city you're better off sticking to public transportation for all but a few of the daytrips.

ACCOMMODATIONS IN AND NEAR PHILADELPHIA:

Unless you live in or around Philadelphia, you'll need a place to stay. Although the city has many fine hotels, they're often heavily booked, making advance **reservations** advisable. Discount **package deals** that combine transportation with hotel rooms are offered by several airlines as well as by Amtrak. Many hotels offer deeply discounted **weekend packages**; check your travel agent about this. Visitors can save a considerable amount of money and avoid traffic by staying at an inn or motel in the **suburbs**, such as Fort Washington or King of Prussia, both on the Pennsylvania Turnpike. Many of these are close to commuter train stations, which makes getting downtown easy.

For adventurous travelers, **Bed & Breakfast** stays are becoming an increasingly popular way of cutting costs while enjoying a much more personalized service. Ask the tourist office for a current list of booking agencies. Short of sleeping in a park, hostels are probably the least expensive of all accommodations. A favorite is the **Hostelling International-AYH Bank Street Hostel** at 2 South Bank Street in Old City, ☎ 215- 922-0222.

PENNSYLVANIA DUTCH COUNTRY:

Although all of the daytrips in the Pennsylvania Dutch Country can be made from Philadelphia, you'll find it much more convenient—and economical—to base yourself in Lancaster or the countryside surrounding this historic town. Accommodations here are plentiful, and offer a friendly experience. The regional tourist office (see page 206) will happily supply you with plenty of current information regarding places to stay.

CHOOSING DESTINATIONS

With fifty trips to choose from, and several attractions for each trip, deciding which are the most enjoyable for you and yours might be problematic. You could, of course, read through the whole book and mark the most appealing spots, but there's an easier way to at least start. Just turn to the index and scan it, looking out for the special-interest categories set in **BOLD FACE** type. These will immediately lead you to choices under such headings as Art Museums, Restored Historic Villages, Revolutionary War Sites, Boat Trips, Children's Activities, Railfan Excursions, and many others.

The elements of one trip can often be combined with another to create a custom itinerary, using the book maps as a rough guide and a good road map for the final routing.

Some of the trips, listed in the index as **SCENIC DRIVES**, are just that—they are primarily designed for the pure pleasure of driving, with just enough attractions along the way to keep things lively. These are especially enjoyable if you are blessed with a car that's fun to drive.

GETTING AROUND

The driving directions for each trip assume that you're leaving from either Philadelphia or Lancaster. Chances are, however, that you live (or are staying) elsewhere in the Delaware Valley or Pennsylvania Dutch Country, so you'll need to modify the routes a bit.

The route **maps** scattered throughout the book show you approximately where the sites are, and which main roads lead to them. In many cases, however, you'll still need a good, up-to-date road map. An excellent choice for a single-sheet map that covers all of the destinations is the *Northeastern United States Area Map* published by Gousha. AAA members can get a free single-sheet *New Jersey/Pennsylvania* road map for the entire area. The free maps distributed by state tourist offices vary greatly in quality, so if the one they give you isn't clear enough, head for your bookstore and look over their selection.

The majority of daytrips in this book are designed to be made by **car**, and do not really lend themselves to public transportation. If you've arrived without wheels, you'll have to rent, borrow, buy, or steal a vehicle; or else limit yourself to those 10 trips that *can* be done *easily* by **subway**, **train**, or **bus**. Besides the trips within Philadelphia itself, these are: Valley Forge, North of Philadelphia, Doylestown, Princeton, and Atlantic City. Of course, a true public transit fanatic will find ways of getting *anywhere* by train or bus, but unless you're willing to spend over two hours each way just arriving at a destination, and then walking long distances, it isn't recommended.

Specific information about transportation within Philadelphia will be found in Section II. In addition, each daytrip has a "Getting There" section outlining the most practical routes and, when applicable, public transportation services.

FOOD AND DRINK

Several choice restaurants that make sense for daytrippers are listed for each destination in this book. Most of these are long-time favorites of experienced travelers, are open for lunch, are on or near the suggested tour route, and provide some atmosphere. Many feature regional specialties not generally found elsewhere. Their approximate price range is shown as:

$ —   Inexpensive.
$$ —   Reasonable.
$$$ —   Luxurious and expensive.
X: —   Days closed.

If you're really serious about dining you should consult an up-to-date restaurant and hotel guide such as the annual *Mobil Travel Guide— Northeast* or the appropriate AAA TourBooks, issued free to members.

Fast-food outlets are, of course, nearly everywhere, and have the advantage of not taking up much of your sightseeing time. In warm weather, why not consider a **picnic**? Many of the attractions have picnic facilities that you can use; these are indicated in the practical information for those sites.

PRACTICALITIES

WEATHER:
The Philadelphia region (Delaware Valley) and the Pennsylvania Dutch Country has a temperate climate, with generally warm summers and moderately cold winters. Exceptions to this do occur, such as a few hot, humid days in July and August, and a few, short bitter-cold spells in winter.

Late spring, summer, and early fall are the best seasons for the entire region, and therefore the most popular. This is a good time to explore the less-famous attractions in the outlying countryside.

OPENING TIMES, FEES, and FACILITIES:

When planning a daytrip, be sure to note carefully the **opening times** of the various sites—these can sometimes be rather quirky. Anything unusual that you should know before starting, such as "don't make this trip on a Monday," is summarized in the "Practicalities" section of each trip.

Entrance fees listed in the text are, naturally, subject to change—and they rarely go down. For the most part, admissions are quite reasonable considering the cost of maintaining the sites. Places with free entry, especially those not operated by governments, are usually staffed with unpaid volunteers and have a donation box to help keep the wolves from the door. Please put something in it.

Any special **facilities** that a site may offer are listed in the *italicized* information for that site, along with the address and phone number. These often include restaurants or cafeterias, cafés, information counters, gift shops, tours, shows, picnic facilities, and so on. **Telephone numbers** are indicated with a ☎; the full 10-digit number including area code must be used—even for local calls in most of southeastern Pennsylvania. Calling ahead, always a good idea, is especially convenient if your car or pocket is equipped with a cell phone. Many of the attractions now have their own **Internet Sites**, where you can **preview their offerings** and get (hopefully) up-to-date information. These are listed wherever known, but bear in mind that site addresses are constantly changing and new ones added every day. Any good search engine such as AltaVista or Yahoo will be able to track them down.

HANDICAPPED TRAVELERS:

Access varies with each individual's needs and abilities, so no firm statement can be made about any site. Those that are generally accessible without much difficulty are indicated with the symbol ᕙ but when in doubt it is always best to phone ahead.

GROUP TRAVEL:

If you're planning a group outing, *always* call ahead. Most sites require advance reservations and offer special discounts for groups, often at a substantial saving over the regular admission fee. Some sites will open specially or remain open beyond their scheduled hours to accommodate groups; some have tours, demonstrations, lectures, and so on available only to groups; and some have facilities for rental to groups.

SUGGESTED TOURS

Two different methods of organizing daytrips are used in this book, depending on local circumstances. Some are based on **structured itineraries** such as walking tours and scenic drives that follow a suggested route, while others just describe the **local attractions** that you can choose from. In either case, a town or area **map** always shows where things are, so you're not likely to get lost. Numbers (in parentheses) in the text refer to the circled numbers on the appropriate map.

Major attractions are described in one or more paragraphs each, beginning with practical information for a visit. **Additional sites** are worked into the text, along with some practical information in italics. All are arranged in a logical geographic sequence, although you may want to make changes to suit your preferences.

Walking tours, where used, follow routes shown by heavy broken lines on the accompanying map. You can estimate the amount of time that any segment of a walking tour will take by looking at the scaled map and figuring that the average person covers about 100 yards a minute.

Trying to see everything at any given destination could easily lead to an exhausting marathon. You will certainly enjoy yourself more by being selective and passing up anything that doesn't catch your fancy, and perhaps planning a repeat visit at some other time.

Practical information, such as opening times and admission fees, is as accurate as was possible at the time of writing, but will certainly change. You should always check with the sites themselves if seeing a particular one is crucially important to you.

* OUTSTANDING ATTRACTIONS:

An * asterisk before any attraction, be it an entire daytrip or just one exhibit in a museum, denotes a special treat that in the author's opinion should not be missed.

TOURIST INFORMATION

The addresses, phone numbers, and Internet sites of local and regional tourist offices as well as major sights are given in the text whenever appropriate. These are usually your best source for specific information and current brochures. On a wider scale, state tourist offices offer free "vacation planning kits," maps, and brochures that are often useful. You can contact them at:

Pennsylvania Office of Travel & Tourism
Room 456, Forum Bldg., Harrisburg, PA 17120
☎ (800) VISIT-PA or (717) 787-5453, FAX (717) 787-0687
Internet: www.state.pa.us/visit

New Jersey Division of Travel & Tourism
20 W. State St., Trenton, NJ 08625
☎ (800) JERSEY 7 or (609) 292-2470
Internet: www.state.nj.us/travel

Delaware Tourism Office
99 King's Highway, Dover, DE 19903
☎ (800) 441-8846 or (302) 739-4271, FAX (302) 739-5749
Internet: www.state.de.us/tourism/intro.

Section II

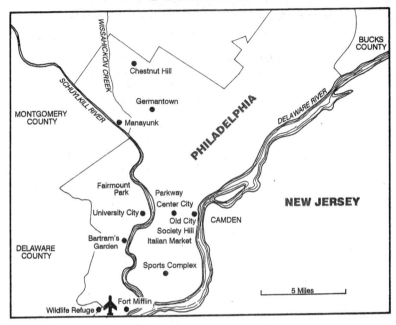

DAYTRIPS WITHIN
PHILADELPHIA

Beffore heading off on daytrips in the Delaware Valley, to the Poconos, to the Jersey Shore, or to the Pennsylvania Dutch Country, you'll probably want to explore some of Philadelphia itself. The five walking tours and three driving tours described in this section can guide you to both the most famous sites and also to some rather obscure attractions—always by means of enjoyable routes. The walks average less than three miles in length and each should take roughly four hours or so to complete, assuming that you visit some of the museums and other attractions along the way.

The "City of Brotherly Love," once the butt of bad jokes, has gone through an astonishing renaissance during the past decade. Even more developments are in the works at this very moment, and others are on the drawing board. This is a city that is determined to recast itself as a major tourist attraction at whatever the cost. Fortunately, it has the raw material to do just that. With its blend of historic preservation, world-class culture, ethnic traditions, and a leading position in sports, education, business, and medicine, the city is drawing far more visitors than ever before. Come and join the fun, and be a witness to the reawakening of a major American city!

GETTING AROUND PHILADELPHIA

Although most of the tours are designed for walking, you'll still need to use some form of transportation to get to their starting points, and then back home. Here are the options:

SEPTA:

The **Southeastern Pennsylvania Transportation Authority** operates a vast network of buses, subways, and street cars. Cash fare on most routes within the city is $1.60, and transfers are 40¢ (exact change required). During off-peak hours, seniors 65+ ride buses and streetcars free, or trains for $1. You can save quite a bit by buying several tokens at a time at SEPTA ticket offices and commercial outlets. You can save even more by purchasing a **Day Pass** for $5 at the Visitors Center at 16th Street and JFK Boulevard, near City Hall. You can also get current **route maps** and **schedules** there and at SEPTA sales offices. While at the Visitors Center, pick up the current Philadelphia Official Visitors Guide, a free magazine that clarifies everything. For further information about SEPTA ☎ 215-580-7800, Internet: www.septa.com.

Bus Route 76 is especially useful for tourists. It runs from Society Hill along Market Street and the Benjamin Franklin Parkway to the Museum of Art and the Philadelphia Zoo in Fairmount Park. Bus Route 42 connects the Center City with University City. The Broad Street Subway connects Center City with South Philadelphia and the Sports Complex area.

SEPTA COMMUTER RAIL:

Although primarily for trips to and from the suburbs, the commuter rail service is also useful for visits to Chestnut Hill and Manayunk. Buy tickets at the stations, or on board if the ticket office is closed and the vending machine doesn't work. All trains stop at the three major Center City stations: Market East (near the Convention Center), Suburban (near the Visitors Center and City Hall), and 30th Street Station (Amtrak connection). For further information ☎ 215-580-7800, Internet: www.septa.com.

PHLASH:

These small purple buses operate on a continuous loop connecting most of the key tourist destinations. They run daily at ten-minute intervals from 10 a.m. to 6 p.m. One-way rides are $1.50, a Day Pass costs only $3, and you'll arrive in style aboard one of the purple monsters. For further information ☎ 215-4-PHLASH.

PATCO:

The Port Authority Transit Corporation, a.k.a. PATCO HiSpeedline, operates a commuter rail line that primarily goes to New Jersey, but is also useful for travel in Center City, where it runs underground along Locust Street from 16th Street east to 9th, then north to Market and 8th Street before crossing the Ben Franklin Bridge. For further information ☎ 215-922-4600, Internet: www.drpa.org/patco.

BY CAR:

You certainly won't need a car for the first five trips, and in fact you'll be much better off without one. The daytrips to Fairmount Park, Germantown/Chestnut Hill/Manayunk, and South Philadelphia, however, are considerably easier to make with your own wheels as they take you far from Center City and cover large areas. Some of the attractions on them can only be reached by private car.

TOURIST INFORMATION

For further information about Philadelphia, contact the **Philadelphia Convention & Visitors Bureau**, 1515 Market St., Suite 2020, Philadelphia, PA 19102, ☎ 215-636-1666 or (888) 90-PHILA; TDD 215-636-3403, Internet: www.libertynet.org/phila-visitor. Be sure to stop at their **Visitors Center** at 16th Street and JFK Boulevard, near City Hall, for current information, maps, and brochures. It's open every day except Thanksgiving and Christmas, from 9 a.m. to 5 p.m., closing at 6 p.m. in summer.

If you plan on visiting most of the major museums, consider purchasing a **CityPass**, which includes actual tickets to the Museum of Art, the Franklin Institute, the Academy of Sciences, the Zoo, the Independence Seaport Museum, and the New Jersey State Aquarium. It is valid for nine days from the first date of use, and is sold at the entrance to each of the attractions. Current prices are: Adults $27.50, seniors 65+ $23.75, and children (3-11) $20. This represents a 50% saving over individual entrances to all six of the sites. For information ☎ 215-235-SHOW, Internet: www.city pass.net/philly.

All **telephone calls**, including local calls, must include the area code as southeastern Pennsylvania now uses ten-digit numbers. If you're calling from outside the 215, 267, 610, or 484 areas, or to an 800 or 888 number, add a 1 first.

*Old City

America's independence was born right here in Philadelphia's Old City, the historic core that boasts an extraordinary wealth of 18th- and 19th-century streetscapes. With a layout dating back to William Penn's time, this is the home of Independence Hall, the Liberty Bell, Benjamin Franklin's digs, the oldest continuously-occupied residential street in America, and dozens of restored historic structures that may be visited. It was also the capital of the infant United States from 1790 until 1800, and the birthplace of both the Declaration of Independence and the U.S. Constitution.

Much of the area is beautifully restored to its Colonial appearance, especially the large, rambling sections that comprise the Independence National Historical Park operated by the National Park Service. Entrance to its holdings is free, courtesy of the taxpayers, so your exploration will not only be fascinating, it will also be cheap. This indeed is one of the most rewarding daytrips that can be made in the region, and an experience no American should miss. The sights along the way are varied enough to appeal to everyone from school-age children to the most sophisticated of adults. Besides its historical interest, Old City is also a fashionable neighborhood of delightful cafés, restaurants, shops, and galleries.

GETTING THERE:

Philadelphia's Old City lies only a few blocks east of the downtown business district, within easy walking distance of many major hotels.

By car, the most convenient parking for this walk is in the underground facility at Independence Mall. There are entrances on both 5th and 6th streets, between Market and Arch. Another handy spot is in the garage behind the Visitor Center, with an entrance on 2nd Street between Chestnut and Walnut.

By subway, take the Market-Frankford line to 5th Street.

By bus, take routes 9, 21, 38, 42, 44, 76, or 121 to 5th Street.

By Phlash, get off at 6th and Market streets.

By SEPTA commuter train, get off at Market East Station and walk four blocks east on Market Street.

By PATCO commuter train, get off at 8th and Market street and walk two blocks east on Market Street.

See page 18 for more details on transit options.

PRACTICALITIES:

Although it can be taken at any time of the year, consider making this daytrip during the off-season, after Labor Day and before May, when there are no waiting lines for the sights. Nearly all of the attractions are open daily, but a few minor ones close on Mondays and some holidays. See the individual listings for details.

For further information, contact the **Philadelphia Visitors Center** at 16th Street & John F. Kennedy Blvd., Philadelphia, PA 19102, ☎ 215-636-1666 or 1-888-90-PHILA, Internet: www.libertynet.org/phila-visitor; or the Superintendent, **Independence National Historical Park**, 313 Walnut St., Philadelphia, PA 19106, ☎ 215-597-8974, TTY 215-597-1785, Internet: www.nps.gov/inde. Another interesting web site to check is: www.ushistory.org

FOOD AND DRINK:

Philadelphia's Old City offers a wide selection of restaurants. Some of the best choices, all open for lunch, are:

City Tavern (2nd & Walnut streets, a block southeast of the Visitor Center) Traditional American cuisine in a reconstructed 18th-century tavern, served by staff in period costume. Indoor/outdoor dining. For reservations ☎ 215-413-1443. $$$

Old Original Bookbinders (125 Walnut St. at 2nd St.) A landmark restaurant since 1865, serving seafood and meats. ☎ 215-925-7027 for reservations. X: Sun. lunch. $$$

New Mexico Grille (50 South 2nd St., between Chestnut and Market) A good value in Southwestern and Mexican cuisine. ☎ 215-922-7061. $$

DiNardo's (312 Race St., a block northwest of Elfreth's Alley) Famous for its steamed hard-shell crabs, also serves other seafood and meat dishes. ☎ 215-925-5115. X: Sun. lunch, holidays. $$

Society Hill (301 Chestnut at 3rd St.) Burgers, sandwiches, omelettes, salads, and the like at the outdoor café or indoor pub. ☎ 215-925-1919. $ and $$

Sassafras (48 South 2nd St., a block east of the Visitor Center) Fancy burgers, salads, omelettes. ☎ 215-925-2317. $ and $$

The Bourse Food Court (215 North 5th St., across from the Liberty Bell) A variety of fast-food outlets in a beautifully restored 19th-century commodities exchange, the nation's first. X: Sun. in winter. $

If the weather's fine, you can save time and money by purchasing a sandwich or salad from one of the many **sidewalk vendors** between the Liberty Bell and Independence Hall, and eating in the adjacent park.

SUGGESTED TOUR:

Numbers in parentheses correspond to numbers on the map.
Begin your walk by strolling into the **Independence National Historical Park**, starting at the:

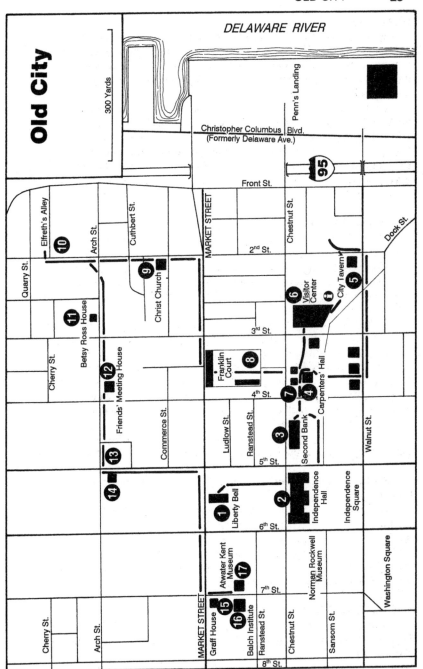

Old City

300 Yards

DELAWARE RIVER

Penn's Landing

Christopher Columbus Blvd.
(Formerly Delaware Ave.)

95

Front St.

Elfreth's Alley

Arch St.

Cuthbert St.

MARKET STREET

2nd St.

Chestnut St.

City Tavern

Dock St.

10

9

Christ Church

Quary St.

6 Visitor Center

5

Betsy Ross House

11

3rd St.

8

Franklin Court

Carpenters' Hall

Cherry St.

Friends' Meeting House

12

7 **4**

4th St.

Commerce St.

Ludlow St.

Ranstead St.

3

Second Bank

Walnut St.

13

5th St.

14

Liberty Bell

1

2

Independence Hall

Independence Square

6th St.

Atwater Kent Museum

17

Norman Rockwell Museum

Washington Square

7th St.

Cherry St.

Arch St.

MARKET STREET

Graff House

15

16

Balch Institute

Ranstead St.

Chestnut St.

Sansom St.

8th St.

*LIBERTY BELL PAVILION (1), Market St. between 5th & 6th streets, on Independence Mall. *Open daily 9–5; early July to early Sept. 9–8. Free.* &.

Housed in its own glass pavilion, the very symbol of American freedom is silhouetted against Independence Hall. There, on July 8, 1776, it was tolled to announce the first public reading of the Declaration of Independence, signed just four days earlier. The bell was originally cast in England in 1751 to commemorate the 50th anniversary of William Penn's Charter of Privileges guaranteeing certain freedoms for Pennsylvania residents. Recast in Philadelphia in 1753 after a defect was discovered, it carries the Biblical quotation "Proclaim liberty throughout all the land, unto all the inhabitants thereof" (Leviticus 25:10). Its famous crack appeared well after the Revolution, and the bell has remained silent since 1846. *NOTE: There are plans to move the Liberty Bell closer to Independence Hall, and house it in a more appropriate structure.*

Stroll south on Independence Mall to the:

*INDEPENDENCE HALL (2), Chestnut St. between 5th & 6th streets. *Open daily 9–5; early June to early Sept. 9–8. Visit by free guided tours only.* &.

Built between 1732 and 1756 as the Pennsylvania State House, this elegant structure is where the Declaration of Independence was adopted in 1776, the Articles of Confederation were ratified in 1781, and the Constitution of the United States framed in 1787. Tours through its beautifully-restored interior take you first to the old **Pennsylvania Supreme Court Chamber**, arranged in the British manner with a bench for the judges, two jury boxes, and a prisoner's dock. The state coat of arms above the judges replaced that of King George III, which was dragged through the streets and burned following the public reading of the Declaration of Independence.

You will then visit the ***Assembly Room**, where those momentous events of American history actually took place. Most of the original furnishings, both here and throughout the building, were destroyed by the occupying British in 1777; what you see today are authentic antiques similar to what would have been here. One of the few original pieces is the "Rising Sun" chair used by George Washington during the Constitutional Convention in 1787, which Benjamin Franklin said depicted a rising, not a setting, sun—surely a good omen for the new nation. The lovely silver inkstand in front of it was the one actually used to sign both the Declaration and the Constitution.

On the second floor is the **Long Gallery**, an enormous light-filled room that served in Colonial days as a banqueting hall, during the British occupation as a prison for captured American officers, and later as an art gallery.

Flanking Independence Hall are, to the west, the **Congress Hall** where the U.S. Congress met from 1790 to 1800 (House of Representatives on the first floor, Senate upstairs) and, to the east, the **Old City Hall** that housed both local government and the U.S. Supreme Court until the latter moved to Washington in 1800. *Both buildings open at various times. Free.* &.

Independence Square, the park behind the hall, is where the Declaration of Independence was first read in public. Near its northeast corner is **Philosophical Hall**, headquarters of the American Philosophical Society, a scholarly organization founded in 1743 by Benjamin Franklin. *Not open to the public.*

Walk east past the reconstructed **Library Hall** *(open to scholars only)* and turn left to the:

SECOND BANK OF THE UNITED STATES (3), 420 Chestnut St. *Open on a varying schedule. Adults $2.*

Built between 1819 and 1824 to house the government's central bank, this handsome Greek Revival structure was modeled after the Parthenon in Athens. From 1845 until 1935 it served as a customs house, and in 1974 was restored as an art gallery. Step inside to see some 90 portraits of the founders of the United States, both the famous and the obscure, and be sure to examine the life-size wooden statue of George Washington by William Rush.

Just across 4th Street is:

CARPENTERS' HALL (4), 320 Chestnut St., ☎ 215-925-0167. *Open Tues.–Sun. 10–4, closed Mon. and also Tues. in Jan.–Feb. Free.*

Still owned and operated by the Carpenters' Company, a trade guild founded in 1724 to promote construction skills, this Georgian structure was the setting for the First Continental Congress in 1774. It was here that the colonists' grievances against the king were first aired and a declaration of rights sent to him, and it was here that the boycott against English goods began. Today, the hall houses changing exhibitions, models, period furniture, and a display of Colonial carpenters' tools.

Follow the map south through the 18th-century garden. Next to this, at the corner of 4th and Walnut streets, is the **Todd House**. This typical 18th-century middle-class home was the residence of Dolley Todd, who after her husband's death became the wife of James Madison, the fourth President of the United States. *Ask at the Visitor Center, below, about a tour that includes this house.* A few steps east on Walnut Street brings you to another row of modest 18th-century houses. To the right of it is the **Bishop White House** of 1787, an ornate, upper-class residence where many of the nation's leaders were entertained. *Ask at the Visitor Center, below, about a tour that includes this house.*

The large Greek Revival structure at the corner of 3rd and Walnut streets is the former **Philadelphia Merchants' Exchange**, a center of commerce in the 19th century. It now houses offices of the National Park Service. *Not open to the public.* Continue on to the:

CITY TAVERN (5), 2nd and Walnut streets, ☎ 215-413-1443. *Open for patrons, daily 11:30 a.m.–10 p.m., closing at 11 on Fri. and Sat. and 8 on Sun.*

This was the favorite eating and drinking place for the nation's Founding Fathers during the 18th century. First built in 1773, it was demolished in 1854 and completely reconstructed in 1975. Once again operating as a restaurant, it is furnished with period reproductions and features mostly Colonial dishes served by staff in 18th-century dress. Reservations are suggested.

Catercorner from the tavern is **Welcome Park**, the site of William Penn's home and the spot where in 1701 he granted the famous Charter of Privileges to Pennsylvania residents. It is now arranged as a rather uninspired outdoor museum that describes the founding of Pennsylvania. From here follow the map to the:

VISITOR CENTER (6), 3rd and Chestnut streets, ☎ 215-597-8974, Internet: www.nps.gov/inde. *Open daily 9–5. Free.* ♿.

A large, modern structure operated by the National Park Service, the center features a free, 28-minute film, entitled *Independence*, on the founding of the nation. There is a self-operated interactive computer exhibit, information desks for both the park and the City of Philadelphia, free brochures and maps, and a bookstore. The Bicentennial Bell in the center's 130-foot tower was presented to the American people in July, 1976, by Britain's Queen Elizabeth II.

Follow the map past the **First Bank of the United States**, which from 1797 until 1811 was the central bank of the new nation. The pediment decorations above the Corinthian columns are carved in mahogany, and are among the very few such outdoor wooden sculptures to have survived from the 18th century. *Not open to the public.* Just beyond this, a right turn leads to the:

NEW HALL MILITARY MUSEUM (7), Carpenters' Court. *Opening times vary. Free.*

This reconstruction of a 1791 building once used by the War

Department now houses a museum devoted to the history of the U.S. Army, Navy, and Marine Corps from 1775 to 1805. Opposite this is the **Pemberton House**, another Colonial reconstruction that is currently home to the National Parks Museum Shop.

Cross Chestnut Street and continue straight ahead to:

*FRANKLIN COURT (8), 316 Market St. *Open daily 9–5. Free. Museum* &.

Little is known about the exact design of Benjamin Franklin's last Philadelphia home, which was torn down in 1812. Its foundation has, however, been unearthed and today a simple steel frame represents the house in its original setting. Adjacent to this a ramp leads down to the **Underground Museum**, where Franklin's amazingly varied achievements are celebrated through a collection of antiques, reproductions, and documents. A room full of high-tech gadgetry allows you to access opinions about the man, and a 20-minute film on his life is shown at frequent intervals.

The adjoining **row of houses** along Market Street were either built by or owned by Franklin. At number 322 is the restored office of *The Aurora*, a newspaper published by his grandson. Next door to this is an exhibit on Franklin's early career as a printer, followed by architectural and archaeological exhibitions. The **U.S. Post Office** at number 316 commemorates his role as postmaster by canceling stamps with the old postmark "B. Free Franklin." Authentically restored in the Colonial style, it is the only post office in the nation that does not display the U.S. flag.

Now follow the map and turn left on 2nd Street to:

CHRIST CHURCH (9), 2nd St. between Market and Arch streets. ☎ 215-922-1695. *Open for tourists Mon.–Sat. 9–5, Sun. 1–5. Closed New Year's, Thanksgiving, Christmas, Mon.–Tues. in Jan. & Feb. Free.* &.

Fifteen signers of the Declaration of Independence worshiped at this Georgian-style church, as did many prominent citizens. President George Washington had his own entrance door and box pew, and other pews were reserved for the Penn family, Benjamin Franklin, and other notables. Fully restored, the church serves an Episcopal congregation with Sunday services at 9 and 11, and a Communion service on Wednesdays at noon.

Continue up 2nd Street to:

ELFRETH'S ALLEY (10), 2nd St. between Arch and Race streets. ☎ 215-574-0560. *Alley always open, museum open March through Dec. Tues.–Sat. 10–4, Sun. noon–4. Alley is free; museum $2, children under 12 $1.*

Dating from 1702, this is thought to be the oldest continuously-occupied residential street in America. Its 30 small houses were built between

1728 and 1836, and are today highly desirable city residences. The one at number 126, open to the public as a museum, is furnished in the Colonial style. Don't miss tiny Bladens Court, off to the left near the east end of the alley.

Now follow the map to the:

BETSY ROSS HOUSE (11), 239 Arch St., ☎ 215-627-5343, Internet: www.ushistory.org/betsy. *Open Tues.–Sun., 10–5. Donation.*

According to tradition, Betsy Ross, a seamstress who probably lived in this house, is credited with sewing the first American flag. However accurate the story, the house is certainly filled with interesting memorabilia that makes it worth a visit.

Continue down Arch Street to the:

FRIENDS' MEETING HOUSE (12), Arch and 4th streets, ☎ 215-627-2667. *Open Mon.–Sat., 10–4. Donation.* &.

Built in 1804 to accommodate an annual meeting of the Society of Friends, this Quaker meeting house still serves its original purpose. There is a small exhibition and a slide show recalling the life of William Penn.

CHRIST CHURCH BURIAL GROUND (13), Arch and 5th streets. *Open by appointment, but Franklin's grave is visible from Arch St.*

Benjamin Franklin and four other signers of the Declaration of Independence are buried in this oasis of quiet in the middle of town. Toss a penny on his grave for good luck.

Cross 5th Street to the:

FREE QUAKER MEETING HOUSE (14), Arch and 5th streets. *Opening times vary. Free.*

Rejecting their principle of pacifism, a group of "free," or "fighting," Quakers answered the call to arms during the Revolution. This caused them to be disowned, so they built their own meeting house in 1783. Later reconciled into the mainstream Quaker faith, their story is told here by exhibits and a slide show.

If time permits, you may want to finish off this walk with the next three attractions:

GRAFF HOUSE (15), Market and 7th streets. *Opening times vary. Free.* &.

In May, 1776, Thomas Jefferson rented two furnished rooms here in what was then the outskirts of Philadelphia. It was here that he drafted the Declaration of Independence, adopted with only a few changes on July 4th. The house you visit today is a total re-creation as the original was demolished in 1883. Jefferson's historic role is portrayed in a short film, and his rooms have been re-created with both period and reproduction furnishings.

Almost next door is the:

BALCH INSTITUTE FOR ETHNIC STUDIES (16), 18 South 7th Street, ☎ 215-925-8090. *Open Mon.–Sat. 10–4. Adults $2; seniors, students & children under 12 $1.* ♿.

Philadelphia is nothing if not ethnically diverse, so it's perfectly fitting that America's immigrant heritage should be celebrated here. A multicultural museum, library, archive, and educational center focuses on the national ethnic, racial, and immigration experiences from both the historical and contemporary perspective.

Directly across the street is the:

ATWATER KENT MUSEUM (17), 15 South 7th Street, ☎ 215-922-3031. *Open Wed.–Mon., 10–4. Closed holidays. Adults $3, children 3–12 $1.50.*

This is the museum of Philadelphia's history from the earliest days to the present. Filled with an enormous collection of artifacts, it is especially noted for its temporary exhibitions. The museum is named for its benefactor, the famous early manufacturer of radios.

Midtown to Penn's Landing

You've strolled all over Philadelphia's Old City, taking in the great historic sights; and you've ambled out along the Parkway to visit some of its world-class museums. Perhaps you've even gone to a ball game or enjoyed a night at the opera. So what else is there to do? Plenty.

The area stretching from Midtown east to the Delaware River abounds in a variety of cross-cultural attractions—starting with one of the best museums of American art anywhere, to a veritable temple of architectural styles. The exciting Reading Terminal Market offers a colorful way to sample ethnic foods and snacks from around the globe before taking a stroll through Chinatown to the pioneering African-American Museum. Short side trips from here lead to the National Museum of American Jewish History, or to the Edgar Allan Poe House. You can also watch money being made at the U.S. Mint, or poke around inside an old restored firehouse.

Down by the river is Penn's Landing with its fascinating Independence Seaport Museum, boats to board, and boats to take you across the Delaware to the Camden Aquarium. From here you can relax at one of the many restaurants, cafés, bars, or entertainment complexes along Christopher Columbus Boulevard or nearby South Street. Or you might want to continue on with some of the attractions described in Tour 3, or return to Center City via bus or Phlash.

GETTING THERE:

By car, you're best off parking in a commercial lot or garage near City Hall or the nearby Convention Center. The walking tour ends down by the river, from which you can return by bus, Phlash, cab, or on foot.

By subway, **bus**, or **Phlash**, take any route to City Hall and walk two blocks north to the Museum of American Art.

By SEPTA commuter train, get off at Suburban Station and walk four blocks northeast to the Museum of American Art.

By PATCO commuter train, get off at 12th/13th Street Station and walk seven blocks northwest to the Museum of American Art.

PRACTICALITIES:

Major attractions are open daily, although some smaller ones close on Sundays or Mondays; others on Saturdays or Tuesdays. Most are closed on major holidays. Check the individual listings to match the tour with your interests.

The suggested walk is about three miles long, virtually level all the way. If you get tired, buses operate frequently along Market, Chestnut, and Walnut streets. At the end, return buses may be boarded at Penn's Landing, or you can take the Phlash from either Penn's Landing (on Christopher Columbus Boulevard) or South Street.

For further information, stop by at the friendly **Philadelphia Visitors Center** at 16th Street & John F. Kennedy Blvd., Philadelphia, PA 19102, ☎ 215-636-1666 or (888)-90-PHILA, Internet: www.libertynet.org/phila-visitor.

FOOD AND DRINK:

Moshulu (Pier 34, south end of Penn's Landing) Have lunch, diner, or Sunday brunch aboard a four-masted sailing ship restored as a turn-of-the-century luxury liner. Wonderful views, Continental cuisine. Reservations advised, ☎ 215-923-2500. $$$

DiNardo's (312 Race St., between the Mint and Fireman's Hall) Famous for its steamed hard-shell crabs; also serves other seafood and meat dishes. ☎ 215-925-5115. X: Sun. lunch, holidays. $$

Imperial Inn (142 N. 10th St., between Race and Cherry streets) A traditional Chinese restaurant; mostly Szechuan but also offering Mandarin and Cantonese dishes. ☎ 215-627-5588. $ and $$

Rangoon (12 N. 9th St., between Arch and Cherry streets) A great place for spicy Burmese cuisine. ☎ 215-829-8939. $ and $$

Harmony (135 N. 9th St., between Race and Cherry streets) Purely vegetarian Chinese food, good for your soul and your health. ☎ 215-627-4520. $

Reading Terminal Market (12th and Arch streets, next to the Convention Center) You haven't been to Philly if you haven't visited the old market under the former Reading Railroad train shed, now part of the Convention Center. Dozens of ethnic lunch counters offer a cornucopia of eating experiences; mostly good and mostly cheap. ☎ 215-922-2317. X: evening, Sun. $

SUGGESTED TOUR:

Numbers in parentheses correspond to numbers on the map.

Begin your walk about two blocks north of City Hall, at the marvelous:

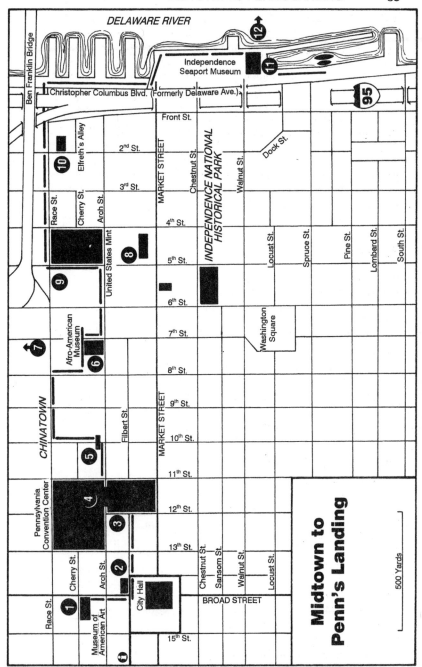

*MUSEUM OF AMERICAN ART (1), Pennsylvania Academy of the Fine Arts, 118 North Broad St., Philadelphia, PA 19102, ☎ 215-972-7600, Internet: www.pafa.org. *Open Mon.–Sat. 10–5, Sun. 11–5. Free Sun. 3–5. Closed New Year's, Thanksgiving, Christmas. During May, most galleries are devoted to the Annual Student Exhibition. Adults $5.95, seniors & students with ID $4.95, children under 12 $3.95. Gift shop. Café. Tours on weekends at 12:30 and 2.* &.

Before entering, cross Broad Street and take a good look at the fabulous **Pennsylvania Academy of the Fine Arts**, home of both the museum and a renowned art school. The building itself is a gem, a true masterpiece of the exotic High Victorian Gothic style and long a Philadelphia landmark. Designed by the noted architect Frank Furness (1838–1912), it was completed in 1876, the year of the great Centennial Exhibition. Passers-by have been stunned by its appearance ever since.

Inside, visitors are treated to a sweeping survey of major works by American artists from Colonial times right up to today's latest trends. Founded in 1805 and modeled after Britain's Royal Academy, this is the oldest museum and school of art in the nation, and remains one of the most important—a "must-see" for any art lover.

Just two blocks south on Broad Street, opposite City Hall, stands another fantastic structure, the **Masonic Temple** (2) of 1873. Its seven lavishly-decorated interior lodge halls each represent a different architectural style—Oriental, Egyptian, Ionic, Corinthian, Norman, Gothic, and Renaissance. They may be seen on guided tours that also include Masonic treasures once owned by George Washington, Benjamin Franklin, Andrew Jackson, the Marquis de Lafayette, and other notables. ☎ *215-988-1917. Tours on weekdays at 10, 11, 1, 2, and 3; on Sat. at 10 and 11. Closed Sun., Sat. in July and Aug., and major holidays. Free.* &.

Stroll three blocks east on Filbert Street to experience an old Philadelphia tradition, the **Reading Terminal Market** (3). When the now-defunct Reading Railroad opened its great station in 1892, it leased out the space beneath the then-world's-largest train shed to a variety of food vendors as a sort of farmers' market for city folk. In 1984 the trains, now operated by SEPTA, moved underground to the new Market East Station, but the food merchants remained as the train shed above them became part of the new Pennsylvania Convention Center. Heroic efforts were made to insure that the market would not deteriorate into yet another sterile "food court," so that today it is still a bustling, boisterous nosher's heaven where you can sample wonderful delicacies from around the world while basking in its friendly (and ever so slightly seedy) ambiance. Don't miss this special Philly treat, and be sure to stop at Bassett's to sample America's best ice cream. ☎ *215-922-2317. Open Mon.–Sat. 8–6.* &.

Adjoining—and above—the market place is the impressive **Pennsylvania Convention Center** (4), opened in 1993. Actually a rather nice piece of architecture, this is among the largest facilities of its type in the nation. Its location in the heart of Center City and its wide-open design successfully integrate conventions into the daily life of the city itself, making visitors feel right at home. *Free tours on Tues. & Thurs. at 11:30, 12:30, 1:30, and 2:15, depart from northwest corner of 12th and Arch streets. Call first to confirm,* ☎ *215-418-4728.*

Like New York, Washington, and San Francisco, Philadelphia has its very own **Chinatown** (5), a colorful neighborhood filled with good places to eat. The first Chinese laundry opened here in 1870, and the first restaurant in 1880. Amble in under the delightful **Chinese Friendship Gate** at 10th and Arch streets, erected in 1983 by artisans from Philly's sister city of Tianjin in the People's Republic.

Following the route shown on the map will soon bring you to a celebration of a different culture at the:

AFRICAN-AMERICAN MUSEUM IN PHILADELPHIA (6), 701 Arch St., ☎ 215-574-0380. *Open Tues.–Sat. 10–5, Sun. noon–5, closed Mon. and major holidays. Adults $6, seniors and children 6-17 $4. Crafts shop. Bookshop.* ঙ.

African-American history, arts, and culture are well represented in this large, modern museum. Exhibitions begin with early African roots and take visitors on a trip through slavery, emancipation, and the slow integration of blacks into mainstream American life. There are, of course, changing exhibitions and a variety of special events.

If you're really energetic, you might want to make an interesting side trip by following the map a little over a half-mile north to the **Edgar Allan Poe National Historic Site** (7), which includes the house where the strange poet lived from 1843–44. It was while residing here that some of his best stories were published, including "The Tell-Tale Heart," "The Gold Bug," and "The Black Cat." A sense of foreboding fills the empty house, which only enhances the atmosphere, and at night the shadow of a raven falls across it. There's a short slide show on his life, a reading room, and a collection of his works. *532 N. 7th St.* ☎ *215-597-8780. Open June–Oct., daily 9–5; Nov.–May Wed.–Sun. 9–5. Closed New Year's, Thanksgiving, Christmas. Call ahead to make sure it's open. Free. Partially* ঙ.

Another, and considerably shorter, side trip can be made to the **National Museum of American Jewish History** (8). The American Jewish experience, from the 17th century to the present, is thoroughly explored in this unique museum—the only one of its kind in the nation. Exhibits include art, artifacts, documents, and religious articles. The museum is especially well known for its temporary exhibitions, special events, films, and cultural affairs. *55 N. 5th St.,* ☎ *215-923-3811, Internet: www.nmajh.org. Open Mon.–Thurs. 10–5, Fri. 10–3, Sun. noon–5. Closed Sat. Adults $2.50, seniors, students, and children 6-18 $1.75.* ঙ.

Back on the main route, you might want to pause for awhile to watch money being made at the **United States Mint** (9). Well, coins at least. Here, in the world's largest mint, visitors can view the activities from an enclosed gallery, and examine rare coins in a museum. Don't expect free samples, though, and don't try to enter carrying a camera or video gear. *5th and Arch streets,* ☎ *215-408-0114. Open July–Aug., daily 9–4:30; May–June, Mon.–Sat. 9–4:30; Sept.–April, Mon.–Fri. 9–4:30. Closed major holidays. Coin-making machines do not usually operate on weekends, nor from just before Christmas until after New Year's. Free.* ♿.

Head east on Race Street, turning a few steps south on 2nd to visit the **Fireman's Hall** (10). The Philadelphia Fire Department has restored an authentic 1876 firehouse and turned it into a marvelous museum of firefighting, complete with an 1815 hand pumper and a horse-drawn steamer from 1907. You can see how the firemen lived, board the wheelhouse of an actual fireboat, and watch a film on the history of firefighting. *149 N. 2nd St.,* ☎ *215-923-1438. Open Tues.–Sat., 9–4:30. Closed holidays. Free. Gift shop.* ♿.

Return to Race Street, turn right, and continue downhill under the traffic roar of Highway I-95. At the bottom is Christopher Columbus Boulevard, known to locals only by its former name of **Delaware Avenue**. Once a downtrodden waterfront of rotting piers, this busy street now hums with stylish cafés, restaurants, nightclubs, and upscale entertainment venues. There's also a great view of the Benjamin Franklin Bridge. Turn south to **Penn's Landing**, a vast open waterfront park that has brought new life to an old commercial district. Here you will find, among other attractions, the marvelous:

*INDEPENDENCE SEAPORT MUSEUM (11), 211 S. Columbus Blvd. at Walnut St., ☎ 215-925-5439, Internet: www.libertynet.org/seaport. *Open daily 10–5, closed New Year's, Thanksgiving, Christmas. Admission to museum and historic ships: Adults $7.50, seniors $6, children 4–12 $3.50. Museum only: Adults $5, seniors $4, children $2.50. Museum, historic ships, NJ State Aquarium, and ferry to the aquarium: Adults $15, seniors $12, children $10. Gift shop.* ♿.

The former Philadelphia Maritime Museum has changed its name and moved into much larger quarters, right on the waterfront. Walk beneath a three-story replica of the Benjamin Franklin Bridge as you enter **Home Port: Philadelphia**, an exciting interactive exhibit that explores the events shaping one of America's most historic urban ports. Unload a giant container ship, experience a general quarters drill aboard the bridge of a naval destroyer, try your hand at welding, hop in a simulated scull and row along the Schuylkill River, and then have an undersea adventure in **Divers of the Deep**. You can even watch boats being built in the **Workshop on the Water**. Lots of fun for all, especially kids, and you'll even learn something.

Just outside, and associated with the Seaport Museum, are two historic naval vessels that may be boarded:

U.S.S. *OLYMPIA* and U.S.S. *BECUNA*, Penn's Landing, ☎ 215-922-1898. *Open daily except Christmas and New Year's, 10–4:30. Admission to both vessels: Adults $3.50, children under 12 $1.75. Joint admission with Seaport Museum available. Ship's store.*

The cruiser *Olympia* was Commodore Dewey's flagship in the Philippines during the Spanish-American War in 1898. Fully restored and open to your inspection, it is the only surviving capital ship from that era. Docked next to it is a World War II submarine, the U.S.S. *Becuna*, whose interior may be explored.

If time permits, you might want to take the **Riverbus** ferry across the Delaware River to the foreign shores of New Jersey to visit the:

NEW JERSEY STATE AQUARIUM AT CAMDEN (12), ☎ 856-365-3300 or (800) 616-5297, Internet: www.njaquarium.org. *Open daily 9:30–5:30, closing at 5 in the off season. Reservations suggested for peak periods. Admission to Aquarium only: Adults $10.95, seniors and students with ID $9.45, children 3–11 $7.95. Riverbus ferry: Adults $5, children $3. Bargain joint ticket to Seaport Museum, historic ships, Aquarium, and Riverbus ferry available. Gift shop. Food service.* ♿.

New Jersey's thoroughly modern State Aquarium has been vastly improved as its horizons were expanded to embrace more exotic subjects than the fish of the Garden State. Visitors can now marvel at a Caribbean outpost, see a submerged wreck, say hello to the sharks, and learn all about the creatures of the deep. The interactive exhibits are especially attractive to kids, and perhaps to adults as well.

Penn's Landing has other attractions and activities, enough in fact to finish off your day here. When it's in port, the ***Gazela of Philadelphia***, a square-rigger built in Portugal in 1883, welcomes visitors aboard to explore the oldest and largest vessel of its kind that still puts out to sea. *For information,* ☎ *215-923-9030.* Other historic boats make appearances here, and some may be boarded. There are also a variety of special events, concerts, festivals, and exhibitions throughout the year. ☎ *215-629-3200 for current programs.* Other attractions include the **Columbus Monument and International Sculpture Garden** and the **Philadelphia Vietnam Veterans' Memorial.**

NOTE: The new Family Entertainment Center at Penn's Landing, now under construction, will make major site changes and offer new amenities.

You can return to downtown via bus from Penn's Landing at Chestnut Street, or head south to the new walkway above Interstate 95 to South Street (see page 42), where you can catch the Phlash visitor bus. Or hike back—it's not that far.

Society Hill to Rittenhouse Square

There are no really great "must-see" sights along this leisurely walking tour, but don't let that deter you. From historic Society Hill to swinging South Street, from the bustling Italian Market to the burgeoning Avenue of the Arts, and on the elegant Rittenhouse Square, the three-mile route—level all the way—leads you through a wide variety of distinctive neighborhoods and experiences. Along the way you'll encounter numerous "off-the-beaten-path" attractions, have unusual shopping opportunities, and pass a tremendous number of enticing places for lunch. For the more ambitious, several side trips to unique destinations have been included.

Society Hill once had a hill, but that's long gone. The land was granted by William Penn to a group called the Society of Free Traders, hence the name. Over the years the neighborhood deteriorated, but beginning around 1960 gentrification set in and Society Hill became a fashionable place to live. Nearly a thousand 18th- and 19th-century houses have been lovingly restored, and new ones built in harmonious styles. Much of the area's charm lies in its hidden mews and courtyards, and of course you'll find cobblestone streets, brick sidewalks, narrow alleys, and antique street lamps.

South Street, on the other hand, is very much a youthful place of today. Once the southern limit of Penn's original city, it now throbs with activity—funky and otherwise—both day and night. Below it lies South Philadelphia, a largely Italian neighborhood that is becoming more ethnically diverse. The area is particularly noted for its colorful food markets, and for a few off-beat museums.

A stroll up the Avenue of the Arts, otherwise known as Broad Street and still very much a work-in-progress, eventually leads around to Rittenhouse Square. This lovely urban park is the perfect place to end your walk, perhaps visiting the nearby museums or shops.

GETTING THERE:

Society Hill, the starting point of this walk, lies immediately south of Independence Hall, within walking distance of the major hotels.

By car, you'll almost surely have to use a commercial parking facility such as the underground one serving Independence Mall, with entrances on both 5th and 6th streets, between Market and Arch.

By subway, take the Market-Frankfort Line to 8th Street.

By bus, take routes 21, 42, or 76 to 6th Street.

By Phlash, get off at 6th and Market streets.

By SEPTA commuter train, get off at Market East Station and walk a block east on Market, then two blocks south on 7th.

By PATCO commuter train, get off at 9–10th Street Station and walk two blocks east on Locust Street.

See page 18 for more details on transit options.

PRACTICALITIES:

Since there are no major attractions along the way, you can really take this walk on any day in fine weather. You might, however, want to check the individual listings to see if any appeal to you, and when they are open. Those intending to probe the Italian Market should note that it is closed on Sundays and Mondays, and busiest on Fridays and Saturdays.

For further information, stop by the friendly **Philadelphia Visitors Center** at 16th Street & John F. Kennedy Blvd., Philadelphia, PA 19102, ☎ 215-636-1666 or 888-90-PHILA, Internet: www.libertynet.org/phila-visitor.

FOOD AND DRINK:

You won't go hungry along this route. Even the most modest budget can satisfy your appetite at one of the countless eateries you'll pass. Of the many outstanding establishments, here's just a sampling:

Dickens Inn (421 S. 2nd St. at Head House Sq.) An English pub in an 18th-century building. ☎ 215-928-9307. $$

Downey's (526 S. Front St., at South St.) An Irish pub with Irish food and a lively atmosphere. ☎ 215-625-9500. $$

South Street Souvlaki (509 South St., between 5th and 6th) Great, classic Greek cuisine served in a modest taverna. ☎ 215-925-3026. $ and $$

Jim's Steaks (400 South St., at 4th) Genuine Philadelphia cheesesteak sandwiches, tasty and cheap. ☎ 215-928-1911. $

Famous Deli (700 S. 4th St., at Bainbridge, a block south of South St.) This traditional Jewish deli has been serving corned beef sandwiches and egg creams since 1923. ☎ 215-922-3274. $

Pat's King of Steaks (1237 E. Passyunk Ave., between 9th and Wharton, 4 blocks south of the Italian Market) Legendary cheesesteaks; a bit out of the way but a real Philly experience. ☎ 215-468-1546. $

Geno's Steaks (1219 S. 9th St., at E. Passyunk Ave., 4 blocks south of the Italian Market) Long a favorite haunt for Philly cheesesteak fans. No phone. $

SUGGESTED TOUR:

Numbers in parentheses correspond to numbers on the map.

Washington Square (1) was one of the original five parks laid out in William Penn's "Greene Country Town" plan, a street layout of 1682 that survives practically intact today. The Quakers called it "Southeastern Square" because they believed it vain to name places after people. Others referred to it as "Congo Square" after its slave market, which flourished until 1780. This was also a burial ground for victims of a yellow fever epidemic, and also for both British and American soldiers killed in the Revolutionary War. Today, they are remembered with an eternal flame at the Tomb of the Unknown Soldier of the Revolution.

Just east of the square, on 6th Street, stands the **Athenaeum**, a private library founded in 1814. Its present home dates from 1847 and was the nation's first major building in the Italian Renaissance Revival style. Its splendid interior, filled with decorative arts from the early 1800s as well as changing exhibitions, may be visited on request. ☎ *215-925-2688. Open Mon.–Tues. and Thurs.–Fri. 9–5, Wed. noon–8. Closed holidays. Free.*

Head east on Locust Street, turning left on 4th Street. **Old St. Joseph's Church** (2), on Willings Alley to your right, is the oldest Roman Catholic church in Philadelphia, having been founded by the Jesuits in 1733. In a way, this could be considered the birthplace of religious freedom in America, as it was the only place in the colonies (or in England!) where Catholic services were permitted under British law. Even in this Quaker city there were more than a few bigots, which is why the original building was so unassuming, as is the present 1838 structure. ☎ *215-923-1733. Visitors welcome. Masses Mon.–Sat. at 12:05, Sun. at 7:30, 9:30, and 11:30.*

Turn right on Walnut Street, passing the **Polish American Cultural Center Museum** (3). Polish contributions to world culture and history are celebrated here, especially in portraits of famous Poles from Pulaski and Kosciuszko to Lech Walesa and Pope John Paul II. ☎ *215-922-1700. Open Mon.–Sat. 10–4, closed Sat. from Jan.–Apr. Free.*

Head south on 3rd Street to the **Powel House** (4), a pre-Revolutionary War townhouse with an adjoining formal garden. Philadelphia's mayor before, during, and after the war, Samuel Powel, built this gem of a Society Hill mansion in 1765 as his residence, and here entertained the likes of George Washington and other notables. Today it's nicely restored (after escaping a slum-clearance wrecking ball in 1930) and used for a variety of social functions, receiving visitors for tours when not in use. *244 S. 3rd St.,* ☎ *215-627-0364. Normally open Sept.–May, Thurs.–Sat. Noon–4, Sun. 1–4; June–Aug., Thurs.–Sat. Noon–5, Sun. 1–5. Adults $3, seniors and students $2, under 6 free.*

Follow the map through some back alleyways to **Old St. Mary's Church** (5), Philadelphia's second-oldest Roman Catholic church and the first cathedral of the Diocese. Established in 1763, it served as the main Catholic church during the Revolution. The graveyard is particularly interesting, containing the tombs of Commodore John Barry and other Colonial notables. *252 S. 4th St.,* ☎ *215-923-7930. Open Mon.–Sat. 9–4:30, Sun. 8:15–1. Masses Sat. at 5, Sun. at 9, 10:30, and noon.*

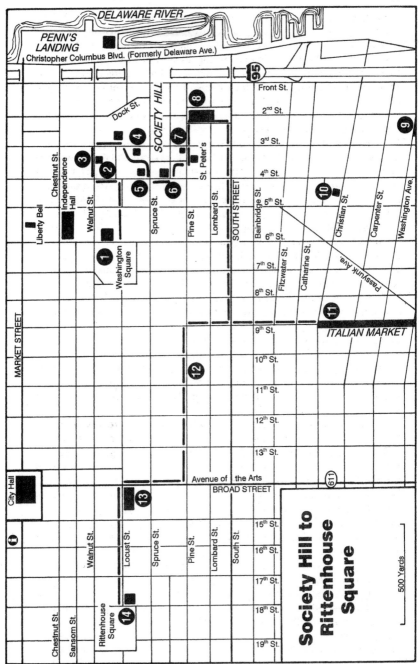

Just a block south stands the **Hill-Physick-Keith House** (6), a freestanding Federal mansion built in 1786. This was once home to Doctor Philip Syng Physick (1768–1837), the acknowledged "Father of American Surgery" and physician to notables. Its unusually elegant interior has been beautifully restored, as has the lovely walled garden. *321 S. 4th St.,* ☎ *215-925-2251. Open Sept.–May, Thurs.–Sat., 11–2; June–Aug., Thurs.–Sat. Noon–4, Sun. 1–4. Adults $4, seniors and students $2.*

Follow the route around **St. Peter's Episcopal Church**, erected in 1761. Several signers of the Declaration of Independence worshiped here. Right down Pine Street is the **Thaddeus Kosciuszko National Memorial** (7), a small townhouse in which the great Polish patriot lodged from November, 1797, until May, 1798, while pursuing a pension from Congress for his heroic aid during the Revolutionary War. The restored interior displays some of his personal possessions and features a short audiovisual presentation in English and Polish. *Third and Pine streets,* ☎ *215-597-9618. Normally open daily 9–5, but hours may be reduced. Free.*

Head House Square (8) is a block farther east on Pine Street. A busy market, meeting place, and community center ever since the early 18th century, its most prominent landmark is the Head House of 1804, which served as both a market and a firehouse. Behind this trails a block-long pavilion that kept Colonial shoppers and merchants dry. Today, the colorful square abounds in crafts shops, boutiques, restaurants, and the like. At its end is **South Street**, a vibrant shopping and entertainment strip with a decidedly youthful ambiance. More than one hundred unusual small stores here feature far-out fashions, health foods, strange books, and even stranger merchandise.

A left on South Street leads to a pedestrian overpass across busy I-95 and into Penn's Landing, described on pages 36-37.

From here, you might possibly be interested in making one or more side trips to enjoy some of Philadelphia's more esoteric attractions. Continuing down 2nd Street for about a half-mile brings you to the **Mummers Museum** (9), dedicated to Philadelphia's old tradition of Mummery, which finds its annual outlet in the very strange Mummers Parade held on New Year's Day. With their roots in pagan celebrations, European heritages, African dance, and more, dozens of participating groups vie with one another to produce the most outlandish costumes, music, and acts. It's all a lot of fun, and you can watch videos of parades past, listen to the music, and examine the costumes right here any time of the year. *Second St. at Washington Ave.,* ☎ *215-336-3050. Open Tues.–Sat. 9:30–5, Sun. noon–5. Closed Mon., Sun. in July–Aug., and some holidays. Adults $2.50, seniors and children $2. Gift shop.* ♿.

Another side trip can be made by heading south on 4th Street to Queen Street, about a quarter-mile, to visit the **Mario Lanza Museum** (10). Located at the scene of the famous tenor's first public recognition, the tiny museum celebrates the life of Mario Lanza (1921–59), one of South Philly's many gifts to the musical world. Personal effects, memorabilia, photos, film clips, and of course records are featured. *Settlement Music School, 416 Queen St.,* ☎ *215-468-3623. Open Mon.–Sat., 10–3:30. Closed Sat. in July–Aug. Free.* ♿.

Gourmets and gourmands alike will surely want to flock south on 9th Street to feast their eyes on the ***Italian Market** (11), a sidewalk cornucopia of things edible. For many, this is the ultimate Philadelphia experience. Billed as the world's largest outdoor market and dating back over 125 years, its sights, smells, and tastes beguile them into returning again and again. Enjoy. *Ninth St. between Wharton and Christian streets,* ☎ *215-922- 5557. Open Tues.-Sat., early morning until late afternoon, best on Fri. and Sat.*

When you're done probing the South Street area, head north on 10th Street for two blocks, then turn left on Pine. Known as **Antique Row** (12), the next three blocks are home to some two dozen antique shops offering quality collectibles. Broad Street, one of the city's main thoroughfares, is today being promoted as the **Avenue of the Arts**, although as such it is more a work-in-progress than an accomplished fact. This is supposed to be the cornerstone of Philadelphia's revitalization, and eventually it will be that, especially when the spectacular Regional Performing Arts Center opens in 2001. As you stroll north on it, you can't miss the marvelously Victorian architecture of the **Academy of Music** (13). Opened in 1857, this has long been home to the world-renowned Philadelphia Orchestra (and will remain so until their new concert hall is finished), as well as to the opera and the ballet. Tours of the facility are offered, but you must make reservations well in advance. Better still, stop by the box office to get tickets for a performance! ☎ *215-893-1935.*

Turn left on Locust Street for four blocks, passing the famed **Curtis Institute of Music**, whose graduates include such luminaries as Leonard Bernstein, Gian-Carlo Menotti, and Samuel Barber. Free student recitals are given every Monday, Wednesday, and Friday during the school year. ☎ *215-893-7902.* Opposite this is **Rittenhouse Square** (14), one of the most urbane of urban parks anywhere. This is Philadelphia at its most gracious—a corner of civility where the ideals of William Penn's "Greene Country Towne" still survive, despite the upscale shops and high-rise apartment buildings surrounding it. It is also a wonderful place to sit down and relax after a rather long but intriguing walk.

Along the Parkway

A merica's Champs-Élysées stretches for over a mile from the nation's most stunning municipal building to one of its very best art museums. Along the way you can gaze down from City Hall's tower, stroll the length of the great boulevard, visit some of the finest museums on Earth, enjoy hands-on science experiences, relax in an elegant park, and savor taste delights at a variety of restaurants and cafés. If you come on the right day, you can even visit the most influential prison in history, built in 1829 and abandoned in 1971. And then escape back into the sunshine!

GETTING THERE:

By car, you're best off parking in a commercial lot or garage near City Hall or the nearby Convention Center. All of the attractions are within walking distance of there. Cars parked illegally are quickly ticketed and towed away!

By subway, take any route to City Hall.

By bus, take any one of many routes to City Hall.

By Phlash, get off at City Hall.

By SEPTA commuter train, get off at Suburban Station and walk two blocks east to City Hall.

By PATCO commuter train, get off at 12th/13th Street Station and walk five blocks northwest to City Hall.

PRACTICALITIES:

The Rodin Museum and the Philadelphia Museum of Art are closed on Mondays and certain holidays, while City Hall is closed on weekends and holidays. The historic Eastern State Penitentiary receives guests from about May through October, but check the schedule. Try to make this tour on a Tuesday, Wednesday, Thursday, or Friday if possible.

The suggested walk is slightly over three miles long, level all the way. If you get tired, buses operate frequently along the Parkway and other midtown thoroughfares.

For further information, stop by the friendly **Philadelphia Visitors Center** at 16th Street & John F. Kennedy Blvd., Philadelphia, PA 19102, ☎ 215-636-1666 or 888-90-PHILA.

FOOD AND DRINK:

Some excellent restaurant choices along the walking route are:

Swann Lounge & Café (Four Seasons Hotel, Ben Franklin Parkway at 18th St.) Light, contemporary American cuisine in luxurious surroundings overlooking the Parkway. ☎ 215-963-1500. $$$

Jack's Firehouse (2130 Fairmount Ave., 5 blocks north of the Rodin Museum) An adventure in creative, even daring, American cuisine; including unusual game dishes. The setting is dramatic, too—it's an old firehouse. Reservations suggested. ☎ 215-232-9000. $$$

Museum Restaurant (in the Art Museum) This delightful full-service museum restaurant serves light American cuisine. ☎ 215-684-7990. $$

Dock Street Brewery (2 Logan Sq., 18th & Cherry streets) Beer mavens will savor the tasty brews made fresh on the premises, served along with an eclectic menu of innovative dishes. ☎ 215-496-0413. $ and $$

Marathon Grill (1617 J.F.K. Blvd., near the Visitors Center) Great burgers, salads, and the like. A cut above fast-food places. ☎ 215-564-4745. $

In addition, you might try **Ben's Restaurant** in the Franklin Institute (accessible without paying museum entrance), the **Skyline Cafeteria** in the Free Library, or the **Art Museum Cafeteria**. All are inexpensive. There are many **street vendors** near the Visitors Center, an area featuring plenty of park benches for an enjoyable alfresco lunch. For the most part, these stands serve sandwiches, sausages, cheesesteaks, and fruit salads, but if you look around you can find more exotic fare at both locations, including Chinese, vegetarian, and Middle Eastern specialties. Prices are quite low.

SUGGESTED TOUR:

Numbers in parentheses correspond to numbers on the map.

Where better to begin your walk than at **City Hall** (1)? This extraordinary structure stands at the center of nearly everything in Philadelphia and is visible for miles around. The largest (and most elaborate) city hall in the United States, it is also the world's tallest self-supporting masonry structure, built completely without a steel frame. Until 1987, an unwritten gentleman's agreement prohibited any other building in town from exceeding its 548-foot height, but during that pivotal year Philadelphia finally entered the Skyscraper Age—and with a vengeance!

Construction on City Hall began in 1871 and was not completed until the turn of the century. It was then topped off with a 37-foot-high statue of *William Penn* by Alexander Milne Calder, whose son and grandson were both born in Philadelphia and were also destined to become renowned sculptors. While you're at the base, swing around to see an entirely different kind of carving, Claes Oldenburg's pop-art masterpiece

Clothespin—a 45-foot-high 1976 rendering in steel of just that.

For a fabulous *view of Center City and way beyond, enter City Hall from the north side and take any elevator to the seventh floor, then follow arrows and take an escalator to the ninth floor, where you'll board a tiny elevator for the **Tower** and **Observation Deck**. You can make reservations for later if necessary, as the tower can only accommodate a few people at a time. ☎ *215-686-2840. Open weekdays except certain holidays, 9:30–4:15. Free. An interior tour is also offered on the same days at 12:30.*

Now follow the map to **John F. Kennedy Plaza** (2), a large open area commanding vast urban vistas. In its southwest corner is the circular **Philadelphia Visitors Center** whose friendly staff will patiently answer your questions while loading you down with free maps and brochures. ☎ *215-636-1666. Open daily except Thanksgiving and Christmas, 9–5, closing at 6 in summer. Gift shop.*

Just west of this stands **Suburban Station**, once the headquarters of the Pennsylvania Railroad and now a busy stop for all SEPTA commuter trains. With its many sidewalk vendors and plentiful park benches, J.F.K. Plaza is a great place for an outdoor lunch or snack. Don't miss Robert Indiana's often-copied sculpture, *Love*, a 1976 piece of typography-as-art framing the glorious view down the Parkway.

Cross 16th Street and head northwest on *Benjamin Franklin Parkway, a magnificent boulevard in the tradition of Europe's most elegant cities. Surely America's answer to the Champs-Élysées, it was laid out in 1918 as relief from the rigid grid pattern imposed on the town by William Penn in the 17th century. Running nearly a mile northwest from City Hall, the Parkway provides a grand entrance to the world's largest municipal park.

Passing numerous hotels and cafés, you will soon come to **Logan Circle** (3). In the center of this lovely open area is the **Swann Memorial Fountain**, whose waters spout some 50 feet into the air from a centerpiece enlivened with three reclining nude statues representing the three great rivers of Philadelphia—the Delaware, the Schuylkill, and the Wissahickon (the latter is really only a creek). The figures were sculpted by Alexander Stirling Calder, son of the creator of the William Penn statue atop City hall and father of Alexander Calder of mobile statuary fame, whose works are well represented in the Art Museum.

Adjoining the Circle on the east is **Sister Cities Plaza**, which celebrates Philadelphia's links to Florence and Tel Aviv, as well as to Tianjin (China), Inchon (South Korea), Douala (Cameroon), and Tourn (Poland). Overlooking the entire scene is the old **Cathedral of Saints Peter and Paul**, begun in 1846 when this was still the boondocks. It is the head church of the Philadelphia Archdiocese, seats nearly 2,000 worshipers, and was designated a Basilica in 1976. ☎   *215-561-1313. Open to visitors daily 9–3:30. Weekday masses at 7:15, 8, 12:05, and 12:35; Sundays at 8, 9:30, 12:15, and 5.*

Parkway

500 Yards

Ridge Ave.

11th St.
12th St.
13th St.

US 30
676

Convention Center

BROAD STREET

611

Callowhill St.

15th St.

16th St.

17th St.

18th St.

Hamilton St.

19th St.

Library

20th St.

Spring Garden St.

Rodin Museum

21st St.

22nd St.

BENJAMIN FRANKLIN PARKWAY

23rd St.

Green St.

24th St.

Pennsylvania Ave.

Fairmount Ave.

25th St.

Philadelphia Museum of Art

Eakins Oval

26th St.

FAIRMOUNT PARK

Franklin Institute

Vine St.

Race St.

Cherry St.

Arch St.

City Hall

1

2

Suburban Station

Cathedral

12

3

4

11

9

10

J.F.K. Blvd.

MARKET STREET

3

3

Market Street

SCHUYLKILL RIVER

30

76

30th Street Station

5

6

7

8

Use side entrance.

Just north of the Circle stands the **Free Library of Philadelphia** (4), one of a pair of matching neoclassical buildings modeled after the famous twin palaces on the Place de la Concorde in Paris. The library has millions and millions of books and other reference materials, and also features changing exhibitions on many subjects. Its Rare Book Department, shown on daily tours, is among the finest on Earth. And for a great view of the Parkway, visit the library's rooftop **Skyline Cafeteria** for lunch or just a snack. ☎ *215-686-5322. Open daily with the exception of Sun. in summer. Free. Gift shop. Tours. ♿, ramp entrance at 20th and Wood streets.*

Continue up the Parkway to the:

*RODIN MUSEUM (5), 22nd St. and Ben. Franklin Parkway, ☎ *215-763-8100. Open Tues.–Sun. 10–5. Donation requested. Gift shop. ♿, use rear driveway and buzz.*

You don't have to travel to Paris to examine the works of Auguste Rodin (1840–1917), one of the greatest artists of all time. His powerful sculptures transcend style, bridging the gap between Romanticism and modern art while capturing the most fleeting, ephemeral moments of life. Because several casts were made of his greatest works, each as much an original as the others, they can be seen in Paris, London, and a few other places besides Philadelphia—but this is the largest collection to be found outside of France.

A cast of *The Thinker* beckons visitors into the tranquil gardens, at the end of which is a 1929 reproduction of the château that Rodin had built for himself outside Paris. Just before the entrance is the fabulous **Gate of Hell* with over a hundred sculpted figures emerging from its 21-foot height. Inside, you'll see the renowned **Burghers of Calais* as well as nearly 200 sculptures and other works of art by the master.

Keep heading northwest on the Parkway until you come to **Eakins Oval**, beyond which is the old rise of "Faire Mount," a low hill once topped by the city's reservoir. Today a broad set of steps—made famous by the film *Rocky*—leads up to the neoclassical pile of the:

*PHILADELPHIA MUSEUM OF ART (6), 26th St. and Ben Franklin Parkway, ☎ *215-763-8100, Internet: www.philamuseum.org. Open Tues.–Sun., 10–5, until 8:45 on Wed. Closed Mon. and legal holidays. Adults $8; seniors, students, and children 5–17 $5. Additional charge for special shows. Free to everyone on Sun. 10–1. Gift shop. Tours. Cafeteria and restaurant. ♿, ramp entrance on south side by special parking places.*

Even if you detest art museums, you should at least walk around the outside of this 1920's complex to admire the superb *views of Philadelphia, the Schuylkill River, and Fairmount Park that it offers.

Inside, you'll be treated to one of the greatest art collections on Earth. More than 200 galleries cover some 10 acres, but it's not necessary (or possible) to see them all in order to uncover those treasures that appeal to you most. Just pick up a diagram of the museum at the entrance and head off towards such masterpieces as Poussin's *Birth of Venus*, Van Eyck's *St. Francis Receiving the Stigmata*, Ruben's *Prometheus Bound*, Renoir's *The Bathers*, Van Gogh's *Sunflowers*, Charles Willson Peale's *Staircase Group*, Benjamin West's *Benjamin Franklin Drawing Electricity from the Sky*, Picasso's *Three Musicians*, and Claes Oldenburg's *Giant Three-Way Plug*. And that's just for starters. There's also the most extensive collection of works by Marcel Duchamp anywhere, weapons, tapestries, a medieval French cloister, a stone Hindu temple from India, a Japanese Buddhist temple and ceremonial teahouse, a 17th-century Chinese palace hall, and much, much more. Visit the period room settings from France, England, and early America. And, if you get tired, you can always relax over lunch or snacks in the cafeteria or restaurant.

Amble around to the rear of the museum (or exit from its west entrance) for some truly glorious views. From the gazebo just beyond the parking lot you can gaze down on the marvelous **Fairmount Waterworks** (7) of 1812, looking for all the world like a group of misplaced Greek temples. A National Historic Engineering Landmark, this fantastic complex on the edge of the Schuylkill River once used steam power to pump water up to a reservoir on the site of the present Museum of Art. Several outbreaks of typhoid caused the city to lose confidence in the river's water, so pumping stopped in 1911. Until 1962 the waterworks were used as an aquarium.

From here on stretches **Fairmount Park**, the largest landscaped city park on Earth. Over 100 miles of trails snake through its more than 8,700 acres, with a multitude of historic, cultural, and recreational attractions along the way. These are described on the daytrip beginning on page 57, which can be partially taken by public transportation, or more thoroughly by car. The truly energetic might want to do it by bicycle.

Return to the front of the Museum of Art. An interesting side trip can be made from here to the nearby **Eastern State Penitentiary** (8). This massive, grim fortress revolutionized the way convicts were rehabilitated by solitary confinement when it first opened way back in 1829. By 1971, however, it was abandoned. Although such renowned guests as Al Capone and Willie Sutton spent much more than a day there, you can stop by for a shorter visit, perhaps taking the guided tour. ☎ *215-236-3300, Internet: www.easternstate.com. Open May, Sept., and Oct., Sat.–Sun. 10–5;*

June–Aug. Wed.–Sun. 10–5. Adults $7, seniors $6, students $5, children 7–18 $3, under 7 not admitted. Gift shop. ♿.

Head back down the Parkway to 20th Street. Here you might want to stop at the world-renowned:

*FRANKLIN INSTITUTE (9), 20th St. and Ben Franklin Parkway, ☎ 215-448-1200, Internet: www.fi.edu. *Open daily 9:30–5, with the Futures Center and Omniverse Theater remaining open on Thurs.–Sat. until 9 and Sun. until 6. Closed July 4, Thanksgiving, Dec. 24, Christmas, and New Year's. Basic admission: Adults $9.50, seniors and children 4–11 $8.50, under 4 free. Additional charges for Omniverse Theater and Fels Planetarium. Combination tickets available. Gift shops. Parking garage. Cafeteria and restaurant. ♿, use ramp at Winter St. entrance.*

Step from the past into the next century in this hands-on science museum, considered by many to be the best of its kind in the world. Here you can learn all about the fundamentals of science, then explore the possibilities of tomorrow through state-of-the-art exhibits that you manipulate yourself. These attractions are contained in the **Science Center** and the dazzling new ***Futures Center**, while the ***Omniverse Theater** surrounds its audience with enormous wraparound images of thrilling scientific escapades. The **Fels Planetarium** uses its Digistar projector to simulate time travel throughout the Universe.

You can easily spend days at the Franklin Institute, but even a short visit of an hour or two will prove to be both entertaining and enlightening. And, if you only have a few moments, at least pop into the **Benjamin Franklin National Memorial** *(free admission from the 20th Street entrance)* for a look at scientific artifacts and personal mementoes of the great man in a hall dominated by his huge statue.

Needless to say, a visit to the Franklin Institute is a delight for the younger set and an enjoyable one for the young-at-heart of all ages. Don't miss it.

Behind the Institute, at 21st and Race streets, is the **Science Park**. This large urban park is filled with learning opportunities and things that are just plain fun for children and adults alike, including a maze and three-dimensional optical illusions. *Open May through Oct. Free with admission to either the Franklin Institute or the Please Touch Museum, below.*

If you happen to have any small kids (age 7 or younger) in tow, you might want to treat them to the **Please Touch Museum** (10) where everything from Nature's Nursery to a TV studio can be climbed over, played on, tried out, or otherwise explored. Foodtastic Journey follows edibles from the farm to the kitchen, while Sendak is an interactive exhibit of characters from the children's books by illustrator Maurice Sendak. *210 North 21st St.* ☎ *215-963-0667, Internet:www.libertynet.org/~pleastch. Open daily 9–4:30. Admission $6.95, under 1 free.* &.

Another nearby attraction is the **Goldie Paley Gallery** of the **Moore College of Art and Design** (11), which features changing exhibitions of art, architecture, crafts, photography, and design. Sometimes the works of yet-to-be-discovered artists, these shows are often provocative and always worthwhile for those with an interest in art. *20th St. and Ben Franklin Parkway,* ☎ *215-568-4515. Open Tues.–Fri. 10–5, Thurs. until 7, weekends noon–4, closed holidays. Free.*

Dinosaur fans and other nature lovers can saunter a block east to the:

ACADEMY OF NATURAL SCIENCES (12), 19th St. and Ben Franklin Parkway, ☎ 215-299-1000, Internet: www.acnatsci.org. *Open weekdays 10–4:30, weekends and holidays 10–5. Closed Thanksgiving, Christmas, New Year's. Adults $8.50, seniors $7.75, children 3–12 $7.50, under 3 free. Gift shop.* &, *level entrance on 19th St.*

America's oldest museum of natural history has been greatly modernized in recent years, and of late has been focusing its attention on everyone's favorite monsters, the dinosaurs. More than a dozen of these awesome creatures, or at least their bones, inhabit a hall that re-creates their prehistoric world and uses the latest technology to answer your questions. In addition, there's a hands-on nature center, mummies, gem exhibitions, stuffed animals in realistic dioramas, and everything else you'd expect to find in a leading natural history museum. Live butterflies flit about a tropical paradise that you can enter and, for kids under 12, there's a touch museum with live little creatures.

From here it's a short stroll back to City Hall.

Trip 5
Philadelphia

University City

J ust across the Schuykill River from Center City lies Philadelphia's "Other City," a tree-lined world of ivy-covered Victorian buildings, a lovely campus, great museums, and wonderful places to eat. This is the home of the University of Pennsylvania, an Ivy League school founded in 1740, and of Drexel University, founded in 1890.

The west bank of the river remained a remote country retreat for wealthy Philadelphians until the mid-19th century, when new bridges and the development of mass transportation opened it up to the middle classes. Crowds poured in for the Centennial Exposition of 1876, and in their wake came the speculative building of townhouses. Around the same time, the University of Pennsylvania moved here from Center City, and in 1891 Drexel University dedicated its main building. Today, the area around the first part of this walking tour retains its distinctive Ivy League character, a delightful escape from the city's hustle.

GETTING THERE:
On foot, energetic travelers can head west on Walnut Street, crossing the river and turning south on 33rd Street. It's just a bit over a mile from Rittenhouse Square.

By car, head west on either Market or Walnut Street, then south on 34th to the Civic Center area just south of the hospital. There are several parking lots around here.

By subway, take the Market-Frankford Line to the 34th Street station, then walk south on 34th Street.

By bus, take the Route 42 bus to the U. of P. Hospital stop on 34th Street.

By SEPTA commuter train, take the R-1, R-2, or R-3 line to the University City Station.

PRACTICALITIES:
Avoid making this trip on a Monday, a holiday, or a Sunday in summer, when the superb University Museum is closed. The Institute of Contemporary Art is also closed on Tuesdays. In general, you're better off coming on a Wednesday, Thursday, or Friday during the school year.

For **Campus Tours** contact the University of Pennsylvania Office of Undergraduate Admissions, 1 College Hall, ☎ 215-898-1000, open Monday to Friday, 8:30–4:30.

For further information, stop by the friendly **Philadelphia Visitors Center** at 16th Street & John F. Kennedy Blvd., Philadelphia, PA 19102, ☎ 215-636-1666 or 888-90-PHILA, Internet: www.libertynet.org/phila-visitor.

FOOD AND DRINK:

You can eat inexpensively and well in University City, especially on or near the Penn campus. Here are a few suggestions:

White Dog Café (3420 Sansom St., between Chestnut and Walnut, between 34th and 35th streets) This is *the* place to dine in University City; what with its eclectic decor featuring canine memorabilia, and its highly creative American cuisine. Reservations recommended. Sunday brunch. ☎ 215-386-9224. $$

Palladium (3601 Locust Walk on campus) Excellent Continental cuisine in an elegant, club-like atmosphere. Reservations suggested, ☎ 215-387-3463. X: Sun. $$

The Restaurant School (4207 Walnut St.) Want real haute cuisine at bargain prices? Philadelphians flock to this finishing school for aspiring restauranteurs to taste what the students are up to. Open for dinner only. Reserve, ☎ 215-222-4200. X: Sun., Mon. $ and $$

Tandoor India (106 S. 40th St., between Chestnut and Walnut) Northern Indian cuisine at bargain prices. ☎ 215-222-7122. $

Museum Café (in the Archaeology Museum) A handy cafeteria with homemade foods. ☎ 215-898-4089. $

Food Court at 30th Street Station (south hall, main level) It's at the very end of the walking tour, but not to be overlooked if you're hungry. A surprisingly eclectic variety of eateries is featured. ☎ 215-349-1821. $

SUGGESTED TOUR:

Numbers in parentheses correspond to numbers on the map.

Begin your walking tour at the intersection of 33rd and Spruce streets, where you'll find the:

*UNIVERSITY OF PENNSYLVANIA MUSEUM OF ARCHAEOLOGY AND ANTHROPOLOGY (1), 33rd and Spruce Sts., Philadelphia, PA 19104, ☎ 215-898-4000, Fax 215-898-0657, Internet: www.upenn.edu/museum *Open Tues.–Sat. 10–4:30, Sun. 1–5. Closed Mon., holidays, and Sun. from Memorial Day to Labor Day. Adults $5, students $2.50, free on Sun. Museum shop. Cafeteria.* ♿.

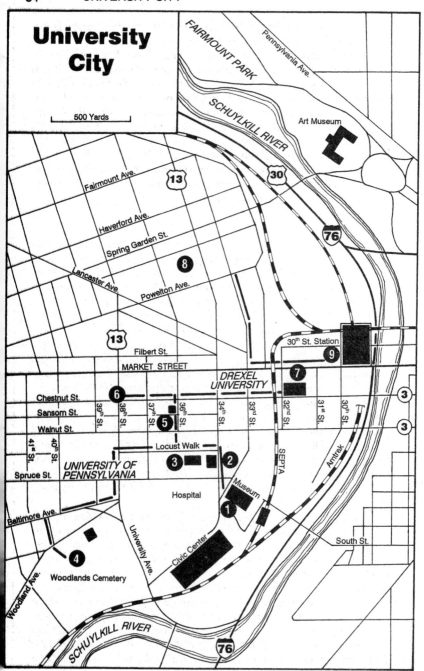

University City

500 Yards

FAIRMOUNT PARK

Pennsylvania Ave.

SCHUYLKILL RIVER

Art Museum

Fairmount Ave.

13

30

Haverford Ave.

Spring Garden St.

76

Lancaster Ave.

Powelton Ave.

8

13

Filbert St.

30th St. Station

9

MARKET STREET

DREXEL
UNIVERSITY

7

Chestnut St.

6

3

Sansom St.

39th St.

38th St.

37th St.

36th St.

34th St.

33rd St.

32nd St.

31st St.

30th St.

3

Walnut St.

41st St.

40th St.

5

SEPTA

3

Locust Walk

UNIVERSITY OF
PENNSYLVANIA

3

2

Amtrak

Spruce St.

Museum

Baltimore Ave.

Hospital

1

South St.

Civic Center

University Ave.

4

Woodlands Cemetery

Woodland Ave.

SCHUYLKILL RIVER

76

Since 1887 the museum has been a leader in archaeological and anthropological research, sponsoring hundreds of expeditions to all corners of the inhabited world. In the course of all those diggings they have brought back well over a million objects, the best of which are on display in these stunning galleries. This is, in fact, one of the finest museums of its kind anywhere, and a must-see for anyone interested in mankind's past. Among the treasures are the ancient Egyptian palace of Merenptah, a 12-ton sphinx of Rameses II from around 1200 BC, mummies, a Kifwebe mask from Zaire, the feathered cloak of an Hawaiian noble, a Mayan stela from Guatemala, and a huge cloisonne lion from China. There's much, much more from ancient Egypt, Mesopotamia, Mesoamerica, Asia, and especially from the Greco-Roman world, along with artifacts of the native peoples of North America, Africa, and Polynesia.

Stroll up 34th Street a short distance to the **Arthur Ross Gallery** (2), the University of Pennsylvania's official art gallery. Housed in the richly-ornamented Fine Arts Library of 1890, an architectural masterpiece by Frank Furness and now a National Historic Landmark, the gallery features changing exhibits from the university's vast art collection along with traveling shows. ☎ *215-898-2083, Internet: www.upenn.edu/ARG. Open Tues.–Fri. 10–5, Sat.–Sun. noon–5. Closed Mon. & some holidays Free.*

Turn left into the campus on *Locust Walk, a delightful pedestrian route through the university. To your left stands the splendidly Victorian **College Hall** (3), a Gothic pile completed in 1873. A persistent legend maintains that this was the inspiration for Charles Addam's spooky house for the "Addams Family," a rumor denied by the famous cartoonist even though he was a student here in the 1930s.

As you wander around the campus, you'll come across a statue of Benjamin Franklin sitting on a park bench. The seat aside of him is vacant, so why not rest for a moment and join Ben in a chat? Others statues scattered nearby include works by Claes Oldenburg ("Split Button," 1981), Alexander Calder ("Jerusalem Stabile," 1979), and Tony Smith ("We Lost," 1975).

You might want to stroll south on 38th Street for a little **side trip** to a picturesque block of Italianate villas and an outstanding Victorian cemetery. Turn right on Baltimore Avenue to a bit beyond 40th Street, then south on **Woodland Terrace** to examine this well-preserved grouping of semi-detached garden houses from 1861. The **Woodlands Cemetery** (4) is just south of this. Established in 1843 on the grounds of the estate of a noted Colonial horticulturist, this the permanent residence of several prominent Victorian Philadelphians. Its curvilinear walkways are also part of a National Recreation Trail, so you're welcome to come for a stroll and a look at the 1789 mansion. *4000 Woodland Ave.,* ☎ *215-386-2181. Grounds open daily, mansion open Mon.–Fri. 9–5. Free. Guided tours by advance* *appointment, charge for tours.* &.

Turning north of Locust Walk on 36th Street soon brings you to the **Institute of Contemporary Art** (5), a facility associated with the University of Pennsylvania. Stop in to see tomorrow's art today in one of the constantly changing exhibitions on a variety of subjects such as photography, digital art, performance art, or just plain painting and sculpture. *118 S. 36th St. at Sansom,* ☎ *215-898-7108, Internet: http://www.upenn.edu/ica. Open Wed.–Fri., noon–8, Sat.–Sun., 11–5. Adults $3, seniors, students and artists $2, free on Sun. mornings.* &.

Continue up 36th Street. To your left, on Chestnut Street at 38th, stands the **Cathedral Church of the Savior** (6), built in 1889 for a congregation of elite Episcopal Victorians. Today it's the Cathedral of the Episcopal Diocese of Philadelphia, and features a lavishly decorated interior as well as an asymmetrical exterior of Romanesque and Gothic elements. ☎ *215-386-0234. Tours by appointment.*

Heading east on Chestnut Street leads to **Drexel University**, founded in 1890 as the Drexel Institute of Art, Science and Industry to teach technical skills to working-class youth. Most of its structures are mundane and utilitarian, but the **Main Building** (7) of 1891 is something else again. Now a National Historic Landmark, this classic Renaissance building with outstanding decorative touches in terra cotta and a stunning interior court also houses the **Drexel Collection**, located on the third floor. Nineteenth-century art, antique furniture from Europe and America, porcelains, and an historic Rittenhouse clock are among the treasures on display. ☎ *215-895-2424. Open Mon. 11–5, Tues.–Wed. 9–10:30 and 1:30–5, Thurs.–Fri. 1:30–5, closed school holidays. Free.*

Before ending your walk, you might take a stroll through nearby **Powelton Village** (8), a turn-of-the-century upper-middle-class neighborhood of large Italianate and Victorian homes and mansions. Some of these are now dilapidated, but others have been lovingly restored by their new owners, bringing fresh vitality to a delightful urban scene.

Walk east on Market Street to **30th Street Station** (9), a gem of a railroad station built in 1933 by the mighty Pennsylvania Railroad. The Pennsy is long gone, having merged first into the unloved Penn Central and finally into Amtrak, but the beautifully-restored station remains as busy as ever, with the constant coming and going of trains bound for New York, Pittsburgh, Washington, Florida, Boston, Montreal, wherever. The station is also a stop for all of SEPTA's commuter trains, for Transit of New Jersey trains to Atlantic City, and for subways and buses to whisk you back to Center City. There's a wonderful **food court** here, with quite a variety of tempting eateries for a well-earned snack after your walk.

Fairmount Park

Beginning in 1812 with five acres of land on William Penn's "Faire Mount," Philadelphia's magnificent Fairmount Park has grown over the years into the nation's largest landscaped city park, encompassing over 8,900 acres on both sides of the Schuylkill River (*pronounced SKU-kill*). The statistics are quite impressive: over a hundred miles of hiking trails and bridle paths, millions of trees, two scenic waterways, over five miles of forested gorge, and all manner of public amenities such as golf courses, ballfields, tennis courts, swimming pools, amphitheaters, and the like. Of primary interest to visitors, though, are the numerous Colonial mansions, America's first zoo, the splendid horticultural gardens and the intriguing Japanese House, a National Historic Engineering Landmark of the first order, and the atmosphere of a vanished age.

Not far from the park, and just over the border in Montgomery County, is the Barnes Foundation with its incredible collection of French Impressionist art, a must-see attraction for any art lover and in itself a compelling reason to visit Philadelphia.

Because you can't possibly see everything here in a single day, and because the range of interests is so great, this trip is presented in a nonstructured way with site descriptions and a map to help you find those attractions you find the most intriguing.

GETTING THERE:

Getting to most of the sites on this trip requires a car, or at least a bicycle. Two of the major attractions, however, can be reached by public transportation. These are the Philadelphia Zoo, served by the Number 76 bus from Center City; and the Barnes Foundation, reached by either the Number 44 bus or SEPTA's Route R-5 commuter train to Merion.

PRACTICALITIES:

The Philadelphia Zoo is open every day except Thanksgiving, December 24, 25, and 31, and New Year's. The Japanese House is open on Tuesdays through Sundays from May through August, and on weekends from September through October. Its exterior and garden can be seen at any time, however. Fairmount Park's historic houses follow a complex schedule—refer to the individual listings and call ahead to be sure. The

Barnes Foundation is sometimes a bit problematical, so be certain to give them a ring before making the trip.

For further information, stop by the friendly **Philadelphia Visitors Center** at 16th Street & John F. Kennedy Blvd., Philadelphia, PA 19102, ☎ 215-636-1666 or 888-90-PHILA, Internet: www.libertynet.org/phila-visitor.

FOOD AND DRINK:

Fairmount Park is the perfect spot for a picnic, and the perfect place for this is the Chamounix Picnic Grounds on the west side across the Strawberry Mansion Bridge. The Philadelphia Zoo has a McDonald's.

There are several nearby restaurants, just east of the Waterworks, or on City Line Avenue (US-1), and one in the northernmost reaches of the park itself. You might also check the listings for Manayunk (see page 65).

The Marker (in the Adam's Mark Hotel, City Line Ave. at Monument Rd., just west of the Schuylkill Expressway) Superb, creative American cuisine in a romantically elegant setting. Reservations suggested, essential for Sunday Brunch. ☎ 215-581-5010. $$ and $$$

Valley Green Inn (Springfield Ave. and Forbidden Drive, in the northern part of the park on Wissahickon Creek, between Chestnut Hill and Roxborough) Creative American and French cuisine in an historic inn from 1850; a lovely setting and a romantic experience. Reserve and ask for directions, ☎ 215-247-1730. $$ and $$$

Marabella's (401 City Line Ave., at Monument Rd., in Bala Cynwyd) A casual Italian eatery with both full and light meals. ☎ 610-668-5353. $$

Café Flower Shop (2501 Meredith St., off 25th St. between Fairmount Ave. and Aspen St.) Eclectic homestyle dishes served amid the posies, indoors or outdoors. Saturday and Sunday brunch. ☎ 215-232-1076. X: Mon., Tues. lunch. $ and $$

Lloyd Hall Café (1 Boathouse Row, on the Schuylkill River) Sandwiches, burgers, salads and the like at a most convenient location for park visitors. Open daily for breakfast and lunch. ☎ 215-334-3472. $

LOCAL ATTRACTIONS:

Numbers in parentheses correspond to numbers on the map.

FAIRMOUNT WATERWORKS (1), Schuylkill River near North 25th Street, ☎ 215-685-0144.

No, it's not a misplaced Greek temple, although it certainly looks like one. This National Historic Engineering Landmark was built in 1812 to pump some four million gallons of water a day from the Schuylkill River to a reservoir atop Faire Mount, where the Art Museum stands today. The first steam-powered pumping station of its kind in the nation, the Waterworks remained in use until 1911, when it was abandoned due to

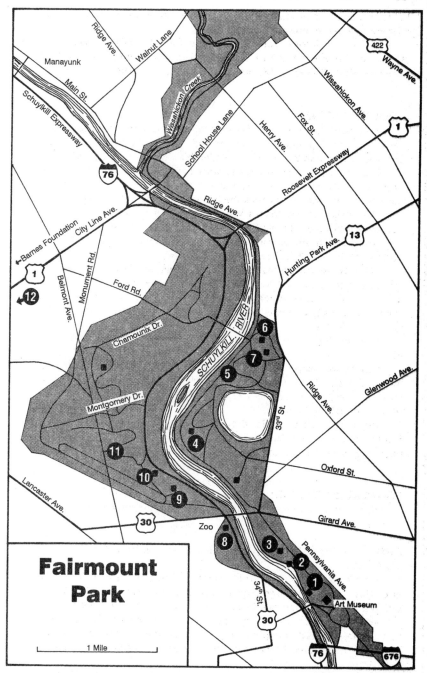

Fairmount
Park

1 Mile

river pollution. Until 1962 the buildings housed an aquarium, and since the 1980s have been undergoing a restoration. Hopefully this will some-day be finished, but in the meantime you can still stop by for a look.

BOATHOUSE ROW (2), Kelly Drive off Sedgely Drive, ☎ 215-978-6919.

The "Schuylkill Navy," a group of rowing clubs that add so much color to the calm, sheltered waters of the Schuylkill River, operates out of these classic 19th-century Tudor structures. Races take place on ten weekends from spring through late fall, with the major events being the Dad Vail Regatta in May, the Independence Day Regatta, and the Frostbite Series in November. Even when the boats are not in the water, the houses are quite a sight.

LEMON HILL (3), Poplar Drive, off Kelly Drive, near Boathouse Row, ☎ 215-232-4337. *Usually open Wed.–Sun., 10–4. Adults $2.50, under 12 $1.50.*

This Federal-style mansion was built in 1800 and named for the lemon trees that once blossomed here. Its three *oval salons are exceedingly rare; the only other examples known to exist in the eastern United States are in the White House, at the University of Virginia, and in a private club in Boston.

MOUNT PLEASANT (4), Fountain Green at 35th St. and Columbia Ave., ☎ 215-763-8100. *Usually open Tues.–Sun., 10–4. Adults $2.50, under 12 $1.*

A wealthy Scottish privateer—a pirate working for the British Crown—built this Georgian mansion in 1761, and in 1779 sold it to the trai-tor Benedict Arnold, who fled town before he could move in. John Adams called it "the most elegant seat in Pennsylvania."

LAUREL HILL (5), East Edgely Drive, ☎ 215-235-1776. *Usually open Wed.–Fri., 9–4. Adults $2.50, under 12 $1.25.*

Built in the Georgian style in 1760 and later expanded in the Federal style, this summer estate features an unusual octagonal room.

STRAWBERRY MANSION (6), near 33rd and Dauphin Streets, ☎ 215-228-8364. *Usually open Tues.–Sun., 10–4. Adults $2.50, under 12 $1.*

The largest of the Fairmount Park mansions, this spacious house was begun in 1798 in the Federal style and completed in the 1820s in the Greek Revival style. Its name comes from the strawberries that were once served there. Today, it's been fully restored with period furnishings and features a splendid collection of antique toys.

WOODFORD MANSION (7), 33rd and Dauphin Street, ☎ 215-229-6115. *Usually open Tues.–Sun., 10–4. Adults $2.50, under 12 $1.*

Both Patriots and Tories lived in this stately Georgian home, but not at the same time. It was built in 1756, and now houses an excellent collection of Colonial furnishings and decorative art.

*PHILADELPHIA ZOO (8), 3400 West Girard Ave., ☎ 215-243-1100, Internet: www.phillyzoo.org. *Open April–Oct., Mon.–Fri. 9:30–4:45, Sat.–Sun. 9:30–5:45; Nov. & March, daily 9:30–4:45; Dec.–Feb. daily 10–4. Closed Thanksgiving, Dec. 24, 25, and 31, and New Year's Day. Adults $10.50, seniors 65+ and children 5-11 $8, children 2–4 $5. Parking $4. Picnic facilities. McDonald's restaurants. Rides. Zoo Shop.* ఉ.

America's first zoo is still among the most popular, especially with children. Opened in 1874 and greatly modernized in recent years, the Philadelphia Zoo is home to more than 1,700 animals, who live as much as possible in re-created natural habitats. Visitors can see the new ***Primate Reserve**, America's first pride of white lions, its only giant river otters, frolicking polar bears, exotic rainforest animals, strange wild pigs, a pack of African wild dogs, and many, many other friendly creatures. Visits might begin with an overview at treetop level on the **Monorail Safari Ride** and/or a ride on a camel, elephant, or pony *(all Apr.–Sept., weather permitting, extra charge)* and, for kids, include a climb and a swing in the **Treehouse** *(extra charge)*. There's also a **Children's Zoo** where barnyard animals can be petted and fed. Other features include a five-acre African Plain and a Victorian picnic grove. You can easily spend several hours here, or even a whole day.

SWEETBRIAR MANSION (9), Lansdowne Ave. north of Girard Ave., ☎ 215-222-1333. *Usually open Mon., Wed., and Sun., 10–4. Adults $2.50, under 12 $1.*

Built in 1797 in the Federal style, Sweetbriar is noted for its period furnishings, and especially for the grand view from its floor-to-ceiling windows.

CEDAR GROVE (10), Lansdowne Drive, ☎ 215-684-7922. *Usually open Tues.–Sun., 10–4. Adults $2.50, under 12 $1.25.*

This Quaker farmhouse was originally built in 1748 in Frankford, and moved here in 1927. According to legend, a resident ghost came along with it. Five generations of Quakers lived in the house, and left behind the furnishings you see today. Its "open Bible" doors and porch are similar in style to those found on Quaker meetinghouses.

*JAPANESE HOUSE AND GARDEN (11), Horticultural Center, off Montgomery Drive at Belmont Mansion Drive, ☎ 215-878-5097, Internet: www.libertynet.org/jhg. *Open May–Aug., Tues.–Sun. 11–4; Sept.–Oct., weekends 11–4; closed holidays. Adults $2.50, seniors and students $2, under 12 $1.*

No, you haven't wandered through some strange space/time warp into 17th-century Kyoto. This is still Philadelphia, although the setting is so authentic you'd swear that you're in ancient Japan. The **Pine Breeze Villa**, as it's called, was built in 1953 in Nagoya, then disassembled and exhibited at the Museum of Modern Art in New York from 1954 to 1955. In 1958 it was reassembled on the current site which, oddly enough, has had a Japanese structure and landscaping almost continuously since the Centennial Exposition of 1876.

The tranquil beauty of a residence such as this one in the late-16th-century *shoin-zukuri* style would have been appropriate for a member of the educated upper class, such as a government official or high-ranking priest. Today's visitors can walk through its elegant interior and then enjoy the serene harmony of the surrounding garden, enlivened with colorful carp playing under a gentle waterfall.

The Japanese House and its garden are a part of the surrounding **Horticultural Center**, a lovely place for a stroll through the gardens and woods. Also nearby is **Memorial Hall**, the centerpiece of the Centennial Exposition of 1876 and one of the few surviving structures from that great national celebration. Until 1928 it was also the home of the Philadelphia Museum of Art, and now serves as the Fairmount Park headquarters.

*THE BARNES FOUNDATION (12), 300 N. Latch's Lane, Merion, PA 19066, ☎ 610-667-0290. *Gallery hours: Fri.–Sat. 9:30–5, Sun. 12:30–5, Sept.–June. Summer hours vary. Admission $5, audio tour $5. Hours and admission policies subject to change. Limited capacity, call ahead. Individual reservations* ☎ *610-664-7917, for groups of 10 or more* ☎ *610-664-5191.* ⑤.

If you love art, you should make every possible effort to experience The Barnes Foundation, even though visits there can be problematic. The first thing to understand about The Barnes is that it is an educational institution, not a museum. Within its walls, however, resides one of the finest collections anywhere on Earth of Post-Impressionist and early French modern art, including absolutely first-rate works by Renoir, Cézanne, Matisse, Picasso, Modigliani, Seurat, Monet, and Manet. As the noted Paris art dealer Ambroise Vollard said, "A visit to The Barnes Foundation is in itself worth the trip to America." Or at least to Philadelphia. In addition to the famed French artists, there are wonderful examples of African art, antique furniture, ceramics, wrought iron, and Native American jewelry.

Dr. Albert Barnes (1872–1951) was born in a working-class Philadelphia neighborhood, became an M.D., and later developed an antiseptic product, Argyrol, that earned him a vast fortune. His interests in psychology, philosophy, and art led him to form his own theories about art appreciation. This, combined with his strong social convictions and respect for the common man, resulted in the creation of The Barnes Foundation in 1922, to which he devoted his full time after 1929. A visit here is enhanced by the surrounding 12-acre arboretum, which supplements the educational programs of the Foundation.

Germantown, Chestnut Hill, and Manayunk

hree very distinct neighborhoods—villages, really—lie clustered together in the northwestern reaches of Philadelphia. Each has its own atmosphere, its own treasures, and its own reason for being. All three offer first-rate attractions that are a bit off the beaten path, and combine to form the focus of an enjoyable daytrip experience.

Germantown Avenue, the "Great Road" of Colonial times that stretches from the Delaware River's edge out into the northwestern suburbs, was once an Indian trail. The area known as Germantown was first settled in 1683 by 13 German families, the first community of Germans in the colonies. By the mid-18th century, wealthy city dwellers began building large summer estates on this hill to escape the heat and congestion of Philadelphia. In 1793 George Washington moved the United States government here for a month to avoid a yellow fever epidemic in town. Washington was here earlier, during the 1777 Battle of Germantown, which he lost. New battles rage today; despite its glorious history and its being a National Historic Landmark, Germantown Avenue has sadly declined and now fights off the encroachments of crime and poverty. Still, the great mansions of history remain, many fully restored and open to visitors.

Heading north on Germantown Avenue brings you to Chestnut Hill, the highest point in Philadelphia, where the scene changes dramatically. This is one of the finest residential neighborhoods in the city, well known for its exclusive shops, galleries, and restaurants, as well as for a thoroughly charming village atmosphere. It is also home to the Morris Arboretum, perhaps the star attraction of this trip.

Manayunk, all the way down on the banks of the Schuylkill River, thrived as an industrial mill town until recent times. Fortunately, it was saved by its colorful canal and riverside location—attracting many young professionals to this newly-fashionable address. Trendy Manayunk's many delightful restaurants and cafés make it the perfect place to end your daytrip.

GETTING THERE:

The only *really* practical way to make this trip is by car. Take Germantown Avenue from its intersection with PA-611 (Broad Street) or US-1 (Roosevelt Boulevard) and follow it northwest past the various sites and into Chestnut Hill. Along the way Germantown Avenue becomes US-422. Continue on this past the Woodmere Museum, crossing the Wissahickon Creek and turning right on Northwestern Avenue to the Morris Arboretum. Return via Wissahickon Drive and Green Lane to Manayunk. Main Street and Ridge Avenue will bring you back to Center City.

It is possible to visit some—but not all—of the sites via public transportation. Bus Route 23 runs from Center City up Germantown Avenue as far as Chestnut Hill, which is also served by the R-7 and R-8 commuter rail lines. Manayunk is a stop on the R-6 commuter rail line.

PRACTICALITIES:

The historic sites of Germantown follow an erratic schedule. Check the listings carefully, and then call ahead to be certain. An exception is Cliveden, which is closed on Mondays through Wednesdays, and January through March. The Woodmere Museum is closed on Mondays and holidays. The Morris Arboretum is open every day of the year except Thanksgiving, December 24–31, and New Year's Day. Chestnut Hill and Manayunk can be visited virtually any time.

For further information, stop by the friendly **Philadelphia Visitors Center** at 16th Street & John F. Kennedy Blvd., Philadelphia, PA 19102, ☎ 215-636-1666 or 888-90-PHILA, Internet: www.libertynet.org/phila-visitor. The **Chestnut Hill Visitor Center** is at 8426 Germantown Ave., ☎ 215-247-6696, Internet: www.chestnuthillpa.com. For **Manayunk** information ☎ 215-482-9565, Internet: www.manayunk.com.

FOOD AND DRINK:

Chestnut Hill offers quite a few good restaurants, and Manayunk is a diner's paradise. From an embarrassment of riches, here's just a few choices:

In Chestnut Hill:

Rollers (8705 Germantown Ave., at Bethlehem Pike, in Top-of-the-Hill Plaza) Superb, creative cuisine in a bright, bustling little bistro. ☎ 215-242-1771. X: Mon., Sun. in summer. $$

Cresheim Cottage Café (7402 Germantown Ave. Near Mt. Airy) Traditional American cuisine in a 1748 cottage. ☎ 215-248-4365. $$

Cafette (8136 Ardleigh St., a block east of Germantown Ave., at Abington Ave.) A good value for light lunches, vegetarian and otherwise. ☎ 215-242-4220. $

Best of British (8513 Germantown Ave. Near Highland St.) Light lunch in a tearoom. ☎ 215-242-8848. $

In Manayunk:

Sonoma (4411 Main St., between Gay and Levering) An extremely popular place for "Italifornia" cuisine — modern American combined with classic Italian. Sunday brunch. ☎ 215-483-9400. $$

Hikaru (4348 Main St. at Grape) Sushi and other Japanese delights in a greenhouse or shoeless on the tatami. ☎ 215-487-3500. X: Weekend lunch. $$

Arroyo Grille (1 Leverington Ave. at Venice Island, off Main St.) Southwestern dishes on an island, indoors or on the deck. Vast selection of tequilas. ☎ 215-487-1400. $$

Café Zesty (4382 Main St.) Greco-Roman specialties, with pizza at lunch. ☎ 215-483-6226. X: Mon., Tues. $ and $$

Le Bus Main Street (4266 Main St., between Cotton & Rector) Classic American dishes with a family orientation. Weekend brunch. ☎ 215-487-2663. $ and $$

LOCAL ATTRACTIONS:

Numbers in parentheses correspond to numbers on the map.

GRUMBLETHORPE (1), 5267 Germantown Ave. at Penn St., ☎ 215-843-4820. *Usually open Apr. to mid-Dec., Tues., Thurs., and Sun. 10–4. Admission $3.*

Germantown's first summer mansion, Grumblethorpe was built in 1744 of local materials by a rich Quaker merchant named John Wister. During the Revolution, it was used by the British to house soldiers; a bloodstain from their General Agnew is still visible. The furnishings are from the mid-18th century, and the garden is maintained as it was at that time.

DRESHLER-MORRIS HOUSE (2), 5442 Germantown Ave., ☎ 215-596-1748. *Usually open April to mid-Dec., Tues.–Sat. 1–4. Closed legal holidays. Adults $1, students 50¢.*

George Washington lived here in the fall of 1793 as a yellow fever epidemic raged in Philadelphia, and liked it so much that he returned for six weeks the following summer. In effect, this was the White House, where many of the affairs of the new United States Government were carried out. Sixteen years earlier, however, it served as headquarters for General Sir William Howe's British command after his victory over Washington at the Battle of Germantown. Now operated by the National Park Service, the house and its lovely garden have been beautifully restored.

GERMANTOWN HISTORICAL SOCIETY (3), 5501 Germantown Ave. at Market Sq., ☎ 215-844-1683. *Open Mon.–Fri. 10–4, Sun. 1–5. Admission $4,*

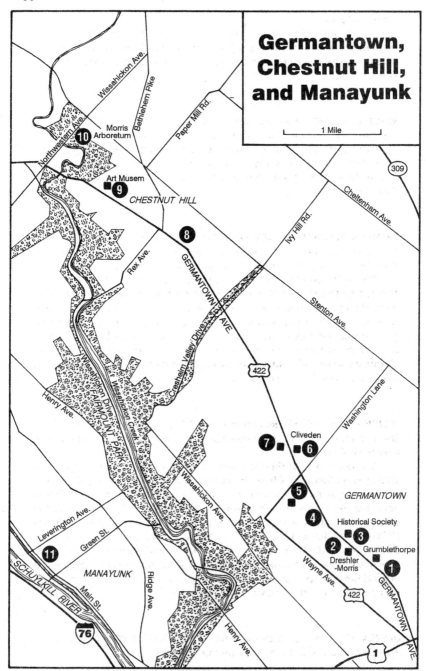

Germantown, Chestnut Hill, and Manayunk

1 Mile

under 13 $2. &.

The history of America's first German settlement, from 1683 to the present, is explored in this museum through its collections of furnishings, costumes, china, silver, tools and farm implements, dolls, toys, and the like.

WYCK (4), 6026 Germantown Ave. at Walnut Lane, ☎ 215-848-1690. *Usually open Apr. to mid-Dec., Tues., Thurs., and Sat. 1–4. Nominal admission.*

Nine generations of the same Quaker family lived here, and left behind their furnishings and heirlooms for you to see. One part of the house dates from about 1700, making it the oldest extant structure in Germantown.

EBENEZER MAXWELL MANSION (5), 200 W. Tulpehocken St. at Greene St., two blocks southwest of Germantown Ave., ☎ 215-438-1861. *Usually open Apr.–Dec., Fri.–Sun. 1–4. Adults $4, seniors $3, ages 3–12 $2.*

Philadelphia's only Victorian house museum was built in 1859 in the Norman Gothic style, with an exuberant mixture of then-popular architectural motifs. The interior is full of exotic faux finishes: slate painted to look like marble, walls papered to resemble stone, and ordinary wood grained like expensive hardwoods. There are, of course, heavy Victorian furnishings, and gadgets from the new Industrial Age, as well as a proper Victorian garden. All in all, this is the perfect haunted house, a scene right out of a Charles Addams cartoon.

***CLIVEDEN** (6), 6401 Germantown Ave., ☎ 215-848-1777. *Open Apr.–Dec., Thurs.–Sun., noon–4. Closed major holidays. Adults $6, ages 6-18 $4. & with advance notice.*

Surely the best of the Germantown mansions, Cliveden was built in 1763 by jurist Benjamin Chew and remained in the Chew family until 1972, when it was given to the National Trust for Historic Preservation. It was here that the Battle of Germantown was fought in 1777, and here that George Washington was defeated by the British. Marks of that battle are still visible, both on the walls and on the garden statuary. The estate occupies six beautifully landscaped acres, complete with stables, coach house, cookhouse, and washhouse. Inside the lavish Georgian-style mansion are original furnishings from over two centuries of the Chew family, including Chippendale furniture and Chinese porcelains.

UPSALA (7), 6430 Germantown Ave., ☎ 215-842-1798. *Usually open Apr.–Dec., Tues. and Thurs. 1–4. Nominal admission.*

The Upsala mansion was built in 1798 on the site where George Washington's troops placed their artillery to fire on the Brits in Cliveden. A fine example of the Federal style, it is filled with period furnishings.

CHESTNUT HILL (8), a haven from the hubbub of Center City, enjoys a village-like atmosphere despite the sophistication of its shops, galleries, and restaurants. This is indeed one of Philadelphia's most desirable residential neighborhoods, and a very pleasant place to visit. Park your car on a side street somewhere near Bethlehem Pike, opposite the Chestnut Hill West SEPTA train station, and stroll up and down Germantown Avenue, making forays into the little streets on either side. *Visitor Center, 8426 Germantown Ave., ☎ 215-247-6696, Internet: www.chestnuthillpa.com.*

WOODMERE ART MUSEUM (9), 9201 Germantown Ave., ☎ 215-247-0476. *Open Tues.–Sat. 10–5, Sun. 1–5. Closed major holidays. Donation. ᕦ by advance notice.*

Especially rich in works by 19th-century American artists such as Benjamin West and Frederick Church, the Woodmere also features sculpture, tapestries, ivories, porcelains, Oriental rugs, and other treasures from the collections of Charles Knox Smith. There are special exhibitions of contemporary artists from the Delaware Valley; call ahead for a schedule.

*MORRIS ARBORETUM OF THE UNIVERSITY OF PENNSYLVANIA (10), 100 Northwestern Ave., between Germantown and Stenton avenues in Chestnut Hill, ☎ 215-247-5777, Internet: www.upenn.edu/morris. *Open daily all year round, 10–4, closing at 5 on weekends from Apr.–Oct. Closed Christmas to New Year's Day. Adults $6, seniors over 65 $5, students with ID $4, under 6 free. Gift shop. ᕦ, main paths are paved, with gentle grades.*

Back in 1887 the brother-and-sister team of John and Lydia Morris, heirs to an industrial fortune, created the summer estate of Compton in Chestnut Hill. Despite poor soil, they managed to surround their mansion with a superb landscape and plant collection devoted to beauty and knowledge. Today, the mansion is gone, but the arboretum lives on, as magnificent as ever. Since 1932 it has belonged to the University of Pennsylvania as an educational resource, and a place of inspired beauty for all who come to visit.

Pick up a map at the Visitor Center and follow the paths through such treats as the ***Rose Garden**, the ***Victorian Fernery**, the **Sculpture Garden**, the **Log Cabin**, the **English Park**, the **Temple of Mercury**, and the **Swan Pond**. In all, more than 9,000 labeled plants are displayed throughout the 92-acre estate, with paths wandering through woods, meadows, past scenic overlooks, and along the Wissahickon Creek.

MANAYUNK (11) is not far in miles, but worlds apart in atmosphere from genteel Chestnut Hill. Located on the banks of the Schuylkill River, its name in the Native American language means "where we go to drink." That name is especially fitting today as smart young Philadelphians flock here to enjoy the booming restaurants, bars, and cafés along its waterfront and Main Street.

Manayunk developed after the construction of its canal in 1819 opened the way to trade and provided the waterpower needed for industrial growth. By the mid-19th century it had become the "Manchester of America," a vital part of Philadelphia's industrial heritage. Today, the town has successfully adjusted to the new economic realities, transforming its watery location and old factories into a smart center for shopping, recreation, and good living. Come and enjoy, and be sure to take a walk along the restored canal.

Beyond South Philadelphia

S outh of South Street, south of the Italian Market, lie several scattered but eminently worthy attractions encompassing a variety of interests. You'll have to pick and choose among them, and plot your route accordingly. Those traveling by car can get at least a taste of each if they wish, or spend more time at just one or two, but there is simply no practical way to link them all together by public transportation.

The sites range from one of America's leading spectator sports complexes to an unusual museum celebrating the culture of the Delaware Valley's first European settlers, the Swedes. A bloody battle of the Revolutionary War is brought to life at isolated Fort Mifflin. Still within city limits, the John Heinz National Wildlife Refuge offers a genuine wilderness experience, while those with a horticultural bend will surely appreciate Historic Bartram's Garden.

GETTING THERE:

By car, just follow Broad Street (PA-611) south to Pattison Avenue for the Sports Complex and the American Swedish Museum.

Continue south on Broad Street to I-95, taking that south to Exit 13. From there follow signs to Island Avenue and Fort Mifflin.

Return to Island Avenue and head north on it to Lindbergh Boulevard. Turn left there to 86th Street and the entrance to the John Heinz National Wildlife Refuge.

Head north on Lindbergh Boulevard to 54th Street for the Historic Bartram's Garden.

By public transportation: The Sports Complex and the American Swedish Museum are easily reached via the Broad Street subway to the end of the line at Pattison Avenue. Fort Mifflin cannot be reached by public transit. It is possible to get to the Wildlife Refuge via Bus Route 37, and to Bartram's Garden via Bus Route 52.

PRACTICALITIES:

The American Swedish Museum is closed on Mondays and holidays, while Fort Mifflin operates from April through November, on Wednesdays through Sundays. All of the other sites are accessible daily.

For the Wildlife Refuge, be sure to wear comfortable walking shoes, and if possible bring binoculars.

For further information, stop by the friendly **Philadelphia Visitors Center** at 16th Street & John F. Kennedy Blvd., Philadelphia, PA 19102, ☎ 215-636-1666 or 888-90-PHILA, Internet: www.libertynet.org/phila-visitor.

FOOD AND DRINK:

There are precious few restaurants in the area covered by this trip, although you are not far from the South Street/Italian Market neighborhood (page 39). Here are a few choices more-or-less near the sports complex:

Jaws (Holiday Inn Philadelphia Stadium, 10th & Packer Ave., just northeast of the sports complex) Steaks, pasta, and seafood with a sports motif. ☎ 215-755-9500. $$

Melrose Diner (1501 Snyder St., Passyunk Ave., a block west of Broad St.) "Everybody who knows goes to Melrose" goes the jingle for this classic American diner that never closes—a Philadelphia institution. ☎ 215-467-6644. $

Tony Luke's (39 E. Oregon Ave., near the Front St. exit of I-95 at the Walt Whitman Bridge) Great sandwiches with an attitude; outdoor tables. ☎ 215-551-5725. X: Sun. $

Celebre's Pizzeria (1536 Packer Ave., near Broad St. at 15th, a few blocks north of the sports complex) Excellent thick-crust pizza in a strip mall with parking. ☎ 215-467-3255. $

If you'd prefer to pack a **picnic lunch**, you'll find places to eat it in the park adjacent to the American Swedish Museum, and at Fort Mifflin.

LOCAL ATTRACTIONS:

Numbers in parentheses correspond to numbers on the map.

Philadelphia has long been renowned as a sports city, with such top professional teams as the Eagles, the Flyers, the 76ers, and the Phillies. These and other pro teams are based at the vast, sprawling **Sports Complex** (1) at the southern end of Broad Street. While you should really come for a game—or the circus, ice shows, rock concerts, or other events—you might just stop by for a look at the three major venues clustered together here. **Veterans Stadium** is home to the **Phillies** (National League baseball, ☎ 215-463-1000) and the **Eagles** (NFL football, ☎ 215-463-5500), as well as the Temple University **Owls** (football, ☎ 215-204-TIXX). The **First Union Spectrum** houses the **Phantoms** (American Hockey League, ☎ 215-465-4522) and the **KiXX** (National Professional Soccer League, (888-888-KIXX). At the southern end, the **First Union Center** features the **Flyers** (National

Hockey League, ☎ 215-465-4500), the **76ers** (National Basketball Association, ☎ 215-339-7600), and the **Wings** (indoor lacrosse, ☎ 215-389-WING).

A short stroll west on Pattison Avenue brings you to the:

AMERICAN SWEDISH HISTORICAL MUSEUM (2), 1900 Pattison Ave., ☎ 215-389-1776, Internet: www.libertynet.org/ashm. *Open Tues.–Fri. 10–4, weekends noon–4. Closed legal holidays. Adults $5, seniors 60+ and students with ID $4, under 12 free.*

Long before William Penn and his Quakers came to Philadelphia, the Swedes were already well established in the Delaware Valley. Over 350 years (1638 to the present) of Swedish culture in the New World are explored in this unique museum, modeled after Eriksberg Castle, a 17th-century Swedish manor house. The museum stands on land that was once part of the original New Sweden Colony. Exhibits here include historical paintings, a Viking sword, a walk-through Swedish farmhouse, household artifacts, achievements by famous Swedish-Americans, and even modern Swedish works of art. Swedish holiday traditions are, of course, celebrated here, including *Julmarknad* (Christmas Market), a winter pea soup dinner, *Valborgsmässoafton* (to welcome spring), *Midsommarfest* (summer festival), and the annual crayfish feast.

FORT MIFFLIN (3), Island Ave. and Fort Mifflin Rd., ☎ 215-492-1881, Internet: www.spiritof76.com/ftmifflin. *Open April through Nov., Wed.–Sun., 10–4. Adults $4, seniors 64+ and students with ID $2. Tours. Picnic facilities. Nature trails.*

The British built this fort in 1772, but in the end it was used against them. For 40 days in the fall of 1777, some 450 patriots fought fiercely to prevent British supply ships from bringing needed munitions to General Howe's redcoat garrison in Philadelphia, buying time for George Washington to lead his troops to safety at Valley Forge. In the end they lost as the fort fell to ruin under ceaseless bombardment, with a total of some 340 brave men giving their lives in the cause of freedom.

Fort Mifflin was rebuilt in the early 1800s and used as a prison for Confederate soldiers, deserters, and political prisoners during the Civil War. It remained in use, mostly as a munitions storage facility, until 1962. Now fully restored, it offers living history demonstrations, militia drills, educational programs, and guided tours.

JOHN HEINZ NATIONAL WILDLIFE REFUGE AT TINICUM (4), 86th St. & Lindbergh Blvd., ☎ 215-365-3118 or 215-521-0662. *Open daily, 8:30–sunset. Visitor Contact Station open daily 9–4. Free. Trails. Fishing (with state*

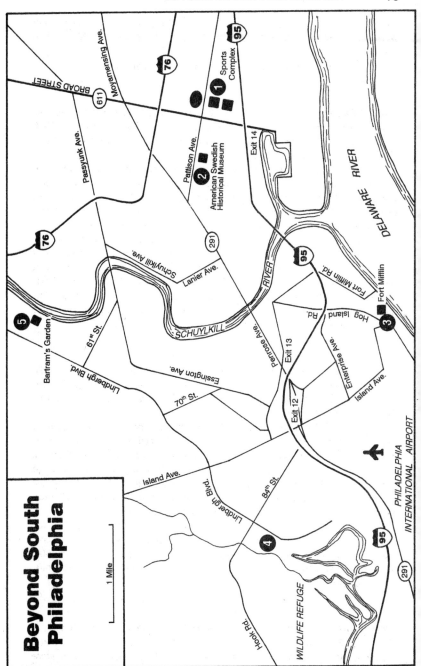

Beyond South
Philadelphia

1 Mile

license). Canoe launch. Bicycling.

Managed by the U.S. Fish and Wildlife Service, this 1,200-acre preserve is practically next door to the Philadelphia International Airport, yet it is a step back into the wilderness that existed before the first Europeans arrived. More than 280 species of birds have been recorded here, with more than 85 species making their nests in the refuge. In addition, numerous small animals such as opossums, raccoons, muskrats, the red-bellied turtle, and the southern leopard frog make this their home.

Visits should begin at the **Visitor Contact Station** near the main entrance, where you can obtain a map. From there you have a choice of some ten miles of trails. The **East Impoundment Trail** is the most popular, leading a bit more than three miles around a 145-acre watery impoundment, with observations areas at strategic points. For the ambitious, other trails extend beyond this into more remote areas.

HISTORIC BARTRAM'S GARDEN (5), 54th St. & Lindbergh Blvd., ☎ 215-729-5281, Internet: www.libertynet.org/bartram. *Garden open daily 9–4. House open April–Dec., Wed.–Sun. noon–4; rest of year Wed.–Fri. noon–4. Grounds free. Tour $3. Partially &.*

John Bartram (1699–1777), the "Father of American Horticulture," traveled widely to gather the native trees, shrubs, and flowers that formed the garden he began in 1728. Two of his sons, William and John Jr., continued the work, maintaining America's first botanic garden and completing the first catalog of American plants. The garden was visited by the likes of Benjamin Franklin, George Washington, Thomas Jefferson, and other notables, and is now preserved much as it was at that time. Bartram's original 18th-century stone house, barn, greenhouse, and dovecote may also be visited on tours.

Section III

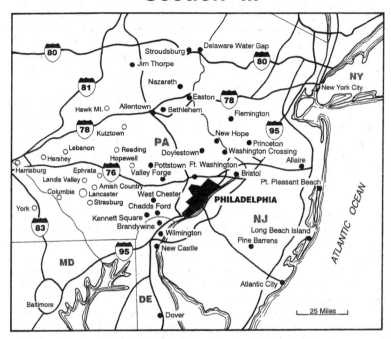

DAYTRIPS FROM
PHILADELPHIA

J ust outside of Philadelphia, and extending for up to a hundred miles in all directions, is one of the greatest concentrations of varied sights in the nation. From the Colonial charms of Chadds Ford to the magnificent estates of the Delaware tycoons, from the unspoiled wilderness of the Jersey Pine Barrens to the glitter of Atlantic City casinos, and from the early industrial sites of Bethlehem to the natural splendor of the Pocono Mountains, this region offers a host of destinations for one-day excursions. Whether your interests lie in history, art, nature, sports, dining, shopping, or simply relaxing on the beach, you'll have no trouble finding just the right daytrip to match your desires with your resources. And, if you have more than a day at your disposal, why not combine several of these trips into a mini-vacation?

All of the Pennsylvania Dutch Country daytrips described in Section IV, beginning on page 203, can also be made from Philadelphia, although you'll find it more convenient to explore them from a base in or near Lancaster.

Chadds Ford

I t's hard to know where to begin when you're exploring Pennsylvania's historic Brandywine Valley. In fact, there are so many attractions that it takes two separate daytrips to really appreciate the area. This trip brings you to Chadds Ford, site of a major Revolutionary War battle, and home to the Wyeth family of artists. The following trip, beginning on page 81, features what many regard as America's finest horticultural gardens as well as a look at the mushroom center of the nation. Trip 33 (pages 181-186) covers the southern part of the valley in Delaware, home to fabulous estates. Since they are only a few miles apart, you could, of course, combine elements of each into your own custom itinerary.

The Brandywine is a special river, both in history and in natural beauty. Not very large, or long, it rises in the Welsh hills of southeastern Pennsylvania and flows some 60 miles south into the Delaware at Wilmington. Its waters powered the mills of early industry, created vast fortunes, and provided the setting for one of the pivotal battles of the American Revolution.

Artists have long been attracted to the valley, capturing its moods in what was to become a uniquely American style of illustration. One of its leading practitioners, Howard Pyle (1853–1911), worked here and helped develop the talents of such younger artists as Maxfield Parrish and N.C. Wyeth. Two succeeding generations of the Wyeth family, Andrew and Jamie, have continued the artistic heritage of the Brandywine Valley, which is best represented at the delightful Brandywine River Museum in Chadds Ford.

GETTING THERE:

By car, Chadds Ford is 25 miles southwest of downtown Philadelphia via US-1.

PRACTICALITIES:

Most of the major attractions are open daily, with some closing on Christmas or on a few holidays. The Brandywine Battlefield closes on Mondays and holidays (except Memorial Day, July 4, and Labor Day). For some of the minor sights, however, you'll have to come on a weekend between May and September. Each listing gives specific details.

For further information contact the **Delaware County Convention & Visitors Bureau**, 200 E. State St., Media, PA 19063, ☎ 610-565-3679 or 800-343-3983., Internet: www.delcocvb.org. Another good source is the **Chester**

County Tourist Bureau, 601 Westtown Rd., Suite 170, P.O. Box 2747, West Chester PA 19380, ☎ 610-344-6365 or 800-228-9933, fax 610-344-6999, Internet: www.brandywinevalley.com. They have a handy **Tourist Information Center** on US-1 at Kennett Square, in an historic Quaker Meeting House of 1885 located next to the entrance to Longwood Gardens.

FOOD AND DRINK:

Some good choices in and around Chadds Ford are:

Crier in the Country (US-1 at Glen Mills) Renowned Continental cuisine in a Victorian mansion. Reserve. ☎ 610-358-2411. X: Mon., weekend lunches. $$$

Chadds Ford Inn (US-1 at PA-100, near the Brandywine River Museum) An historic 18th-century inn noted for its American and Continental cuisine, and Colonial atmosphere. Reservations are advised, ☎ 610-388-7361. X: Fri. and Sat. lunch; brunch on Sun. $$ and $$$

Hank's Place (US-1 at PA-100, near the Brandywine River Museum) Everyone in Wyeth Country comes to Hank's for its simple, homestyle cooking. Nothing fancy here. ☎ 610-388-7061. $

Brandywine River Museum Restaurant (inside the museum) A small and exceptionally pleasant cafeteria overlooking the river, reserved for museum visitors. ☎ 610-388-2700. X: Mon. & Tues. from Jan.–March. $

LOCAL ATTRACTIONS:

Numbers in parentheses correspond to numbers on the map.

BRANDYWINE BATTLEFIELD STATE PARK (1), Route US-1, Chadds Ford, PA 19317, ☎ 610-459-3342. *Open Tues.–Sat. 9–5, Sun. noon–5, grounds remain open until 8 from Memorial Day through Labor Day. Closed Mon. and non-summer holidays. Visitor Center, museum, and grounds free. Tours: Adults $3.50, seniors $2.50, children 6–12 $1.50, under 6 free. Museum. Gift shop. Picnic facilities. &. for Visitor Center & museum. Grounds are hilly with gravel paths.*

General Washington and his Colonial troops may have lost the Battle of Brandywine on September 11, 1777, but they inflicted such damage on the British that the French were convinced into joining the fray and helping to bring about final victory. The whole story is told in an interesting slide show given frequently in the Visitor Center. There's also a museum of artifacts and dioramas that brings the story to life.

Elsewhere in the 50-acre park are the restored **headquarters** of General Washington and the Marquis de Lafayette, looking much as they did in 1777. Their interiors may be explored on guided tours that begin at the Visitor Center, or you can just walk around outside and enjoy the views. This is a fine place for a picnic.

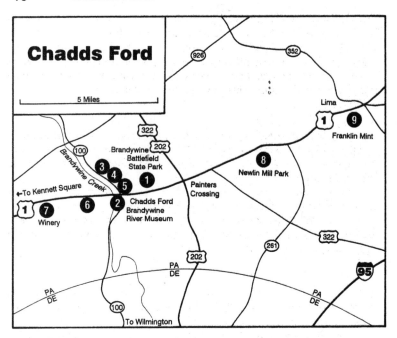

Continue west on US-1 for about a mile to the:

*BRANDYWINE RIVER MUSEUM (2), Route US-1, Chadds Ford, PA 19317, ☎ 610-388-2700, fax 610-388-1197, Internet: www.libertynet.org/bmuse. *Open daily except Christmas, 9:30–4:30. Adults $5, seniors, students, and children 6–12 $2.50, under 6 free. Inquire about tours to nearby N.C. Wyeth Studio, offered Apr.–Nov. Gift shop. Cafeteria, closed Mon.–Tues. from Jan.–March. ♿, use entrance on river side near reserved parking.*

Whether you're an art fan or not, you'll almost certainly enjoy a visit to the Brandywine River Museum. This is the best place to see works of the Brandywine River School, a quintessential American style that bridges the gap between fine art and popular illustration. From the local land-scape paintings of the 19th century to the fantasy worlds created by Maxfield Parrish and N.C. Wyeth in the early 20th, the works shown here appeal to a wide range of tastes. Andrew Wyeth, the latter's son, was born in Chadds Ford in 1917 and became one of America's leading fine artists, a tradition continued by his son Jamie. Both are well represented with major works in this museum, as are other artistic members of the Wyeth family.

The museum, founded in 1971, is housed in a restored gristmill of 1864 set on the banks of the Brandywine. Complementing the original structure is a large, modern wing of 1984, with glass towers that enable visitors to take in the local scenery along with the art. The self-service restaurant is a great place for either lunch or light refreshments.

Be sure to stroll in the riverside garden adjacent to the museum. The **River Trail** is a mile-long nature path leading from here along the water's edge, under Route 1, and on a boardwalk over a marsh to the next attraction, John Chads House. This can also be reached by car.

JOHN CHADS HOUSE (3), Route 100, a quarter-mile north of Route 1, Chadds Ford, PA 19317, ☎ 610-388-7376, Internet: www.de.psu.edu/cfhs. *Open May–Sept., weekends only, noon–5; otherwise by appointment. Adults $3, children $1.*

Eighteenth-century life in the hamlet of Chadds Ford is described by guides in Colonial dress as they show visitors through this stone farmhouse of 1725. You may also get to see baking in the beehive oven. Just across the road is an 18th-century springhouse, used as a schoolhouse in the 1840s. Related material is shown nearby at:

THE BARN (4), Route 100, a quarter-mile north of Route 1, Chadds Ford, PA 19317, ☎ 610-388-7376, Internet: www.de.psu.edu/cfhs. *Open May–Sept., weekends only, noon–5. Adults $3, children $1.*

Headquarters of the Chadds Ford Historical Society, this museum displays local furniture and furnishings from the 18th century. Just to the south is the:

CHRISTIAN C. SANDERSON MUSEUM (5), Route 100, 100 yards north of Route 1, Chadds Ford, PA 19317, ☎ 610-388-6545. *Open weekends, Memorial Day, July 4, and Labor Day; 1–4:30; and by appointment. Donation requested.*

Chris Sanderson was a close friend of the Wyeths, an all-around Renaissance man, and an incurable collector. The latter trait resulted in a house full of all sorts of treasures including works by the Wyeths, but mostly with the strangest mementos that you can possibly imagine. A sample of these includes melted ice from the South Pole, sand from digging the Panama Canal, Easter eggs from 1886, and a piece of the bandage used on President Lincoln after he was shot.

Continue west on US-1 a short distance to the:

BARNS-BRINTON HOUSE (6), Route 1, Chadds Ford, PA 19317, ☎ 610-388-7376, Internet: www.de.psu.edu/cfhs. *Open May–Sept., weekends only, noon–5; otherwise by appointment. Adults $3, children $1. Crafts demonstrations.*

Guides in Colonial dress will take you through this brick tavern of 1714, restored and authentically furnished by the Chadds Ford Historical Society. Listed on the National Register of Historic Places, the structure is noted for its fine interior woodwork and exterior brickwork.

A bit farther west on US-1 is the:

CHADDSFORD WINERY (7), Route 1, Chadds Ford, PA 19317, ☎ 610-388-6221, Internet: www.chaddsford.com. *Open Tues.–Sat. 10–5:30, also Mon. from Apr.–Dec., Sun. noon–5. Wine shop. Special events.* &.

Tasting the local country wines is always interesting, and these are well worth the sampling. You can watch the entire process of making wine, from the crushing of the grapes to the final bottling. Then, after tasting them, you can purchase a bottle or so right from the winemakers.

Continuing west on US-1 takes you into the area described on the next daytrip, Kennett Square. Those returning to Philadelphia may want to make stops at:

NEWLIN MILL PARK (8), 219 South Cheyney Rd., Glen Mills, PA 19342, ☎ 610-459-2359. *Open daily 8–dusk. Adults and children over 5 $1. Picnic facilities & fishing by reservation, hiking trails.*

An operating stone gristmill of 1704 is the highlight of this reconstructed Colonial village, operated by a non-profit foundation. There's also a furnished miller's house of 1739, a springhouse, a blacksmith's shop, and a log cabin—all set in 150 acres of land and forest.

In another three miles you'll come to:

THE FRANKLIN MINT MUSEUM (9), Franklin Center, PA 19091, ☎ 610-459-6168. *Open Mon.–Sat., 9:30–4:30, Sun. 1–4:30. Closed major holidays. Free. Gift shop.* &.

You've seen their ads—now see their treasures. Prized as collectibles by many (and considered high-class kitsch by others), the future heirlooms offered by the Franklin Mint are hard to categorize, but always interesting. There are original works of art by Andrew Wyeth and Norman Rockwell, along with sculptures in porcelain, crystal, pewter, and bronze. Dolls, miniature cars, classic books, coins, philatelics, jewelry, and much, much more round out the collection.

Kennett Square

Another aspect of Pennsylvania's Brandywine Valley can be explored just a few miles down the road from the previous daytrip to Chadds Ford. Here, around Kennett Square, is one of the most magnificent gardens to be found anywhere; one that draws thousands of visitors from all around the globe.

The town is also renowned as the "Mushroom Capital of the World," which makes for some delicious dining as well as for an interesting visit to a museum devoted solely to the fungus. For those able to stay overnight, both this trip and the previous one combine well with the ones to Delaware's Brandywine Valley (page 181) and Wilmington (page 187).

GETTING THERE:

By car, Kennett Square is about 35 miles southwest of downtown Philadelphia via US-1.

PRACTICALITIES:

Anytime is a good time to visit Kennett Square as the Longwood Gardens are open daily throughout the year, and the Mushroom Museum every day except New Year's, Easter, Thanksgiving, and Christmas. For further information, be sure to stop at the friendly **Brandywine Valley Tourist Information Center**, just outside the entrance to Longwood Gardens. Located in a historic Quaker Meeting House of 1855, the center has interesting exhibits and can furnish you with a wealth of free information on each site, and on the many special events held throughout the year. *Route 1, Kennett Square, PA 19348.* ☎ *610-388-2900 or 800-228-9933, Internet: www.brandywinevalley.com. Open daily 10–6, closing at 5 from Oct.–Mar.*

FOOD AND DRINK:

The Terrace (in Longwood Gardens) Both a cafeteria and a full-service restaurant, this delightful spot has both indoor and outdoor tables for garden visitors. Reservations are accepted for the restaurant. ☎ 610-388-6771. Restaurant X: Jan., Feb. $ and $$

Taqueria Moroleon (15 New Garden Shopping Center, on Baltimore Pike, US-1), in Kennett Square) Authentic Mexican cuisine in an unprepossessing setting. ☎ 610-444-1210. $ and $$

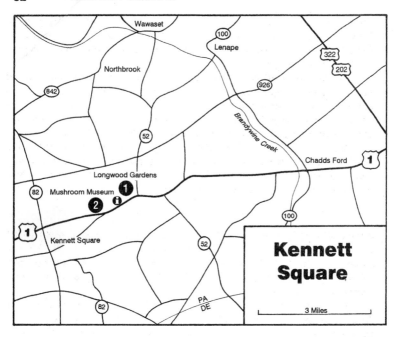

In addition, check out the listings for Chadds Ford (Trip 9), West Chester (Trip 11), and Delaware's Brandywine Valley (Trip 33).

LOCAL ATTRACTIONS:
Numbers in parentheses correspond to numbers on the map.

*LONGWOOD GARDENS (1), Route 1, Kennett Square, PA 19348-0501, ☎ 610-388-1000 or 800-737-5500, Internet: www.longwoodgardens.org. *Open every day of the year, 9–6, closing at 5 from Nov.–March. Conservatories open at 10. Both are frequently open late into the evening for fountain displays and special events. General admission: Adults $12, $8 on Tues.; youths (16–20) $6; children (6–15) $2; children under 6 free. Inquire about prices for special events. Gift shop. Cafeteria and restaurant. &, wheelchairs available free of charge.*

You'd have to travel all the way to Europe to experience the likes of Longwood, since nowhere else in America will you find such a magnificent horticultural estate. Some 350 of its 1,050 manicured acres are open to the public, offering 11,00 different kinds of plants in exquisite settings. Among the highlights is a complex of enormous ***conservatories** where the weather is perfect all year round, an outdoor ***Italian water garden** right out of a Florentine dream, the estate house of Pierre S. duPont, spectacular fountains, waterfalls, a topiary garden of whimsical shapes, a secluded forest walk, formal rose gardens, and an "idea garden" where you can pick up hints on starting your very own Longwood.

William Penn originally sold Longwood to a Quaker family named Peirce in 1700 for agricultural use. Handed down from generation to generation, it slowly became more of a garden and less of a farm. In 1906 the estate was purchased by a wealthy industrialist, Pierre S. duPont, who created the present gardens and set up an endowment to maintain them.

As you enter through the Visitor Center, be sure to pick up a free map of the estate, which shows where everything is and also indicates an easy route suitable for wheelchairs. Allow a minimum of two hours for this visit—you could easily spend the whole day here.

PHILLIPS MUSHROOM MUSEUM (2), Route 1, Kennett Square, PA 19348, ☎ 610-388-6082 or 800-AH-FUNGI, Internet: http://phillipsmushroom place.com. *Open daily except New Year's, Easter, Thanksgiving, and Christmas, 10–6. Adults $1.25, seniors 75¢, children 7–12 50¢, children 6 and under free. Gift shop.* &.

A museum for a fungus? Yes, indeed. Kennett Square is the center of America's mushroom industry, so it's the best place to find out more about these delicious edibles. Their history, folklore, and culinary mystique are explained through films, dioramas, and exhibits before watching the real things grow. The gift shop sells exotic species that you may never have seen before, along with all manner of items with mushroom motifs.

Trip 11

West Chester Area

Yorou'll have to pick and choose from among the many eclectic offerings in the West Chester area. None are very spectacular, but most
are certainly unusual — and they do cover a wide variety of interests.
So, read through the descriptions below and plot a course to those that
appeal most.

Elements of this trip could be combined with the previous ones to
Chadds Ford and Kennett Square, or with the following one to Valley
Forge.

GETTING THERE:

By car, West Chester is about 30 miles west of downtown Philadelphia
via PA-3, which starts out as Market and Walnut streets in the city. From
there you can plot your own itinerary using the locations given for each
attraction, the map on page 86 as a guide, and a good area road map for
detail.

PRACTICALITIES:

Note the opening times of the attractions carefully as some are a bit
quirky or quite limited. A few require advance reservations. Excellent road
maps for this trip are Rand McNally's *Philadelphia Area* and ADC's *50-Mile
Radius Map of Philadelphia*.

For further information contact the **Chester County Tourist Bureau**, 601
Westtown Rd., Suite 170, P.O. Box 2747, West Chester PA 19380, ☎ 610-344-
6365 or 800-228-9933, fax 610-344-6999, Internet: www.brandywine
valley.com. They have a handy **Tourist Information Center** on US-1 at
Kennett Square, in an historic Quaker Meeting House of 1885 located next
to the entrance to Longwood Gardens.

FOOD AND DRINK:

A few suggestions from among the many restaurants in this affluent
suburban area:

General Warren Inne (West Old Lancaster Hwy, PA-29, in Malvern) A
250-year-old Colonial inn with Continental cuisine served in romantic can-
dlelit dining rooms. Reservations suggested, ☎ 610-296-3637. X: Sun., Sat.
lunch. $$$

Durling-Kurtz House (146 S. Whitford Rd., US-30, a mile west of PA-100, in Exton) Traditional American and Continental cuisine in an 1830's inn. Dress nicely and reserve. ☎ 610-524-1830. X: weekend lunch. $$ and $$$

White Horse Restaurant (at the Sheraton Great Valley Hotel, US-30 at US-202, in Frazer) Dine in a restored Colonial farmhouse, in an atmosphere reminiscent of fox hunts. Reservations suggested, ☎ 610-594-2650. $$ and $$$

Margaret Kuo's Mandarin (190 Lancaster Ave., US-30, half a mile west of PA-29, in Malvern) Mandarin and Szechuan specialties in an attractive Chinese restaurant. ☎ 610-647-5488. $ and $$

China Royal (201-30 W. Lincoln Hwy., by the jct. Of US-30 and PA-100, in Exton) An attractive place with an extensive Chinese menu. ☎ 610-363-1553. $ and $$

Magnolia Grille (West Goshen Center, 971 Paoli Pike, in West Chester) Cajun specialties in a bookstore, BYOB. ☎ 610-696-1661. $ and $$

The Restaurant & The Bar (18 Gay St., at the University exit off US-202, in West Chester) Light contemporary cuisine in a classic bar and grill. ☎ 610-431-0770. $ and $$

Bagel Bistro (PA-113, a mile north of PA-100, Lionville, near Chester Springs) Bagels and homemade soup for a light lunch. ☎ 610-363-0288. X: major holidays, evenings. $

Alternatively, why not have a picnic at Ridley Creek State Park?

LOCAL ATTRACTIONS:

Numbers in parentheses correspond to numbers on the map.

CHESTER COUNTY HISTORICAL SOCIETY (1), 225 N. High St., West Chester, PA 19382, ☎ 610-692-4800, Internet: www.chesco.com/~cchs/. *Museum open Mon.–Sat. 9:30–4:30. Library open Mon.–Tues. and Thurs.–Sat. 9:30–4:30, Wed. 1–8. Museum: Adults $5, seniors $4, under 17 $2.50.*

Chester County's rich past is thoroughly explored in the museum's new History Center, with hands-on exhibits, Early American furniture and decorative arts, regional crafts, artifacts, and the like. There is also a research library dealing with local history and genealogy.

AMERICAN HELICOPTER MUSEUM (2). 1220 American Blvd., Brandywine Airport, off Airport Rd., West Chester, PA 19380, ☎ 610-436-9600, Internet: www.helicoptermuseum.org. *Open Wed.–Sat. 10–5, Sun. noon–5. Adults $5, seniors $4.50, students and children under 12 $3.50, under 3 free. Helicopter rides on weekends by advance reservation and extra charge.*

Three out of four major helicopter manufacturers in America can trace their roots back to this region, where the industry continues to prosper. Fittingly, this unique museum is located in a former helicopter plant

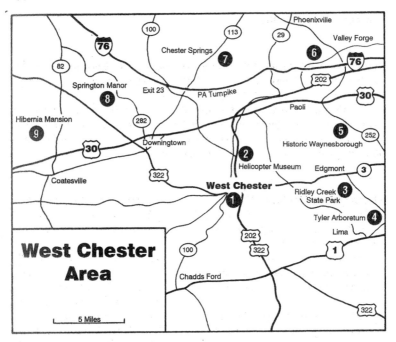

next to the airport. Here visitors can explore the history and technology of vertical flight, and examine (sometimes climbing aboard!) some of the most outstanding helicopters ever built. Among those on display are the second helicopter to successfully fly in America, the prototype of the first mass-produced helicopter, and the world's first commercial machine. Fighting copters from both the Korean and Vietnam wars are on view, augmented with a Bell H-13 in its "MASH" configuration, and a 50-year-old Sikorsky S-51. On weekends you can even go for a *helicopter ride** for an extra charge, but call ahead first.

RIDLEY CREEK STATE PARK (3), Media, PA 19063, seven miles east of West Chester on PA-3, ☎ 610-892-3900, Plantation ☎ 610-566-1725. *Park open daily 8–dusk. Colonial Plantation open Apr.–Nov., weekends only, 10–4. Park free. Plantation: Adults $2.50, seniors and children 4–12 $1.50.*

    This is a great place for a picnic, a hike, a bike ride, or to go fishing. If you happen to come on a weekend in season, you're in for a real treat. That's when the **Colonial Pennsylvania Plantation**, a living history museum located in the park, operates. Here life on a working farm in the 1770s is re-created, with interpreters carrying out the farm chores using the old methods. Even the crops and animals are as authentic as possible, and visitors can even join in the fun.

TYLER ARBORETUM (4), 515 Painter Rd., Media, PA 19063, immediately south of Ridley Creek State Park, ☎ 610-566-5431. *Grounds open daily 8–dusk. Adults $3, children 3–15 $1.*

This historic 650-acre arboretum is renowned for its collection of rare trees, shrubs, and plants. Some 20 miles of hiking trails lead through forests and open fields, and to such features as the fragrance garden, the butterfly garden, and the bird habitat garden.

HISTORIC WAYNESBOROUGH (5), 2049 Waynesborough Rd., Paoli, PA 19301, a mile south of US-30 via PA-252, ☎ 610-647-1779. *Open mid-March to late Dec., Tues. & Thurs. 10–4, Sun. 1–4, closed holidays. Adults $4, seniors and ages 7–18 $3.*

"Mad Anthony" Wayne (1745–96), the Revolutionary War general and hero, was born and lived much of his life here at the Wayne family homestead near Paoli. Seven consecutive generations of the Wayne family have occupied this land since it was first acquired by the general's grandfather in 1724. The present structure, a stately stone house in the Georgian manner, was built a few years later by Wayne's father. Many of the furnishings are contemporary with the general and include his military uniform and various personal possessions. The history of both the family and the house is outlined in an audiovisual presentation.

*WHARTON ESHERICK STUDIO (6), Horseshoe Trail, just west of Valley Forge, P.O. Box 595, Paoli, PA 19301, ☎ 610-644-5822. *Tours by reservation only, Mon.–Fri. 10–4, Sat. 10–5, Sun. 1–5. Closed Jan., Feb., and major holidays. Weekday tours require a minimum charge of $30 per group, but individuals may join a scheduled group. There is no minimum on weekends. Adults $6, children under 12 $3. Call ahead for reservations and directions to the site.*

You'll have to plan ahead for this treat, but it's certainly worthwhile if you have any interest in 20th-century craftsmanship and art. Wharton Esherick (1887–1970) was a leading sculptor, artist, and craftsman who helped create a uniquely American style, ranging from the organic to the Expressionist to the free-form lyrical. It took him 40 years to create this marvelously-sculpted studio, which today is preserved as it was when he lived and worked here. More than 200 of his creations—paintings, woodcuts, sculpture, and furniture—produced between 1920 and 1970 are on open display, where they can be examined closely in a friendly setting that in no way resembles a museum.

HISTORIC YELLOW SPRINGS (7), Art School Rd., P.O. Box 62, Chester Springs, PA 19425, ☎ 610-827-7414. *Open Mon.–Fri. 9–4, closed major holidays. Donation accepted.*

Long before Europeans settled the land, the Lenni Lenape and Susquehanna Indians enjoyed the healing qualities of the mineral-laden waters that bubbled to the surface at Yellow Springs. As early as the 1720, doctors in Philadelphia began sending their patients here to partake of the cure. Within a few decades, the area became a health spa, with bath houses, taverns, and living quarters. During the Revolutionary War, Yellow Springs was used as a hospital for Continental soldiers—in fact, it was the proximity of the springs that helped George Washington to select Valley Forge for his famous winter encampment. After the war, Yellow Springs became more fashionable than ever, attracting the rich, the famous, and the powerful from all over the newly-created United States. No longer used as a spa, the village has been preserved as an historic site and also functions as a notable art center, with many special events throughout the year.

SPRINGTON MANOR FARM (8), 860 Springton Rd., north of US-322, Glenmoore, PA 19343, ☎ 610-942-2450. *Open daily 10–3:30. Free.*

First farmed in the 1730s, Springton Manor is now a demonstration farm where Chester County agricultural practices are displayed, including livestock management and soil conservation. There's a manor house, Victorian gardens, a barn showing the development of farm implements over the years, a petting zoo, a catch-and-release pond, and nature trails.

HIBERNIA MANSION & COUNTY PARK (9), 1 Park Rd., Wagontown, PA 19376, ☎ 610-384-0290. Take PA-82 north from Coatesville for six miles, then turn left on Cedar Knoll Rd. To the park entrance on the left. *Mansion open Memorial Day weekend to mid-Sept., on Sundays from 1–4. Call for tour rates. Park open daily, free.*

During the late 1700s and early 1800s, Hibernia was a prosperous iron plantation with a furnace, forges, rolling mill, and grist mill. Charles Brooke, the owner and ironmaster, built this mansion and the surrounding estate on his considerable profits. It was later sold to one Franklin Swayne, a Philadelphia lawyer who greatly expanded and embellished the property into what you see today, complete with much of Swayne's furniture. The **County Park** features picnicking, fishing, camping, hiking, and playgrounds.

Valley Forge

No battle was ever fought at Valley Forge, yet this encampment is arguably the best-known site of the Revolutionary War. It was here, in the bitter winter of 1777–78, that George Washington's ragtag, hungry army—run out of Philadelphia by the British—set up camp to lick their wounds. Close enough to the enemy to defend against further incursions, their winter quarters occupied easily-defensible high ground protected by hills and the Schuylkill River. Severe weather, disease, and a lack of adequate food and other provisions created almost unendurable hardships, yet for those who survived this was truly the turning point of the war. Baron Friedrich von Steuben, recently arrived from Europe with a letter of introduction from Benjamin Franklin, was employed to train the raw troops into highly disciplined, motivated soldiers. Although the conflict was to last another five years, the lessons learned at Valley Forge proved to be the key to ultimate victory.

In addition to the hallowed ground in the National Historical Park, there are two other outstanding historic sites within a few miles of Valley Forge, both unusual and both uncrowded. And, to finish the day in style, you might want to visit the enormous, upscale shopping malls at King of Prussia.

Not only is this an easy trip, it is also an inexpensive one—courtesy of the National Park Service and Montgomery County with their free admissions to nearly all of the sites. Of course, you *could* blow your budget at the mall, or on a fancy meal!

GETTING THERE:

By car, the Valley Forge National Historical Park is about 20 miles northwest of downtown Philadelphia. Take the Schuylkill Expressway (I-76) north to US-202 (Dekalb Pike) at King of Prussia, then North Gulph Road north into the park, turning left to the Visitor Center parking lot.

Mill Grove/Audubon Wildlife Sanctuary is another three miles to the north. From the Visitor Center go east on PA-23, then quickly north on US-422. Just across the Schuylkill River, turn north on PA-363 (Trooper Road) and almost immediately left on Audubon Road. Turn left on Pawlings Road, then right into Mill Grove.

The Wentz Farm is another nine miles to the north. Pawlings Road becomes Park Avenue, then Valley Forge Road (PA-363). Continue north on that to Skippack Pike (PA-73) and turn right a short distance. The entrance is on the left.

Return on PA-363 (being careful to follow its dogleg at Ridge Pike) to US-422, follow that south, and then go east a short way on US-202 to the King of Prussia mall complex.

By bus, SEPTA provides an hourly Monday-to-Friday service on their Route 125, departing JFK Boulevard near 17th Street in downtown Philadelphia for the one-hour run to the National Historic Park Visitor Center. Stops are made at the King of Prussia malls. Audubon and the Wentz Farm are not accessible by bus. ☎ 215-580-7800.

PRACTICALITIES:

Any day (except Christmas) is a fine day to visit Valley Forge. Winter is especially appropriate as it gives you a better "feel" for its history. Both the Audubon Sanctuary and the Peter Wentz Farmstead are open all year, on Tuesdays through Sundays, but not on some major holidays. The malls throb nearly all the time.

For further information contact the **Valley Forge Convention & Visitors Bureau**, 600 West Germantown Pike, Plymouth Meeting, PA 19462, ☎ 610-834-7969 or 888-VISITVF, fax 610-834-0202, Internet: www.valleyforge.org.

FOOD AND DRINK:

Kennedy Supplee Mansion (1100 W. Valley Forge Rd., PA-23, in the National Historical Park) Luxury dining in an historic mansion, American/Continental cuisine. Dress well and reserve. ☎ 610-337-3777. X: Sun., Sat. Lunch. $$$

The Baron's Inne (499 N. Gulph Rd., near Exit 24 of I-76) American and Continental cuisine in a warm, friendly setting. Reservations suggested. ☎ 610-265-2550. X: Sun., holidays. $$ and $$$

Coppermill Harvest (in the Park Ridge Hotel, 480 N. Gulph Rd., west of Exit 24 of I-76) An attractive, yet casual, place for fine American cuisine. Sunday brunch. ☎ 610-878-1400. $$ and $$$

Carlucci's (795 W. Dekalb Pike, US-202, at Gulph Rd. opposite the mall) Contemporary cuisine with Italian and Californian overtones, including pizza and sandwiches. Sunday brunch. ☎ 610-265-0660. $$

Bertolini's (in The Plaza at King of Prussia mall complex) Creative Italian cuisine. ☎ 610-265-2965. $$

Why not have a picnic in the Valley Forge National Historical Park? There are three picnic areas, available free on a first-come-first-served basis. The Betzwood area has grills.

In addition, the King of Prussia mall complex fairly crawls with eateries. Another good choice is in nearby Skippack, see page 95.

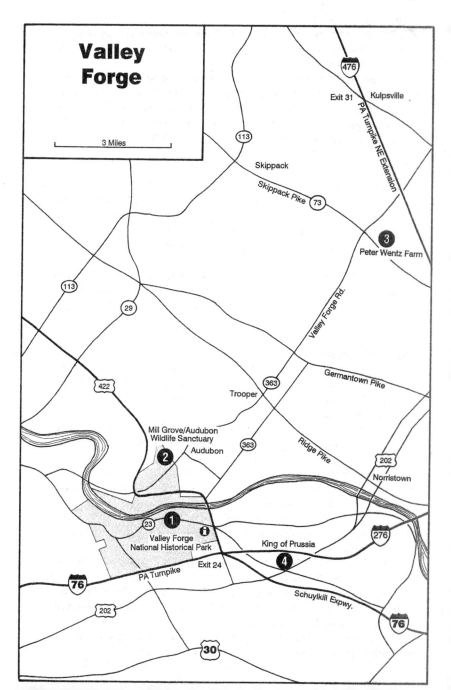

LOCAL ATTRACTIONS:
Numbers in parentheses correspond with numbers on the map.

*VALLEY FORGE NATIONAL HISTORICAL PARK (1), N. Gulph Rd. & PA-23, Valley Forge, PA 19481, ☎ 610-783-1077, Internet: www.nps.gov/vafo, also try: www.libertynet.org/iha/valleyforge. *Open daily except Christmas, 9–5. Free. Entry to Washington's Headquarters from Apr.–Nov.: Adults $2, children under 17 free. Map for self-guided tour available at Visitor Center, along with exhibits, artifacts, and a 15-minute orientation film. Bookstore. Audiotape rentals. Bus tours offered from May to Sept. Picnicking facilities. Hiking, biking, and horse trails; ask for special map. &.*

Begin your tour of the beautiful 3,600-acre site at the **Visitor Center**, where you can obtain maps, watch a short film, and examine artifacts. The suggested route then takes you to the reconstructed huts and defenses of the **Muhlenberg Brigade**, staffed on weekends by costumed interpreters. Passing the National Memorial Arch and Wayne Statue, you will soon arrive at ***Washington's Headquarters**, whose interior may be visited. *Open daily 9–5, closed Christmas. Adult admission $2, free Dec.–Mar.*

Continue on past several redoubts, the Artillery Park, and Varnum's Quarters to the **Washington Memorial Chapel**, a lovely Episcopal church on private property within the park. The church is noted for its stained-glass windows and carillon recitals. *Open Mon.–Sat. 9:30–5, Sun. 12:30–5. Donation.* ☎ *610-783-0120.*

Next to this stands the **Valley Forge Historical Society Museum** with its large collection of artifacts, several of which belonged to George and Martha Washington. *Open Mon.–Sat. 9:30–4, Sun. 1–4:30, closed major holidays. Adults $2, seniors and children 13–15 $1.50* ☎ *610-783-0535.* A new attraction is the adjacent **World of Scouting Museum**, in its own log cabin. *Open Memorial Day to Labor Day, Fri.–Sun. 11–4; rest of year weekends 11–4. Adults $2, seniors and under 18 $1.* ☎ *610-783-5311.* From here it is only a short distance back to the Visitor Center.

MILL GROVE/AUDUBON WILDLIFE SANCTUARY (2), Audubon & Pawlings Roads, Audubon, PA 18407, ☎ 610-666-5593, Internet: www.mont copa.org/culture/history. *House open Tues.–Sat. 10–4, Sun. 1–4. Closed Mon. and major holidays. Sanctuary open Tues.–Sun. 7–dusk. Free.*

John James Audubon (1785–1851), the famous American ornithologist and artist, lived in this elegant 1762 farmhouse from 1803 until 1806. Although still a teenager at the time, being away from his French parents gave him the freedom to pursue what would become his lifelong passion—studying and drawing birds. It was here that the intense young artist experimented with bird banding, and here that he devised the "wire armature" that enabled him to position freshly-killed birds in life-like poses for drawing. This made his renderings far more scientifically accurate and dramatic than those of his contemporaries, inspiring modern artists and conservationists to higher achievements.

The house has now been preserved as a museum of Audubon's works, and the 175-acre plot on which it sits, overlooking the scenic Perkiomen Creek, turned into a wildlife sanctuary with numerous hiking trails. If you like birds, you'll love this place.

PETER WENTZ FARMSTEAD (3), Schultz Rd., off PA-73, Worcester, PA 19490, ☎ 610-584-5104, Internet: www.montcopa.org/culture/history. *Open Tues.–Sat. 10–4, Sun. 1–4. Closed Mon. and major holidays. Free.*

George Washington (and his troops) stayed here twice, both before and after the Battle of Germantown, in October of 1777. This was just before they retreated to Valley Forge for that long, hard winter. It was here that they first learned of the very welcome American victory at Saratoga, which led to a spirited celebration resulting in damage to Peter Wentz's farmstead, for which he was reimbursed.

The son of a German immigrant, Peter Wentz Jr. (1719–93) inherited 300 acres of land on which he built a log house and a stone barn around 1744. With growing prosperity, in 1758 he built the present house, an impressive Georgian-style structure with distinctly German features. Today, only foundations of the log house remain, but the original barn, the main house, and the dependent buildings remain as they were when used by George Washington in 1777, beautifully preserved by the county. Some farming and gardening, as well as animal husbandry, is still carried on in the 18th-century manner, and craft demonstrations by costumed guides are held occasionally. Tours are given throughout the day. Don't miss this special, and unexpected, treat!

THE PLAZA AND COURT AT KING OF PRUSSIA (4), 160 N. Gulph Rd., King of Prussia, PA 19406, ☎ 610-265-5727, Internet: www.shopking.com. *Mall hours Mon.–Sat. 10–9:30, Sun. noon–6.*

Two adjacent malls, The Plaza and The Court, have combined to form the largest shopping complex on the East Coast, and the second largest in the nation. With such upscale names as Bloomingdales, Nordstrom, Neiman Marcus, and Lord & Taylor, this is a class act, but for the less affluent there's also Macy's, J.C.Penney, Sears, and Strawbridges. In total, about 400 separate stores vie for your dollar, and of course there are plenty of restaurants, cafés, and other diversions. What a way to end the day!

Western Montgomery County

You don't have to venture far from Philadelphia to experience an elegant bit of rural splendor. This short drive through the southwestern part of Montgomery County takes you to historic manor houses, a fine collection of antique automobiles with a Pennsylvania heritage, an art museum in a college town, and ends the day in the charming village of Skippack, where you can enjoy fine dining and excellent shopping for antiques. Like the Valley Forge trip, this little excursion includes sites associated with George Washington and the Revolutionary War. And it won't be crowded; everything here is pretty far off the beaten path.

You might prefer to mix and match some elements of this trip with those of the previous one to Valley Forge to form a custom itinerary, as they are very close together.

GETTING THERE:

By car, Pottsgrove Manor is about 40 miles northwest of downtown Philadelphia. Take I-76 (Schuylkill Expressway) northwest to King of Prussia, then US-422 northwest to the PA-100 (Pottstown) exit. Take PA-100 north across the river, exiting onto King Street. To the right is the entrance to Pottsgrove Manor.

From here follow the route in the text, which leads you back towards Philadelphia via a somewhat longer route, making stops at various points of interest.

PRACTICALITIES:

Avoid making this trip on a Monday or holiday, when virtually all of the attractions are closed. The two manor houses open at 1 p.m. on Sundays. For further information contact the **Valley Forge Convention & Visitors Bureau**, 600 West Germantown Pike, Plymouth Meeting, PA 19462, ☎ 610-834-7969 or 888-VISITVF, fax 610-834-0202, Internet: www.valley forge.org.

FOOD AND DRINK:

There are numerous fast-food places around Pottstown and Boyertown, and colorful cafés and restaurants around Skippack. Pennypacker Mills has good picnic facilities if you prefer to bring your own lunch. Some choice restaurants are:

Skippack Roadhouse (4022 Skippack Pike, PA-73, in Skippack) An old favorite for Continental cuisine in an elegant setting. Sunday brunch. Reservations suggested, ☎ 610-584-4231. $$$

Mainland Inn (17 Main St., PA-63, in Mainland, a few miles north of Skippack) A bit out of the way, but a superb place for creative American cuisine in a delightful setting, with service to match. Reserve, ☎ 215-256-8500. $$$

Gypsy Rose (505 Bridge Rd., PA-113, just north of Collegeville, on the way to Skippack) Steak, seafood, veal, and the like in a 19th-century inn overlooking the Perkiomen Creek. Sunday brunch. Reservations suggested, ☎ 610-489-1600. $$

Trolley Stop (PA-73 in the heart of Skippack) Casual dining in an old trolley car or other cozy setting. ☎ 610-584-4849. $$

LOCAL ATTRACTIONS:

Numbers in parentheses correspond to numbers on the map.

POTTSGROVE MANOR (1), 100 West King St., Pottstown, PA 19464, ☎ 610-326-4014, Internet: www.montcopa.org/culture/history. *Open Tues.–Sat. 10–4, Sun. 1–4. Closed Mon. & major holidays. Free, donation accepted. Museum shop.*

John Potts, a Colonial ironmaster and the founder of Pottstown, built this stately sandstone mansion for his family in 1752. At that time it was quite an amazing sight, attracting visitors from as far as Philadelphia, who came to admire the views, the handsome interior, and the overall Quaker sense of restraint. Once again furnished with genuine period pieces, it features a lovely garden, an elegant hall, and even slave quarters.

Return to Route PA-100 and head north about six miles to Boyertown on Route PA-73. Purists will note that the town is actually in Berks County, but only by a few feet. Be sure to visit the:

BOYERTOWN MUSEUM OF HISTORIC VEHICLES (2), 28 Warwick St., Boyertown, PA 19512, ☎ 610-367-2090, relevant Internet site: www.boyertown.net/museum. *Open Tues.–Sun. 9:30–4. Closed major holidays. Adults $4, seniors 60+ $3.50., children 6–18 $2. Museum shop.*

The museum is well hidden in an old industrial building. Take PA-73 (Philadelphia Ave.) to the center of town and turn left on Reading Ave. (PA-562). At the first bend in the road, bear left onto Warwick Street and the museum. There are plans to move the facility to another location in Boyertown in the near future.

Much of America's earliest automotive history took place not in Detroit, but in Pennsylvania—especially around Philadelphia and Reading.

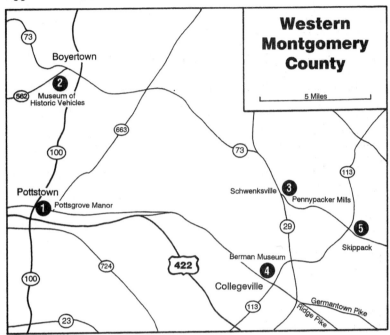

Examples of those rare, first "horseless carriages" are lovingly preserved in the museum along with other carriages, wagons, sleighs, cycles, later motor vehicles, and even some experimental electric cars of today. The oldest actual automobile on display is a 1904 Phaeton, produced in Reading by Charles Duryea (1861–1938). This automotive pioneer created his first successful gasoline automobile in 1893! Another model, his **1907 Buggyaut**, is also shown. Reading produced some other rather weird cars, and some rather elegant ones, before its industry was overtaken by the mass production of Motor City. In all, visitors are treated to over 75 vehicles, most of which are beautifully restored, and many of which are in running condition. If you love cars, you won't want to miss this outstanding exhibition.

Return to PA-73 and head east about 13 miles to Schwenksville. Cross the Perkiomen Creek and turn left into:

PENNYPACKER MILLS (3), Route 73 and Haldeman Rd., Schwenksville PA 19473, ☎ 610-287-9349, Internet: www.montcopa.org/culture/history. *Open Tues.–Sat. 10–4, Sun. 1–4. Closed Mon. and major holidays. Free, donations appreciated. Gift shop. Picnic facilities.*

The mills along the picturesque Perkiomen Creek are long gone, but most of the 125-acre Pennypacker estate is still being farmed, and looks much as it did in the 1700s, when George Washington stayed here. The property and its old Colonial farmhouse were purchased in 1900 by Samuel W. Pennypacker, a wealthy Philadelphia businessman who served as Pennsylvania's governor from 1903–07. He enlarged the house, converting it into a spacious, comfortable Colonial Revival mansion surrounded by 15 acres of natural, English-style landscape. Remaining in the Pennypacker family for decades, the property has now been preserved by Montgomery County as a turn-of-the-century country gentleman's estate, with much of the original furnishings and artifacts intact. This is a great place to see an historic house that's a bit different from most, and one where you won't be bothered by crowds of visitors.

From here, you might want to make a short side trip by following Route PA-29 south about six miles to Collegeville, home of Ursinus College and the acclaimed **Berman Museum of Art** (4). Turn right on Main Street and follow it for about a half-mile to the campus, on the right. Campus Drive leads to the visitor parking lot and the museum. Changing exhibitions feature unusual and challenging works along with more traditional styles, with an emphasis on regional and Pennsylvania artists in a variety of media. *Open Tues.–Fri. 10–4, Sat.–Sun. noon–4:30. Closed Mon., major holidays, and Dec. 24–31. Free.* ☎ *610-409-3500.* &.

A delightful way to end the day is to take a short drive to **Skippack Village** (5), located on Route PA-73 about four miles east of Pennypacker Mills, or Route PA-113 some five miles north of Collegeville. Its main street—Skippack Pike (PA-73)—preserves much of its 18th-century charm, and is lined with antique shops, boutiques, art galleries, crafts emporiums, and the like. And with plenty of restaurants and cafés, it's the perfect place to relax, wander around, and perhaps have dinner. *For information* ☎ *610-584-3074, Internet: www.skippackvillage.com.*

Staying on Route PA-73 will eventually return you to Philadelphia, possibly turning south on routes 309 or 611.

Trip 14

North of Philadelphia

Just north of Philadelphia, in the affluent suburbs of Montgomery County, lies a collection of historic homes and outstanding works of architecture that provide the focus for a pleasant day's excursion. You probably won't want to see all of the sites—or have the time to—on one trip, but you can always come back for more at a later date. So, read the descriptions, make your choices, and head north.

GETTING THERE:

By car, Fort Washington is about 15 miles north of downtown Philadelphia. Take PA-309 north to PA-73, head west to Bethlehem Pike, and north a short bit to Hope Lodge. Continue west on PA-73 a short distance to the Fort Washington State Park and The Highlands.

For Graeme Park, the easiest way is to take the Pennsylvania Turnpike (I-276) from the Fort Washington interchange to Exit 27 at Willow Grove. From there take PA-611 (Easton Road) north beyond the Naval Air Station to County Line Road, then west on that to the entrance.

Follow the map to Bryn Athyn, whose attractions are both located just off PA-232 (Huntington Pike), on Cathedral Road.

The Beth Shalom Synagogue is on PA-611 (Old York Road) at Foxcroft Road in Elkins Park.

By train, SEPTA offers frequent commuter service on its R-5 line to Fort Washington. From the station it's about a mile to Hope Lodge, and another mile to The Highlands. The other sites are more difficult to reach by public transportation.

PRACTICALITIES:

This trip is best made in the middle of the week, but not on a holiday. Note that Hope Lodge is closed on Mondays, The Highlands on weekends, Graeme Park on Mondays and Tuesdays, and the Glencairn on weekends. Reservations are needed for the latter. Reservations are also required to tour the Beth Shalom Synagogue, and then on Sundays through Wednesdays only.

For further information contact the **Valley Forge Convention & Visitors Bureau**, 600 West Germantown Pike, Plymouth Meeting, PA 19462, ☎ 610-834-7969 or 888-VISITVF, fax 610-834-0202, Internet: www.valleyforge.org.

FOOD AND DRINK:

Besides the usual fast-food and chain eateries, this area boasts several notable restaurants:

Nul Bom (Benson Manor at routes 73 and 611, in Jenkintown, near Elkins Park) Innovative Korean and Japanese fare, including sushi. ☎ 215-884-5100. $$ and $$$

Stazi Milano (Jenkintown Train Station, West & Greenwood Aves., at Township Line Rd. in Jenkintown) This smartly decorated, casually elegant Italian restaurant makes good use of the busy, classic train station. ☎ 215-885-9000. $$ •

Alfio's (15 Limekiln Pike, PA-152, at Mt. Carmel Rd., in Glenside) Try the famous Caesar salad at this favorite Italian restaurant. ☎ 215-885-3787. X: Mon., Sat., Sun. lunch, major holidays. $$

Athena (264 Keswick Ave. at Easton Rd., Glenside) Authentic Greek home cooking in a relaxed setting. ☎ 215-884-1777. X: Mon., Sun. lunch. $$

Otto's Brauhaus (233 Easton Rd., PA-611, at Pine Ave. in Horsham) Old-fashioned, Old-World German/American home cooking in a quaint tavern. Vast selection of beers. ☎ 215-675-1864. X: Sun. lunch. $$

Mandarin Garden (91 Old York Rd., PA-611, at Davisville Rd. in Willow Grove) Excellent Chinese cuisine, featuring Peking duck and "Chef's Surprise." ☎ 215-657-3993. X: Sun. lunch. $$

If the weather is nice, you might also consider having a **picnic** at Fort Washington State Park.

LOCAL ATTRACTIONS:

Numbers in parentheses correspond to numbers on the map.

HOPE LODGE (1), 533 Bethlehem Pike, Fort Washington, PA 19034, ☎ 215-646-1595. *Open Tues.–Sat., 9–4, Sun. noon–4. Closed Mon. and some holidays. Adults $3.50, seniors $3, ages 6–12 $1.50.* &.

Surprise! George Washington never slept in this mid-18th-century Early Georgian gem of a mansion, although his surgeon general did use it as a headquarters just prior to the Valley Forge encampment. Hope Lodge was built between 1743 and 1748 by a wealthy Quaker gristmill operator named Samuel Morris. A later owner was one Henry Hope, whose family name also graces the famous diamond. Threatened with demolition in 1921, the house was saved and restored by William and Alice Degn, who lived here until 1953. Authentically furnished with period antiques, Hope Lodge today reflects two distinct time periods: the Colonial era from 1743 to 1770, and the Colonial Revival period, 1922 through 1953.

The original builder, Samuel Morris, had his gristmill nearby on the same property. Rebuilt in 1820, it is now known as the **Mather Mill**, and its exterior remains as it was at that time.

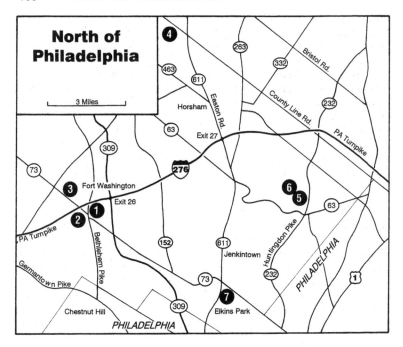

FORT WASHINGTON STATE PARK (2), 500 Bethlehem Pike, Fort Washington, PA 19034, ☎ 215-646-2942, Internet: www.dcnr.state.pa.us. *Open daily, 8–dusk. Free.*

This is a great place for picnicking, or just relaxing between visits to the historic sites. Visitors can also go hiking, fishing, birding, cross-country skiing, or sledding.

THE HIGHLANDS (3), 7001 Sheaff Lane, Fort Washington, PA 19034, ☎ 215-641-2687. *Open Mon.–Fri. 9–4, closed holidays. Reservations advised. Adults $4, seniors $3, ages 6–17 $2.*

Another wealthy Quaker businessman, Anthony Morris (no relation to Samuel Morris of Hope Lodge) built this splendid 32-room Georgian mansion between 1794 and 1801. Poor Anthony didn't get to enjoy its luxury for long; by 1808 he was broke and had to sell.

Once covering over 300 acres, the estate is now some 43 acres in size, but its magnificent ***gardens** are still there for you to enjoy. Along with the thoroughly restored mansion, there is also an unusual two-story octagonal springhouse, a barn, a smokehouse, an icehouse, greenhouses, and cottages.

GRAEME PARK (4), 859 County Line Rd., Horsham, PA 19044, ☎ 215-343-0965. *Open Wed.–Sat. 10–4, Sun. noon–4. Closed Mon., Tues., New Year's, Easter, Thanksgiving, Christmas, and state holidays. Adults $3.50, seniors $3, ages 6–12 $1.50.*

Sir William Keith, the Provincial Governor of Pennsylvania during Colonial times, began this mansion around 1723 as a country retreat and local distillery. After a falling-out with the Penn family, Keith was removed from office and returned to England, where he soon died. Later, his son-in-law, Dr. Thomas Graeme, purchased the estate and remodeled it into an elegant country house with exquisite paneling. Although sparsely furnished, its interior is a treasure of design and ornamentation. This is the only surviving residence of a Colonial governor of Pennsylvania.

BRYN ATHYN CATHEDRAL (5), Cathedral Rd. at Huntington Pike (PA-232), Bryn Athyn, PA 19009, ☎ 215-947-0266. *Tours Tues.–Sun. 1–4. Free.* ♿.

Begun in 1913, the thoroughly Gothic Bryn Athyn Cathedral is the center of the Church of New Jerusalem, a faith based on the teachings of the 18th-century philosopher Emmanuel Swedenborg. Its construction involved the revival of medieval crafts and building techniques, resulting in a structure that evolved organically over the years. The lack of straight lines and right angles contributes to an overall feeling of warmth, enhanced by light filtering in from the spectacular stained-glass windows.

*GLENCAIRN MUSEUM (6), 1001 Cathedral Rd., Bryn Athyn, PA 19009, ☎ 215-938-2600. *Open Mon.–Fri. 9–4. Advance reservations are necessary due to space limitations. Admission charged. Partially* ♿, *call ahead.*

Raymond Pitcairn (1885–1966), who designed the Bryn Athyn Cathedral (above), built this adjacent castle for himself between 1928 and 1939. The same medieval techniques were used by the same craftsmen, resulting in a truly unexpected structure here in the suburbs of Philadelphia. Its ***Great Hall** is fitted with reproductions of the famed stained-glass windows in Chartres Cathedral, and has a charming cloister and gardens next to it. Upstairs, there are treasures from the Pitcairn's collections of Egyptian, Roman, Greek, medieval, and Native American arts and artifacts.

BETH SHALOM SYNAGOGUE (7), Old York and Foxcroft roads, Elkins Park, PA 19117, ☎ 215-887-1342. *Tours by appointment only, Mon.–Wed. 11–3, Sun. 9–1.*

Built in 1959, Beth Shalom was the only synagogue that Frank Lloyd Wright (1867–1959) ever designed, and also his last major work. This unusual, world-famous structure rises from a hexagonal base, with an asymmetrical dome topping out at 110 feet. For fans of Wright's architecture, this is surely a must-see!

Lower Bucks County

This short drive through the southernmost reaches of Bucks County features four unusual historic sites, mostly dating from early Colonial times. You may not have the time to see all of them in one day, but be sure to at least visit Pennsbury Manor, the reconstructed 17th-century riverside country estate of William Penn. The drive itself is hardly scenic as most of it is through slightly seedy industrial areas and somewhat run-down communities, but the attractions will make it all worthwhile.

GETTING THERE:

By car, the farthest point (Fallsington) is about 30 miles northeast of downtown Philadelphia. Take I-95 north to Exit 23, then head south on Linden Avenue, and east (left) on State Road. Turn right (south) on Grant Avenue to Glen Foerd.

Continue east on State Road through Croydon and into Bristol. Bear left and then right onto Old Route 13, making a right on Mill Street to the wharf. The Grundy Museum is nearby on Radcliffe Street.

From Bristol take US-13 north to Tullytown. Turn right through the town and follow Bordentown Road east across a lake for about two miles to Pennsbury Road, where you turn right into Pennsbury Manor.

Leaving Pennsbury, turn right on Bordentown Road, and then left on New Ford Road for about three miles. The entrance to Historic Fallsington is about a half-mile beyond the intersection with US-13, on the right just opposite New Falls Road.

Nearby US-1 will return you to Philadelphia, or you can connect from it to I-95.

PRACTICALITIES:

Check the individual opening times carefully, preferably calling ahead for Glen Foerd and Historic Fallsington. For further information, contact the **Bucks County Visitors Bureau**, 152 Swamp Rd., Doylestown, PA 18901, ☎ 215-345-4552 or 800-836-2825, Internet: www.bucks countycvb.org.

FOOD AND DRINK:

King George II Inn (102 Radcliffe St. at Mill St. in Bristol) An inn since 1765, this waterfront favorite occupies a scenic spot in Historic Bristol. American/Continental cuisine. Reservations suggested, ☎ 215-788-5536. $$$

Fisher's Tudor House (1858 Street Rd., PA-132, at Hulmeville Rd. in Bensalem) A long-time favorite for seafood; also serves meats and pasta. ☎ 215-244-9777. X: Mon. $ and $$

Michael's (3340 Street Rd., PA-132, about 3 miles north of the river, in Bensalem) Comfort food in a nice diner, with a good salad bar. ☎ 215-638-2283. $

Alternatively, **picnic facilities** are available at nearby Neshaminy State Park, and at Pennsbury Manor.

LOCAL ATTRACTIONS:

Numbers in parentheses correspond to numbers on the map.

Glen Foerd (1) is actually still in Philadelphia, but it's right on the Bucks County line and really belongs with this group of attractions. Set in a magnificent 18-acre estate overlooking the Delaware River, this 25-room mansion was built in 1850. Glen Foerd is especially noted for its Victorian architecture, Tiffany-style stained-glass skylights, grand staircase, pipe organ, antique furniture, and art gallery. Guided tours are conducted year round, but call ahead for reservations. *5001 Grant Ave.,* ☎ *215-632-5330, Internet: www.glenfoerd.org. Open Tues.–Fri. 10–2, closed holidays. Tours at 10 and 2 Adults $5, children under 12 free.*

The Bucks County town of **Bristol** (2) was founded in 1681, making it one of the oldest communities in Pennsylvania. Its waterfront, stretching from the delightful **Wharf**, site of a ferry service begun in 1681 and of the first steamboat runs in 1787 by John Fitch, is lined with 18th- and 19th-century buildings of outstanding historic interest. The King George II Inn dates from 1765 and is regarded as the oldest inn in the country to remain in continuous operation. Several of the mansions reflect the wealth generated by the opening of the Delaware Canal (see page 123), which ran from Easton south to its terminus here in Bristol. Adjacent to the wharf is the Bristol Marsh, a nature preserve that can be viewed from an observation deck next to the parking lot.

A stroll up Radcliffe Street soon brings you to the **Margaret R. Grundy Memorial Museum**, an early-19th-century Victorian mansion featuring richly carved oak paneling, furniture, rugs, and art objects. *610 Radcliffe St.,* ☎ *215-788-9432. Open Sept.–June, Mon.–Fri. 1–4 and Sat. 1–3, rest of year Mon.–Fri. 1–4. Free.*

From Bristol, it's only a few miles to the main attraction of this trip:

*PENNSBURY MANOR (3), 400 Pennsbury Memorial Rd., Morrisville, PA 19067, ☎ 215-946-0400, Internet: www.pennsburymanor.org. *Open all year Tues.–Sat. 9–5, Sun. noon–5; closed Mon. and certain holidays. Guided 90-minute tours: Tues.–Fri. at 10, 11:30, 1:30 and 3:30; Sat. at 11, 12:30, 2 and*

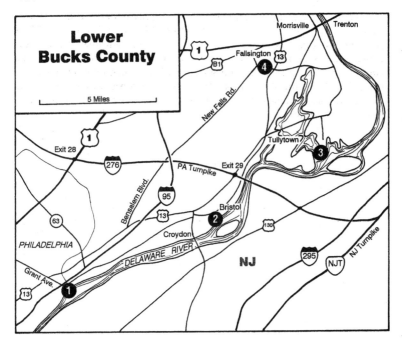

3:30; Sun. at 12:30, 1:30, 2:30 and 3:30. Adults $5, seniors $4.50, children 6–12 $3, family rate $13. Grounds pass $4.50. Picnic facilities. Partially &.

"The Country Life is to be preferr'd; for there we see the Works of God; but in Cities little else but the Works of Men," wrote William Penn, Quaker, diplomat, and founder of Pennsylvania. No wonder he chose to live at Pennsbury, a (now reconstructed) manor house of 1683 on the Delaware River, surrounded by 43 acres of gardens, orchards, and stately trees. The bake-and-brew house, the blacksmith's and joiner's shops, the replica of Penn's **river barge**, and the motley crew of farm animals give you a glimpse of the many activities that sustained the life of this country plantation.

Another site associated with Penn, just a few miles to the north, is:

HISTORIC FALLSINGTON (4), 4 Yardley Ave., Fallsington, PA 19054, ☎ 215-295-6567. Open May–Oct., Mon.–Sat. 10–4, Sun. 1–4, closed major holidays. Hourly tours; reservations recommended. Adults $3.50, seniors $2.50, ages 6-18 $1.

Fallsington, settled in the late 17th century by followers of William Penn, is an unspoiled village that represents an enduring Quaker community and a uniquely American architectural heritage. Many of the houses are still occupied by descendants of the original settlers. Three restored buildings are shown on the tours: the **Moon-Williamson House** (c. 1685), a pioneer log building, one of the oldest in Pennsylvania; the **Burges-Lippincott House**, an elegant, beautifully decorated home built in four stages from 1700 to 1829; and the **Stagecoach Tavern**, in continual operation from the 1790s until Prohibition. The **Gillingham Store**, rebuilt in 1910, is the headquarters of Historic Fallsington, Inc., and has a museum store and information center.

Trip 16

Washington Crossing

A great episode in American history, George Washington's triumphant crossing of the Delaware on that stormy Christmas night in 1776, is brought back to life here at the Washington Crossing Historic Park. By visiting each of the restored sites, you can gain a clear understanding of the strategy and importance of the battle, whose outcome allowed the American Revolution to carry on to ultimate victory. Here is the river, once filled with blocks of ice; here are the banks where the frostbitten Continentals embarked and landed; and here are the houses they used for shelter.

Those planning to stay overnight might want to combine this trip with the previous one to the Bristol/Morrisville area, with New Hope, and with Doylestown.

GETTING THERE:

By car, Washington Crossing is about 34 miles northeast of downtown Philadelphia. Take Route I-95 to Exit 31, then River Road (PA-32) north about three miles.

PRACTICALITIES:

Washington Crossing Historic Park is open on Tuesdays through Saturdays, from 9–5, and on Sundays from noon–5. It is closed on New Year's, Martin Luther King Jr.'s Birthday, Columbus Day, Thanksgiving, and December 24 and 31. Park admission: $1 per private vehicle. Combined admission and tour of all sites: Adults $4, seniors $3.50, children 6–12 $3. The Memorial Building/Visitor Center, Durham Boat House, Thompson-Neely House, and the Wildflower Preserve are ꝺ; other sites are not.

An annual **re-enactment** of the event is held on Christmas Day at 1 p.m., with a less-crowded rehearsal two weeks earlier.

For further information contact the **Washington Crossing Historic Park**, P.O. Box 103, Washington Crossing, PA 18977, ☎ 215-493-4076.

FOOD AND DRINK:

Washington Crossing Inn (River Rd., routes PA-32 and PA-532, adjacent to the park) Continental cuisine in a low-key Colonial atmosphere. Sunday brunch. ☎ 215-493-3634. X: Mon. $$ and $$$

Light lunch and supplies are available at the Taylorsville General Store in the park, and there are numerous picnic facilities throughout the park. Also consider dining up the road a few miles in New Hope (see page 109).

SUGGESTED TOUR:

Numbers in parentheses correspond to numbers on the map.

The park is divided into two sections about four miles apart, starting with the McConkey's Ferry Section at the intersection of routes PA-32 and PA-532. Your tour begins there at the **Memorial Building and Visitor Center** (1), near where the Continentals massed before their raid on the Hessian garrison in Trenton, NJ. Here, in Concentration Valley, the 2,400-odd patriots, beaten back in the disheartening campaigns of 1776, assembled to execute General Washington's bold strategy. At the Memorial Building, which houses the Visitor Center, park offices, a gallery with changing exhibits, and a theater with an exact copy of Emanuel Leutze's famous painting *Washington Crossing the Delaware* (the original hangs in the Metropolitan Museum in New York), you can watch a half-hour documentary film on the crossing.

Near the Memorial Building is the Point of Embarkation. Footpaths lead to a stone marker at the spot on the riverbank where the crossing began in 1776, and where the Christmas Day Re-enactment begins each year. Volunteers in uniform climb into a Durham boat with "General Washington" and paddle across, hopefully under conditions less hazardous than those of 1776. The full-scale reproduction used in the re-enactment is on display at the **Durham Boat House** (2). Durham boats were flat-bottomed barges about 60 feet long used for hauling iron ore on the river. They were propelled by oars or sails.

Not far from the boat house is **McConkey's Ferry Inn** (3), where General Washington may have eaten his Christmas meal before starting across the river. The inn served as a guardpost for the ferry landing during the Continental Army's encampment. In the vicinity of the inn are the **Taylorsville General Store** (4), a.k.a. The Patriot, and several 19th-century houses, including the 1817 residence of Mahlon K. Taylor, one of the founders of Taylorsville, a village now known as Washington Crossing.

Leaving the McConkey's Ferry Section, drive north on PA-32 for about four miles, then turn left on Lurgan Road for about three-quarters of a mile. Here an almost-hidden right turn leads up a steep, twisting lane to **Bowman's Hill Tower** (5). The hill was used by Washington's sentinels to observe enemy activity as it provides an unmatched panoramic sweep of the river valley. A commemorative fieldstone tower, 110 feet high, was built in 1930 and more recently equipped with an elevator. You can ride almost to the top, then climb up steep circular stairs for a marvelous *view. ☎ 215-862-3166. Open Apr.–Oct., Tues.–Sun., 10–5; Nov. weekends 10–5. Admission included in the joint ticket.*

Return to PA-32 and turn left into the Thompson's Mill Section of the park. The **Thompson-Neely House** (6) was headquarters during the crucial month of December, 1776, of General Stirling, who commanded the

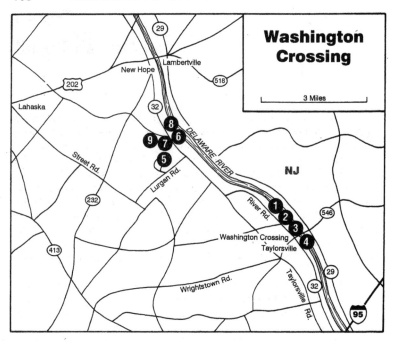

troops stationed along the Delaware to prevent a British crossing. It is a fine example of early-18th-century Colonial architecture, and its beautifully-restored interior may be seen on informative tours. *Open same times as the park; admission included in joint ticket. Partially &.*

Nearby is a restored, operating water-powered **grist mill** (7) built in the 1830s, a restored 18th-century barn and, beyond the Delaware Canal, the **graves** (8) of America's first unknown soldiers. Across the road is the **Bowman's Hill State Wildflower Preserve** (9), a 100-acre sanctuary devoted to the preservation of the native plants of Pennsylvania. It features miles of trails, exhibitions, and special events. The peak season for blooms is April through June. ☎ *215-862-2924. Open Tues.–Sat. 9–5, Sun. noon–5. Free. &.*

New Hope

Artists, writers, actors, musicians, and other creative types have been attracted to the charms of New Hope ever since the early 1900s, forming what amounts to a colony on the banks of the Delaware. In more recent times, hordes of tourists have followed, lured by both the arty atmosphere and the very real attractions the town has to offer.

New Hope began to flourish in the 1720s as a ferry town. It was known as Coryell's Ferry during the Revolutionary War, when the local people aided the Continental Army. The mills operated by Benjamin Parry in the late 18th century and the opening of the Delaware Canal in 1832 made the town a bustling commercial center for a time. Its prosperity was extended in the 1890s by the arrival of the railroad, and again by its growing fame as an art colony.

Today, besides the numerous galleries, boutiques, restaurants, cafés, riverside setting, and historic sites, New Hope offers a wonderfully preserved stretch of the canal complete with rides on a mule-drawn barge, and excursions by steam train into the nearby countryside.

Those lucky enough to be able to stay overnight might consider combining this trip with the ones to nearby Washington Crossing (page 106), Doylestown (page 114), or The Two Rivers and Their Canals, a natural extension if ever there was one (page 119).

GETTING THERE:

By car, New Hope is about 45 miles northeast of downtown Philadelphia. Take Route I-95 north to Exit 31, then Taylorsville Road and PA-32 through Washington Crossing and into New Hope, where it becomes Main Street.

PRACTICALITIES:

Summer weekends bring mobs of tourists; you'll be much better off coming on a weekday, preferably from May through October. Decent weather will enhance this almost-entirely outdoor trip.

New Hope hosts several annual events including the Auto Show in August and the Arts & Crafts Festival in October. For local information contact the **New Hope Borough Information Center**, South Main and Mechanic streets, New Hope, PA 18938, ☎ 215-862-5880, Internet: www.newhopepa.com. Regional information is obtainable from the **Bucks County Visitors Bureau**, 152 Swamp Rd., Doylestown, PA 18901, ☎ 215-345-4552 or 800-836-2825, Internet: www.buckscountycvb.org.

FOOD AND DRINK:

One of the prime reasons to visit New Hope is to dine well. Not cheaply, but well. Here are some suggestions:

La Bonne Auberge (at Village 2, a mile west on Mechanic St.) It's open for dinner only, a bit hard to find, and expensive, but the classic French cuisine is as good as you'll find anywhere in the Philadelphia suburbs. Reservations and jacket required. ☎ 215-862-2462. X: Mon., Tues., some holidays. $$$

Odette's (South River Rd., PA-32, 4 miles south of New Hope) Set by the canal and the river, Odette's has long been a favorite for stylish, elegant Continental dining in a bistro atmosphere. Sunday brunch. Reservations suggested, ☎ 215-862-2432. $$$

Martine's Fine Food (7 East Ferry St. near Main) A romantic hideaway with an interesting, eclectic menu. ☎ 215-862-2966. $$

Havana (105 South Main St.) Creative, contemporary dishes served indoors or out. Very popular. ☎ 215-862-9897. $$

Lambertville Station (11 Bridge St., just south of the bridge, Lambertville, NJ) Creative American cuisine in a restored Victorian railroad station. Sunday brunch. ☎ 609-397-8300. $$

Cock 'n' Bull (Peddler's Village, PA-263 off US-202, Lahaska, PA) Traditional American fare in a Colonial-style setting. Sunday brunch. ☎ 215-794-4010. $$

Spotted Hog (Peddler's Village, US-202 at Street Rd., Lahaska, PA) Standard American fare in a casual country setting. ☎ 215-794-4030. $$

LOCAL ATTRACTIONS:

Numbers in parentheses correspond to numbers on the map.

PARRY MANSION (1), South Main and West Ferry streets, New Hope, PA 18938, ☎ 215-862-5652. *Open May to mid-Dec., Fri.-Sun. 1–5. Adults $4, ages 1-12 $1.*

Benjamin Parry, a wealthy lumbermill owner, built this mansion in 1784, and it remained in the family until 1966, when the New Hope Historical Society purchased it. As a result of the remarkable continuity over five generations, it was restored to reflect the various decorative changes experienced by the Parrys themselves over the years. You can see whitewash yield to wallpaper, candles to oil lamps, and the craze for Victoriana to more severe modern tastes.

*MULE BARGE (2), New Hope Canal Boat Co., 149 S. Main St., New Hope, PA 18938, ☎ 215-862-0758, Internet: www.canalboats.com. *Operates April through October, weather permitting. Departures daily May–Oct. at 12, 1:30, 3 and 4:30; in April on Fri., Sat., and Sun. at 12:30 and 3. Adults $7.95, children under 12 $6.50.* ⅃.

Here's a chance for a relaxing, hour-long ride on the historic Delaware Canal through New Hope and the surrounding countryside. During most of the season a barge musician and historian are aboard to entertain and inform you. Bring your camera, forget your problems, enjoy the ride.

*NEW HOPE & IVYLAND RAILROAD (3), 32 West Bridge St., New Hope, PA 18938, ☎ 215-862-2332. *Operates daily late March to early Apr.; mid-May to early Nov.; and in late Dec.; on Fri. and weekends mid-Apr. to mid-May; and early to late Nov.; and on weekends only from Jan. to mid-March. Santa Claus trains run Thanksgiving until Christmas. Fares: Adults $8.95, seniors $7.95, children 2-11 $4.95, under 2 $1.50. Special evening dinner trains, Sunday bruch trains, and BYOB wine-and-cheese trains. Schedules and fares subject to change; check first.* ♿.

This 9-mile, 50-minute narrated round trip by vintage steam train takes you from the restored New Hope Station of 1891 across the trestle to which Pearl White was tied in the 1914 silent movie classic, *The Perils of Pauline*, and on through woodlands and countryside to Lahaska before returning. The 1920s passenger coaches are usually pulled by a 1925 Baldwin 2-8-0 locomotive, although other engines may be substituted. The New Hope & Ivyland is one of the only steam railroads in the country that allows people the rare opportunity to ***ride in the locomotive** while it's pulling the train! Ask at the ticket office about this special treat. There's a small display of railroad history, as well as a gift shop, at the New Hope Station.

Other attractions in New Hope include **Coryell's Ferry Boat Rides** (4) on the Delaware River aboard a 65-foot Mississippi-style river boat. *Departures every 45 minutes starting at noon, daily in season. Trips last 30 min. Tickets sold at Gerenser's Exotic Ice Cream, 22 S. Main St.,* ☎ *215-862-2050.* The same shop also sells tickets for **Colonial Walking Tours** that bring New Hope's Revolutionary past back to life. If you're in town after dark, you might want to take one of the eerie **Ghost Tours** arranged by a psychic investigator. ☎ *215-957-9988.* New Hope is also famous for its quality **art galleries, antique shops**, and **boutiques** of all kinds; and has a broad choice of inns, restaurants, and cafés.

Another enjoyable diversion is to stroll across the bridge to **Lambertville** (5) in New Jersey, which has a lower-key atmosphere but many of the same type of attractions as New Hope.

Heading west from New Hope on Route US-202, the old Colonial road linking New York with Philadelphia, soon brings you to the **New Hope Winery** (6), where you can taste some of their 30-odd varieties. ☎ *215-794-2331 or 800-592-WINE.* A few miles farther on is the famous:

PEDDLER'S VILLAGE (7), 4 miles west of New Hope on US-202, Box 218, Lahaska, PA 18931, ☎ 215-794-4000, Internet: www.peddlersvillage.com. *Shops open daily except Thanksgiving, Christmas, New Year's.*

This is the star attraction of Lahaska, a village first settled around 1700 by Quakers from England. Originally a collection of barns and chicken coops, Peddler's Village has evolved into 42 acres with 70 specialty shops, eight restaurants, and a country inn arranged as a Colonial village around a common complete with a gazebo and a pond. All kinds of crafts, antiques, and unusual items can be found here; and there are frequent country festivals and special events to entertain you. Its newest attraction is the magnificent **Grand Carousel Ride,** a beautifully restored 1922 carousel from the famed Philadelphia Tobaggan Company, which you can ride. There is also a museum of carousel history. ☎ *215-794-8960. Museum: Adults $3, seniors $2.75, children $2. Museum and carousel ride: $3.50,* *children $2.50. Ride only: $1.50, infants free.*

Lahaska has many other shops as well, especially the upscale **Penn's Purchase Manufacturer's Outlet Village** and the 12 antique dealers in the **Antique Courte.**

For another nearby attraction, continue two miles west on US-202, then two miles south on PA-413 to the **Buckingham Valley Vineyards** (8). Free wine tastings and self-guided tours are offered at Bucks County's first winery. *Open Tues.–Sat. 11–6, Sun. noon–4.* ☎ *215-794-7188.*

Doylestown

E asily one of the most attractive towns in the Philadelphia area, Doylestown offers more than its share of memorable attractions. The best of these are within walking distance of one another, and of the local commuter train station, so you don't even need a car to enjoy the trip.

A family named Doyle took up residence here in the 1730s, opening a tavern around 1745 at the strategic intersection of two rutted Colonial roads, one (now US-202) linking New Hope with Norristown, and the other (now PA-611) running from Philadelphia to Easton. Both tavern and town prospered, and in 1813 Doylestown became the county seat of Bucks County. Today it is a picturesque country town of beautifully-preserved Colonial, Federal, and Victorian houses.

A regional cultural center as well, Doylestown is best known for the works of its resident eccentric, Henry Chapman Mercer (1856–1930), a noted archaeologist, antiquarian, and leader of the Arts and Crafts Movement. You will encounter several of his strange creations and obsessions as you explore the neighborhood. Other noted locals, either by birth or residence, included the authors James A. Michener and Pearl S. Buck.

GETTING THERE:

By car, Doylestown is about 25 miles north of downtown Philadelphia. Take PA-611 (Broad St.) all the way and get off at the Main Street exit just south of Doylestown.

By commuter train, take the SEPTA Route R-5 from Philadelphia's 30th Street, Suburban, or Market East stations. Service operates hourly on weekdays, less frequently on weekends. The ride takes about 75 minutes and leaves you near the main attractions.

PRACTICALITIES:

Most of the sites are open daily (except Thanksgiving, Christmas, and New Year's), but art lovers should note that the outstanding Michener Museum is closed on Mondays and holidays. The Pearl S. Buck House is open from March through December, on Tuesdays through Sundays, but not on major holidays. Advance reservations should be made for the Fonthill Museum as capacity is limited.

For further information contact the **Bucks County Visitors Bureau**, 152 Swamp Rd., Doylestown, PA 18901, ☎ 215-345-4552 or 800-836-2825, Fax

215-345-4967, Internet: www.buckscountycvb.org.

FOOD AND DRINK:

Sign of the Sorrel Horse (4424 Old Easton Rd., northeast of town) Award-winning French cuisine in a 1714 grist mill. Dinner only. Dress nicely and reserve, ☎ 215-230-9999. X: Mon., Tues. $$$

Russell's 96 West (96 W. State St.) Sophisticated New American cuisine, with a seasonal menu. Indoor/outdoor dining. ☎ 215-345-8746. X: Sun. $$$

Café Arielle (100 S. Main St.) A casual French bistro in a lovely setting. Reservations suggested, ☎ 215-345-5930. X: Mon., Tues., no lunch on weekends. $$ and $$$

State Street Café (57 W. State St.) Unusual fare from an adventurous menu; an enjoyable place for lunch. BYOB. ☎ 215-340-0373. $$

Paganini Ristorante (81 W. State St.) Homemade Italian cuisine. ☎ 215-348-5922. $$

Doylestown Inn (18 W. State St.) Hearty American fare in an old-fashioned, comfortable setting. ☎ 215-345-6610. $$

LOCAL ATTRACTIONS:

Numbers in parentheses correspond to numbers on the map.

*MERCER MUSEUM AND SPRUANCE LIBRARY (1), Pine and Ashland streets, ☎ 215-345-0210, Internet: www.libertnet.org/bchs/mm. *Museum open Mon.–Sat. 10–5, Sun. noon–5, closing at 9 on Tues. Library open Wed.–Sat., 10–5, Tues. 1–9. Both closed Thanksgiving, Christmas, New Year's. Adults $5, seniors $4.50, students with ID $1.50, under 6 free. Audio device rental $1. Gift shop. Largely &.*

A stunning concrete structure and National Historic Landmark, The Mercer Museum houses the tools and products of more than 60 trades and crafts. It was established by Henry Mercer to display his collection of over 50,000 examples of Early American furnishings, folk art, and implements. Fortunately for succeeding generations, Dr. Mercer saw these artifacts as the stuff of history rather than yard sales. Henry Ford, a man of strong opinions, called this six-story treasure trove the only museum in the country worth visiting. Don't miss the eerie 19th-century Vampire Killing Kit on the ground floor; or the prisoner's dock, gallows, and coffin in the sixth floor. The new "Inform" audio devices explain everything as you wander around freely in whatever directions your interests take you. For children, there are hands-on stations to try out life in the past. Each year on the second full weekend in May the museum hosts a Folk Fest featuring Early American craft demonstrations, picnics, music, dancing, sheep shearing, quilting, and the like.

The Spruance Library is a gold mine of information on the nation's past. It contains special collections on Bucks County history and genealogy, and on early American technology, culture, and folk art.

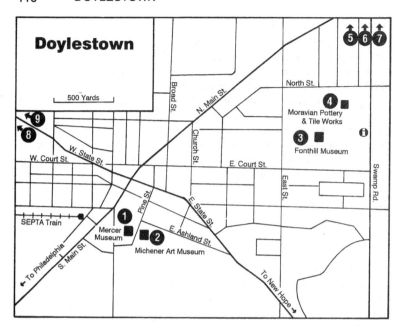

Doylestown

500 Yards

North St.

Broad St.

N. Main St.

Moravian Pottery & Tile Works

Fonthill Museum

Church St.

W. State St.

W. Court St.

E. Court St.

East St.

Swamp Rd.

SEPTA Train

Pine St.

Mercer Museum

E. State St.

E. Ashland St.

Michener Art Museum

To Philadelphia

S. Main St.

To New Hope

*JAMES A. MICHENER ART MUSEUM (2), 138 S. Pine St., ☎ 215-340-9800, Internet: www.michenerartmuseum.org. *Open Tues.–Fri. 10–4:30, weekends 10–5, closed holidays. Adults $5, seniors $4.50, children 12-18 and students with ID $1.50. Museum shop. Café.* ♿

Just across the street from the Mercer Museum stands the old county jail, a handsome structure of 1884. Parts of this were placed on the National Register of Historic Buildings and Sites in 1985, the year the facility closed. In 1988 its preserved sections were converted into an art museum honoring and partly endowed by the late author, James A. Michener, who grew up in Doylestown and later became a noted art collector. Since then, other modern additions have been made, greatly expanding the available gallery space. Permanent collections include a Visual Heritage of Bucks County with regional works of art from Colonial times to the present, the Creative Bucks County multimedia exhibition celebrating the county's rich artistic tradition, and Abstract Expressionist paintings from the collection of Mari S. and James A. Michener. Michener's Bucks County Office, where he wrote "Tales of the South Pacific," has been re-created, and you can visit the Nakashima Reading Room, filled with classic furniture from the studio of the renowned woodworker George Nakashima. Repeat visitors will appreciate the many changing exhibitions, some of which are created by the museum itself.

Follow the map, by car or on foot, to the:

FONTHILL MUSEUM (3), East Court St., ☎ 215-348-9461, Internet: www.lib ertynet.org/bchs/fh. *Open Mon.–Sat. 10–5, Sun. noon–5. Closed Thanksgiving, Christmas, New Year's. Last tour at 4. Reservations are strongly urged as space is limited and tour groups small. Adults $5, seniors $4.50, students with ID $1.50, under 6 free.*

Henry Chapman Mercer designed Fonthill, today a National Historic Landmark, as a home and showcase for his collection of tiles and prints from all over the world. The castle-like structure, begun in 1908, consists almost entirely of poured concrete and was conceived of as a "Castle for the New World." Each of the 40-odd rooms has a highly individual person-ality, with tiles sometimes depicting stories or historic events; and there are warrens, alcoves, and cubicles everywhere you turn on your fascinat-ing tour of Fonthill.

Stroll over to the:

MORAVIAN POTTERY AND TILE WORKS (4), Swamp Rd. (PA-313), ☎ 215-345-6722, Internet: www.libertynet.org/bchs/tw. *Open daily 10–4:45. Last tour at 4. Closed holidays. Adults $3, seniors $2.50, children 7–17 $1.50. Tile shop. Partially &.*

A National Historic Landmark adjacent to the Fonthill Museum and the tourist office, this concrete Spanish-Mission-style tile works was built by Henry Mercer to revive the dying Pennsylvania-German art of tile mak-ing. Today it operates much as it did in Mercer's time, using the original formulas and methods. Over the years the tile works has furnished deco-rations for such notable installations as the Pennsylvania State Capitol (see page 260), the Gardner Museum in Boston, and the John D. Rockefeller Estate in New York.

If you've come by car, you might want to take a short drive to the:

NATIONAL SHRINE OF OUR LADY OF CZESTOCHOWA (5), Ferry Rd., Beacon Hill, ☎ 215-345-0600. *Take Swamp Rd. north a mile or so, then Ferry Rd. west about 2 miles. Shrine and grounds open daily 9–5 all year. Free. Largely &.*

A Polish spiritual and pilgrimage center, established in 1955 by the Pauline Fathers and dedicated to Out Lady of Czestochowa (pronounced "Chen-sto-ho-va") in America. The present structure was completed in 1966 to commemorate the Millennium of Poland's baptism as a Christian nation. It houses a faithful reproduction of the Miraculous Painting of the Holy Mother, which is traditionally attributed to St. Luke and hangs in the Shrine of Czestochowa in Poland. The copy was blessed by Pope John XXIII in 1962.

A 6.5-mile **side trip** northwest of Doylestown on Route PA-313 (Swamp Rd.) takes you to the village of Dublin, where you can turn left on Maple Avenue to Green Hill Farms and the **Pearl S. Buck House** (6). This 1835 farmhouse, now a National Historic Landmark, was the home of the renowned author from 1935 until her death in 1973. Until 1993 the only woman to have ever won both the Nobel and Pulitzer prizes, Peal S. Buck was raised in China and became famous for her classic novel *The Good Earth* in 1934. In 1964 she started a foundation to care for displaced children, which today operates the house and maintains its delightful blend of Asian and Western cultures. *520 Dublin Rd., Perkasie, PA 18944,* ☎ *215-249-0100 or 800-220-BUCK, Internet: www.pearl-s-buck.org. Tours Tues.–Sat. at 11, 1, and 2, Sun. at 1 and 2. Closed Jan.–Feb., and on Mon. and most major holidays. Adults $5, seniors and students $4.*

Another nearby attraction on the way back to Doylestown is the **Peace Valley Winery** (7), where you can taste country wines made from premium grapes grown on the 36-acre vineyard. *300 Old Limekiln Rd., 2 miles west of PA-313 on Stump Rd., then a bit south.* ☎ *215-249-9058. Open Wed.–Sun., noon–6. Free tastings.*

In the mood for some unusual shopping? It's only a few miles west on US-202 to **Byers' Choice** (8), where it's Christmas all year round. Famous for their delightful figurines of carolers, Byers' is one of the largest producers of Christmas decorations in the United States. You can tour the factory, visit the elaborate gallery where over 400 figurines are displayed in winter settings, and perhaps purchase some to put around your tree. *4355 County Line Rd., Chalfont, PA,* ☎ *215-822-0150, Internet: www.byerschoice.com. Take US-202 west beyond Chalfont and turn right on County Line Rd. for a half-mile. Open Mon.–Sat. 10–4, closed Jan. and holidays. Free.*

The Two Rivers and their Canals

Pennsylvania's canal era was brief but glorious, and left behind a legacy that can still be enjoyed today. For nearly a century, from around 1830 until the 1920s, Easton was an important junction of two river systems and three canals. From here the 72-mile-long Lehigh Canal ran northwest to the coal mining regions of Mauch Chunk (see page 144) and White Haven, the Delaware Canal some 60 miles south to Bristol (see page 103), and the inefficient, quirky, and lamented Morris Canal 107 miles east to New York Harbor. While only traces of the latter remain (New Jersey tried to rid itself of even the memory!), portions of the Delaware and Lehigh canals have been fully restored and today carry tourists on mule-drawn boats, plying them with entertaining tales along the way.

Easton, the focus of this daytrip, is also home to Binney & Smith, makers of those colorful crayons. Children will love their Crayola Factory here, a special facility made for creative fun. The same building contains the National Canal Museum, an essential stop for those experiencing the canal boat ride. Finally, people who enjoy gourmet dining in romantic riverside getaways can indulge themselves on the way back, putting a perfect end to a memorable day out.

If you can spend more than a day, why not stay overnight and combine this trip with the ones to New Hope (page 109), Bethlehem (page 124), or the Allentown area (page 131)?

GETTING THERE:

By car, Easton lies some 58 miles north of Philadelphia via Route PA-611 all the way. On the way back, follow the Delaware River on PA-611, then PA-32 through New Hope and south to I-95, leading into Philadelphia.

PRACTICALITIES:

This watery tour is strictly a summer affair, to be made any day from mid-June to Labor Day, on Tuesdays through Sundays from early May to mid-June, and on weekends in September. Although the Canal Museum and the Crayola Factory operate all year round, it won't be as much fun without the canal boat ride.

Those intending to finish the day off with a riverside dinner should make reservations ahead of time or risk possible disappointment.

For further information, contact the **Two Rivers Chamber of Commerce**, 1 South 3rd St., Easton, PA 18044, ☎ 610-253-4211.

FOOD AND DRINK:

Easton offers little more than the usual fast-food outlets, coffee shops, and pizzerias. You might instead pack a picnic lunch to enjoy at Hugh Moore Park. On the way back, however, you will pass a number of enticing, first-rate riverside restaurants—a wonderful way to end the day. Some suggestions are:

Chef Tell's Manor House (1800 River Rd., PA-32, in Upper Black Eddy) The famous TV chef offers eclectic fare along with the standards, all served up in a lovely setting. Sunday brunch. Reservations, ☎ 610-982-0212. $$$

Golden Pheasant Inn (763 River Rd., PA-32, in Erwinna) Classic French cuisine in gorgeously romantic dining rooms. Dinner only, plus Sunday brunch. Reserve, ☎ 610-294-9595. X: Mon. $$$

Cuttalossa Inn (PA-32 in Lumberville) Dine in a 1750 inn on the river, with views of a 30-foot waterfall. American cuisine served indoors and out on the patio. Lunch and dinner. Reservations suggested, ☎ 215-297-5082. X: Sun. $$ and $$$

Black Bass Hotel (3774 River Rd., PA-32, in Lumberville) This 18th-century riverside inn offers contemporary American cuisine, with an outdoor veranda in good weather. Lunch and dinner. Reservations suggested, ☎ 215-297-5770. $$ and $$$

LOCAL ATTRACTIONS:

Numbers in parentheses correspond to numbers on the map.

Begin at Easton's **Centre Square** (1), whose Soldiers' and Sailors' Monument stands on the site of the Old Courthouse of 1765, erected on land rented from the Penn family for the sum of one red rose a year. The town was founded in 1752 by Thomas Penn, a son of William Penn, and shows the elder Penn's influence in its grid layout built around a "Great Square." Its location at the confluence of two great rivers made it an important commercial center from the earliest times, and its industries flourished with the coming of the canals and the later development of railroads. A short stroll around the area reveals many historic houses from those pioneer times.

TWO RIVERS LANDING (1), 30 Centre Square, Easton, PA 18042, ☎ 610-515-8000, Internet: www.crayola.com/factory and www.canals.org/museum.

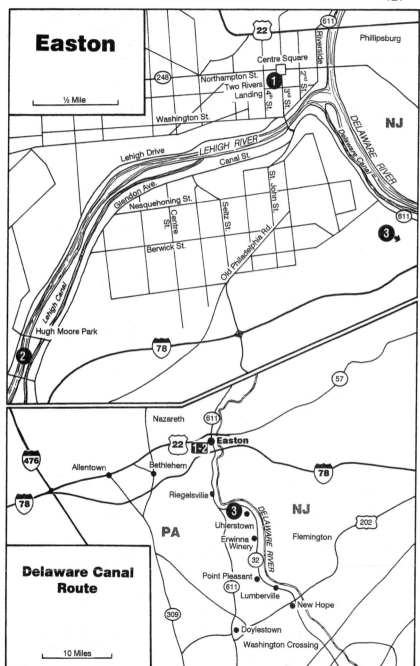

Canal Museum & Crayola Factory open Memorial Day to Labor Day, Mon.–Sat 9–6, Sun. 11–6; rest of year Tues.–Sat. and holiday Mon. 9:30–5, Sun. noon–5. Closed Easter, Thanksgiving, Christmas, and New Year's. Capacity limited, admission on first-come, first-serve basis. Reservations for groups of 10 or more only. Admission to both attractions $7, seniors 65+ $6, under 3 free. &.

Two quite separate attractions make up the Two Rivers Landing, both covered by the same admission. In addition, there is a **Visitors Center** on the ground floor. The **Crayola Factory**, on the second floor, is full of interactive displays telling you—and your kids—all about those colorful crayons so familiar to childhood. There is also a replica factory where you can watch vats of brightly-colored liquid being transformed into crayons, and studios where visitors can exercise their creative impulses with crayons, computer graphics, and other art media.

On the third floor is the **National Canal Museum**, where the history of America's canals is told in great detail. Along with actual artifacts, there are old photographs, models, and a video show. A visit here will surely whet your appetite for the next attraction!

From here head south on South Third Street almost to the bridge, then turn right on Washington Street and Lehigh Drive, following the latter along the river and crossing a bridge onto the island park. The route is well marked with signs to:

HUGH MOORE PARK/*CANAL BOAT RIDE (2), P.O. Box 877, Easton, PA 18044, ☎ 610-515-8000. *Park open year-round, dawn to dusk. Free. Canal Boat rides early May to Labor Day, Tues.–Sun., also on weekends in September and Mondays in summer. Adults $5, children 3–15 $3. Fare includes admission to historic Locktender's House. Boat and Bike rentals. Hiking and biking trails, towpath, picnic facilities, fishing, playground. Shop and snack bar. Ride and parts of park are* &.

Climb aboard the canal boat *Josiah White* for a leisurely ***mule-drawn ride** along a restored section of the Lehigh Canal. Led by a costumed interpreter, the cruise lasts between 40 and 45 minutes, but takes you back well over a century in time to a quieter, gentler era. Begun in 1817 to bring anthracite coal from northeastern Pennsylvania some 150 miles to the coastal cities, the canal declined after the development of railroads but continued limited operations until a disastrous flood in 1942. Along with the ride you can also visit a restored locktender's house and view other fascinating artifacts of 19th-century industry.

Exit via a small bridge to Glendon Avenue, turn left and follow Canal Street to Route PA-611 South. This heads back towards Philadelphia, running alongside the:

DELAWARE CANAL STATE PARK (3), 11 Lodi Hill Rd., Upper Black Eddy, PA 18972, ☎ 610-982-5560, Internet: www.dcnr.state.pa,us. *Open daily during daylight hours. Free. Hiking, mountain biking, cross-country skiing on towpath, canoeing on watered sections of canal. Picnic facilities.*

Stretching some 60 miles from Easton south to Bristol, the Delaware Canal linked the Lehigh Canal with the Philadelphia area from the early 19th century until being abandoned during the 1930s. It is still in good condition and is fully watered in selected sections. The entire length is now a state park, albeit a rather narrow one, with a restored towpath for hiking, biking, and cross-country skiing. Adjacent to the park is River Road (PA-611 and PA-32), a slow, winding two-lane thoroughfare passing through magnificent scenery.

Along the way you'll discover lovely villages noted for their country inns, romantic restaurants, antique shops, and other low-key attractions. Pass through Riegelsville and Kintnersville, bearing left onto PA-32. Here the road narrows as it squeezes between majestic cliffs and the canal. Below Uhlerstown are several points of interest, including Tinicum County Park and the **Sand Castle Winery**, where you can taste the vinifera vintages on cellar and vineyard tours. *755 River Rd., behind the Golden Pheasant Inn, ☎ 610-294-9181 or 800-722-9463. Open daily.*

At **Point Pleasant** visitors can experience the Delaware on canoes, rafts, or tubes. *Daily from May–Sept. Bucks County River Country, ☎ 215-297-5000, Internet: www.rivercountry.net.* Just below here is **Lumberville**, a bit of Colonial charm set alongside the river and canal. Its country store has been around since 1770, and offers sandwiches for waterside picnics, bicycle rentals, and a variety of unusual goods. There are public outdoor tables by the locks, and you can walk along the towpath. A footbridge leads across the Delaware to New Jersey and the **Bull's Island Section**, ☎ 609-397-2949, of the Delaware & Raritan Canal State Park, a haven for picnickers, birds, and birders alike.

Continue south to the intersection with US-202. Immediately south of it is ***New Hope**, whose **canal boat trips**, steam train rides, and other attractions are described on pages 109-112.

Staying on PA-32 takes you past the **Washington Crossing State Park** (see page 106), below which is Route I-95, leading back into Philadelphia.

Bethlehem

A star shines over Bethlehem, as it did over its namesake in the Holy Land so long ago. Founded on Christmas Eve, 1741, by Moravian missionaries under leadership of Count Nikolaus von Zinzendorf, the settlement grew into a mighty industrial giant that has thankfully preserved much of its colorful 18th-century heritage. In addition to the year-round attractions described here, Bethlehem is famous for its Christmas celebrations, Musikfest, Bach Festival, Celtic Classic Highland Games, and other annual festivities.

The town's major industry, Bethlehem Steel, no longer produces steel locally, but its plants and furnaces are now scheduled to become a museum of America's Industrial Heritage, with a vast assortment of historic artifacts on loan from the Smithsonian Institution. When this opens (200?), Bethlehem will become even more attractive as a daytrip destination. In the meantime, there's always enough here to keep you busy all day long.

You might consider staying overnight and combining this trip with the ones to Easton (page 119), the Nazareth Area (page 128), or the Allentown Area (page 131).

GETTING THERE:

By car, Bethlehem lies some 53 miles north of downtown Philadelphia. Take Route PA-309 to Center Valley, then PA-378 into Bethlehem. Cross the bridge over the Lehigh River, bearing right onto the Main Street ramp. Turn left on Main Street and park at a lot. A right on Walnut Street leads to the Municipal Parking Garage. The Visitor Center is nearby, and all in-town attractions are within walking distance.

PRACTICALITIES:

Several of the sights are closed on Mondays, and have reduced hours on Sundays. At least one is closed on Sundays as well. Phone ahead to check for possible closings, especially of the Eighteenth-Century Industrial Area.

Bethlehem is noted for its **festivals**, especially the: **Bach Festival**, held in mid-May, ☎ 610-866-4382, Internet: www.bach.org; **Musikfest**, held in mid-August, ☎ 610-861-0678, Internet: www.musikfest.org; **Celtic Classic Highland Games**, held in late September, ☎ 610-868-9599, Internet: www.celticfest.org; and the **Christkindlmarkt**, which begins the day after Thanksgiving, ☎ 610-861-0678, Internet: www.fest.org.

For further information contact the **Bethlehem Visitors Center**, 52 West Broad St., Bethlehem, PA 18018, ☎ 610-868-1513 or 800-360-8687, Internet: bethtour.org. Another source is the **Lehigh Valley Convention and Visitors Bureau,** ☎ 610-882-9200 or 800-747-0561, Internet: www.lehighvalleypa.org.

FOOD AND DRINK:

For visitors, some especially recommended restaurants are:

Sun Inn (554 Main St.) Traditional American cuisine in an authentic 1758 inn. Reservations suggested, ☎ 610-974-9451. $$

Pane e Vino (1267 Schoenersville Rd., a half-mile south of US-22) A romantic place for traditional Italian cuisine, including pizza. ☎ 610-691-7125. $ and $$

LOCAL ATTRACTIONS:

Numbers in parentheses correspond to numbers on the map.

Begin at the **Bethlehem Visitors Center** (1) at the corner of Broad and Guetter streets, from which you can easily walk to these attractions:

SUN INN (2), 556 Main St., Bethlehem, PA 18018, ☎ 610-866-1758, Internet: www.suninn.org. *Guided tours Mon.–Sat. 11:30–4, also Fri.–Sat. 5–9. Admission $3, $1 if you have a meal there. Restaurant reservations ☎ 610-974-9451. Gift shop.*

George Washington visited this inn, and Martha too, but at different times. Other patrons included Benjamin Franklin, John Adams, Samuel Adams, Ethan Allen, the Marquis de Lafayette, and a host of other notables. Built in 1758 and restored as a living history museum, the inn still serves meals upstairs, and guided tours are conducted through the rest of the historic building.

Continue south on Main Street, making a sharp right downhill just beyond the Hotel Bethlehem, to the:

COLONIAL INDUSTRIAL QUARTER (3), 459 Old York Rd., Bethlehem, PA 18018, ☎ 610-691-0603, Internet: www.historicbethlehem.org/industr. *Exhibits. Tours Mon.–Fri., 8:30–5, schedule varies, call ahead to be sure. Nominal charges.*

Bethlehem was an industrial center centuries ago, long before it became famous for its steel mills. Grouped along the Monocacy Creek, in a valley just below Main Street, are surviving workshops from earlier times, including a tannery, gristmill, miller's house, and waterworks.

Back uphill, you are only steps from the Moravian College campus and the:

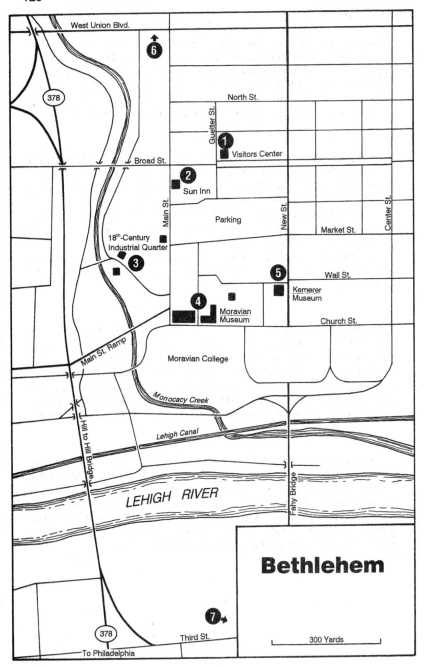

West Union Blvd.

378

North St.

Guetter St.

Broad St.

Visitors Center

Sun Inn

Main St.

Parking

New St.

Center St.

Market St.

18th-Century
Industrial Quarter

Wall St.

Kemerer
Museum

Moravian
Museum

Church St.

Moravian College

Main St. Ramp

Monocacy Creek

Lehigh Canal

Hill to Hill Bridge

Fahy Bridge

LEHIGH   RIVER

Bethlehem

378

Third St.

To Philadelphia

300 Yards

MORAVIAN MUSEUM (4), 66 West Church St., Bethlehem, PA 18018, ☎ 610-867-0173, Internet: www.moravianmuseum.org. *Open Tues.–Sat. 1–4. Adults $5, students $3. Guided tours of museum and historic community.*

Bethlehem's oldest building is the Gemeinhaus of 1741, a remarkable five-story log-structured house that once sheltered workshops, a chapel, and dormitories for the earliest settlers. Little changed over the centuries, it is now used as a museum of early Moravian life.

Continue up Church Street, turning left on New Street to the:

KEMERER MUSEUM OF DECORATIVE ARTS (5), 427 N. New St., Bethlehem, PA 18018, ☎ 610-868-6868, Internet: www.historicbethlehem.org/decor. *Open Tues.–Sun., noon–4, closed major holidays. Adults $5, children under 13 $2. Reservations needed for groups. Museum shop.*

Two hundred and fifty years of folk art, furnishings, paintings, and historical fine arts are gathered together in a lovely old townhouse, where they form one of the finest museums of its type in Pennsylvania.

If you're interested in finding out more about 18th-century Moravian life and can make advance arrangements, you might enjoy a visit to the nearby:

BURNSIDE PLANTATION (6), 1461 Schoenersville Road, Bethlehem, PA 18016, ☎ 610-691-0603, Internet: www.historicbethlehem.org/agri. *Open for self-guided walking tours Mon.–Fri., 9–4. Donation requested.*

Bethlehem's first private residence, the first step away from communal living, was this 1748 farm owned by a Moravian missionary named James Burnside. Currently being restored, the 6.5-acre site features a farmhouse and several outbuildings, a self-guided tour, and special programs.

Just five miles south of Bethlehem, via Route PA-412, are the **Lost River Caverns** (7), where visitors can take a 30-minute guided tour through the stalactites and stalagmites. Along the way, they can also enjoy a tropical garden, various natural history exhibits, and a delightful hodgepodge of museum items. *Durham Street, Hellertown, PA, ☎ 610-838-8767, Internet: www.lostcave.com. Open daily 9–5, until 6 in summer. Closed Christmas, New Year's, and Thanksgiving. Adults $8, children 3–12 $4.*

The Nazareth Area

More than a bit off the beaten path, Nazareth offers several unusual low-key attractions, all located conveniently near the sites on Trips 19, 20, and 24 in the event that you wish to combine them into an overnight mini vacation.

Nazareth was originally part of a large estate owned by the William Penn family. In 1740 it was purchased by the British Methodist evangelist George Whitefield as the site for a proposed school. Construction of this was overseen by a small band of Moravians from Germany, who settled here in 1744 and opened the school in 1755. For more than a century, Nazareth remained exclusively a Moravian settlement. Its school has since merged into Moravian College in nearby Bethlehem, and the area now has a diversity of interests, including a world-famous guitar company that you can visit, an historical museum, a state park with the remnants of an 18th-century village, a winery, and a NASCAR speedway.

GETTING THERE:

By car, Nazareth lies about 64 miles north of downtown Philadelphia. Take PA-309 north to Center Valley, then bear right onto PA-378 through Bethlehem to US-22. Head east on US-22 for about four miles to PA-191, taking that north into Nazareth. Follow 191 as far as Center Street, turning left there for two blocks, and north on North Main Street to the tourist office. They will point the way to the sights, or you can just follow signs.

PRACTICALITIES:

The Martin Guitar Company is closed on weekends and holidays, but most other sites are accessible daily. Calling ahead would be a good idea to avoid disappointment. The winery is open for visitors on Fridays, Saturdays, and Sundays.

For further information contact the **Nazareth Area Visitors Center,** 201 N. Main St., Nazareth, PA 18064, ☎ 610-759-9174 or 888-629-7223. They offer brochures, a video introduction, a gift shop, and tours by prior arrangement.

FOOD AND DRINK:

Newburg Inn (4357 Newburg Rd., at PA-191, 2 miles north of US-22) Beef, seafood, salad bar and the like at a country inn. ☎ 610-759-8528. X:

Sat. lunch, holidays. $ and $$

Barn House Village (7401 Airport Rd., at jct. of PA-987 & PA-329, just southwest of Bath, which is west of Nazareth on PA-248) A country restaurant for American dishes. ☎ 610-837-1234. $ and $$

LOCAL ATTRACTIONS:

Numbers in parentheses correspond to numbers on the map.

Begin your trip at the **Visitors Center** (1), where you can watch a video about the area and get directions to the various sites. *201 N. Main St.,* ☎ *610-759-9174. Open Mon.–Fri. 10–4.* From there follow Center Street east to the **Moravian Historical Society and Whitefield House Museum** (2). This is the spot where Nazareth began in 1740, now operated as a museum that explores the Moravian influence on early American life, music, culture, and history. It also hosts special events and tours; call ahead for a schedule. *214 E. Center St.,* ☎ *610-759-5070. Open daily, 1–4.*

Also in town is the **Martin Guitar Company** (3), a world-renowned manufacturer of handcrafted guitars since 1833. A one-hour guided tour, offered at 1:15 on Mondays through Fridays, takes you through the entire process of creating a top-quality guitar, from planing the wood to stringing the finished instrument. A small museum displays outstanding and unusual guitars crafted by Martin over the last 160 years, along with musical memorabilia. *510 Sycamore St.,* ☎ *610-759-2837, Internet: www.mguitar.com. Open Mon.–Fri., 9–5. Tours at 1:15. Closed weekends, holidays, week of July 4, and Christmas week. Free.*

The **Nazareth Speedway** (4), on PA-191 just south of town, is the site of NASCAR and CART racing events. *P.O. Box F, Nazareth, PA 18064,* ☎ *610-759-8800 or 888-629-RACE, Internet: www.penskemotorsports.com.*

Continue north of town on PA-191, turning left on PA-33 to **Jacobsburg State Park** (5). Along with the usual amenities, the park features an **Environmental Education Center** sited around the remains of an 18th-century village and a historic gun factory. There are also more than seven miles of hiking trails, five miles of equestrian trails, a creek for fishing, and winter trails for cross-country skiing. *835 Jacobsburg Rd., Wind Gap, PA 18091,* ☎ *610-746-2801, Internet: www.dcnr.state.pa.us/stateparks/parks/jburg. Free.*

A short distance northwest of Nazareth is the **Slate Quarry Winery** (6), founded in 1988 and known for its hybrid and vinifera wines. This is a fine place to end your day with a tasting tour, and perhaps to purchase some bottles. *460 Gower Rd.,* ☎ *610-759-0286. From Nazareth take High Street northwest for a mile or so, then turn left onto Gower Rd. Open Fri., Sat., and Sun. 1–6.*

The Allentown Area

J ust an hour north of Philadelphia, the Allentown area offers a wonderful old amusement park renowned for its world-class roller coasters, an outstanding art museum whose quality may surprise you, and an enormous game preserve where visitors can observe bison and elk in their natural habitat as well as other wildlife in a modern zoo. Then, too, there are historic sites, a restored mill, a center of Indian culture, unusual museums, and a scenic drive taking you over covered bridges. You can't see all of these in a single day, of course, but you can pick and choose the ones that interest you most, and perhaps stay overnight or come back another day for the remainder. If you are overnighting, you might want to combine this area with the tours to Bethlehem, Easton, Nazareth, or even Kutztown.

GETTING THERE:

Allentown lies a bit over 50 miles north of Philadelphia. The easiest drive is via the I-76 Schuylkill Expressway to I-476, then continue north as this becomes the Northeast Extension of the Pennsylvania Turnpike (toll). Take this north to Exit 33, Lehigh Valley, then US-22 east for five miles to PA-145, which brings you into downtown Allentown. This total route is 62 miles from center Philadelphia. Note that some of the best attractions are much closer to the turnpike exit; check the map. A considerably shorter route (53 miles) is to take the sometimes congested PA-309 north to its merger with I-78, where you continue on PA-145 for downtown Allentown or stay on 309/78 for Dorney Park, the Game Preserve, and other out-of-town attractions. Check the map for details.

PRACTICALITIES:

Check the individual listings for each attraction as schedules vary widely and seasonally.

For further information, contact the **Lehigh Valley Convention & Visitors Bureau**, 2200 Ave. A, Bethlehem, PA 18017, ☎ 610-882-9200 or 800-747-0561, Internet: www.lehighvalleypa.org.

FOOD AND DRINK:

Ambassador Restaurant (3750 Hamilton Blvd., near Dorney Park, just east of I-78 exit 16) Steak, seafood, and Continental cuisine in a Mediterranean setting. ☎ 610-432-2025. X: Sun. $$ and $$$

Brass Rail (1137 Hamilton St., downtown at 12th St.) Homestyle Italian-American cooking, a local favorite for decades. ☎ 610-434-9383. $ and $$

Yocco's (2128 Hamilton St., 2 miles east of Dorney Park, 2 miles west of the Art Museum) The "Hot Dog King" has been serving exceptionally tasty wieners since 1922, and the quality has never varied. Burgers, steak sandwiches, and the like also available. A local institution. ☎ 610-433-1950. $

Dorney Park, of course, offers several eateries, and the Game Preserve has an attractive snack bar with outdoor tables overlooking the zoo.

LOCAL ATTRACTIONS:

Numbers in parentheses correspond to numbers on the map.
Probably nothing draws more visitors to the Allentown area than:

*DORNEY PARK & WILDWATER KINGDOM (1), 3830 Dorney Park Rd., Allentown, PA 18104, ☎ 610-395-3724 or 800-386-8463, Internet: dorney park.com. *Open daily Memorial Day to Labor Day, weekends early May to Memorial Day and Labor Day to early Oct. Parks open at 10 a.m.; closing time varies. Admission includes rides: Adults $29.50, seniors over 59 and children under 48 inches tall $6, under age 4 free. Reduced prices in the early season, spring, fall, and on bonus weekends and hallo weekends. After 5 p.m. adult admission is greatly reduced. Parking $5. Partially ㅅ.*

Easily worth a daytrip in itself, this summer treat is best saved for a time when you can devote a full day to its many attractions. However, if you're pressed for time you can still enjoy a few hours here, especially after 5 p.m. when the admission is reduced substantially.

For true roller coaster fans, Dorney Park is a mecca—what with its classic, world-famous ***Hercules wooden coaster** that still provides thrills, and its **Steel Force**, the longest, tallest, fastest coaster in the Northeast. Add to that two more world-class coasters, a white-water rafting ride, wave pool, sky ride, splashdown ride, 11 top-rated water slides, and the **Dominator**, a tower that blasts riders straight up 15 stories and then drops them back to earth. For kids there are six play areas including **Berenstain Bear Country**, a fantasy village based on the children's books. And for the not-so-adventurous, there's always the classic old-fashioned merry-go-round, a Dentzel of 1921. Now covering some 200 acres, Dorney Park was founded in 1884 and is considered to be one of the best amusement parks in the nation.

On the way into Allentown proper are two other attractions that might interest you. The first, right out of Dorney Park, is the **Haines Mill Museum** (2), an operating grist mill of 1760 that demonstrates milling tech-

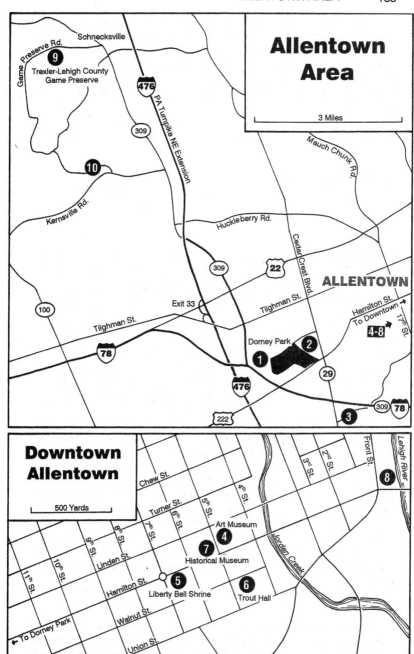

niques at the turn of the century. *3600 Dorney Park Road,* ☎ *610-435-4664. Open May–Sept., weekends only, 1–4. Free.* About two miles south of this, reached via Cedar Crest Boulevard (PA-29), is the **Museum of Indian Culture** (3) of the Lenni Lenape Historical Society. Housed in an 18th-century farmhouse, the museum tells the story of the local Lenape Indians in times gone by. Special events are held on the first Sunday in May, and the second Sundays of August and October. *2825 Fish Hatchery Rd.,* ☎ *610-797-2121, Internet: www.lenape.org. Open Thurs.–Sun. noon–3. Closed major holidays and in bad weather. Adults $3, seniors and children 12 and under $2.*

Downtown Allentown has four worthwhile attractions (and a fifth on the drawing boards), all within easy walking distance of each other. Park as close to Fifth and Hamilton streets as possible to enjoy the:

*ALLENTOWN ART MUSEUM (4), Fifth and Court streets, Allentown, PA 18105, ☎ 610-432-4333, Internet: www.allentownartmuseum.org. *Open Tues.–Sat. 11–5, Sun. noon–5, closed major holidays. Adults $4, seniors $3, students $2, under 12 free. Café. Museum shop.* ♿.

Art lovers will be pleasantly surprised at the overall excellence of this regional museum, featuring world-class European paintings and sculptures from the Gothic, Renaissance, and Baroque periods, along with two centuries of American art, decorative items, textiles, photography, gems, and the like. The museum is especially renowned for its for its Frank Lloyd Wright room, where you can experience an authentic architectural setting by the great master.

Within easy strolling distance of the museum is the **Liberty Bell Shrine** (5), where Philadelphia's famous Liberty Bell was hidden during the British occupation of that city from September, 1777 until June, 1778. There's an exact replica of it here today, along with exhibits and artifacts tracing its history. *Zion Reformed Church, 622 Hamilton St.,* ☎ *610-435-4232. Open Mon.–Sat. noon–4, Sun. by appointment. Closed Mon.–Wed. from Nov.–Apr., and all of Jan. Free.*

Trout Hall (6) is the oldest home in Allentown. Built in 1770 by James Allen, son of the town's founder, it has been beautifully restored and furnished in the style of the period. *414 Walnut St.,* ☎ *610-435-4664. Open Apr.–Nov., Tues.–Sat. noon–3, Sun. 1–4, closed major holidays. Free.* ♿.

The area's rich heritage, from the original Indian inhabitants to the Pennsylvania Dutch traditions and the growth of local industries, is on display in the **Lehigh County Historical Museum** (7) located in the Old Courthouse. *501 Hamilton St.,* ☎ *610-435-4664. Open Mon.–Sat. 10–4, Sun. 1–4. Free.* ♿. One last attraction in downtown Allentown isn't open yet, but hopefully by 2000 you'll be able to visit the proposed **America on Wheels Collection** (8) on the banks of the Lehigh River. Already committed are historical vehicles from Mack Trucks, a local firm, and postal vehicles from the Smithsonian in Washington. More cars, cycles, military vehicles, and even airplanes are being sought.

About ten miles northwest of Allentown is another attraction that's particularly suited to children, as well as to nature lovers of all ages, the:

LEHIGH COUNTY GAME PRESERVE (9), 5150 Game Preserve Rd., Schnecksville, PA 18078, ☎ 610-799-4171, Internet: www.lehigh valleyzoo.org. *Open daily late Apr. through Oct., 10–5. Adults $5, seniors and children 2–12 $3. Outdoor café. Nature store. Picnic facilities. Hiking trails. Partially &. To get there, head north on PA-309 for about 5.5 miles beyond its intersection with US-22 to Schnecksville, turning left there on Game Preserve Road and crossing a delightful covered bridge. The main entrance is about two miles west of Schnecksville, on the left.*

General Harry Trexler founded this 1,200-acre wildlife sanctuary way back in 1909, when the very existence of North American bison, elk, and the like was threatened. They've prospered ever since in the protected natural habitat, and are now joined with a thoroughly modern zoo complete with more exotic animals such as camels and zebras. For the kids, there are pony rides, a petting zoo, and an exploration station. Outside of the zoo area are some nature trails, a creek to ford in your car, picnic areas, and a drive of over two miles through the wildlife preserve, where you can observe herds of bison and elk in their natural setting.

Covered bridge mavens should return to PA-309 by a slightly longer route. Exiting the preserve, they can again cross the Jordan Creek on Schlicher's Bridge of 1882. Continue beyond the preserve entrance, then turn left on Rhueton Hill Road, and again left on Jordan Road. This takes you over the scenic **Rex Covered Bridge** (10) of 1858, a beautiful barn-red span if ever there was one. Continue east on Old Packhouse Road, which returns you to PA-309 just south of Schnecksville.

You can either return to Philadelphia by heading south on PA-309 all the way, or by connecting with the Northeast Extension of the Pennsylvania Turnpike (I-476)(toll) via US-22.

Trip 23
Delaware Water Gap

This glorious one-day excursion meanders in and out of the 35-mile-long Delaware Water Gap National Recreation Area, taking you through some of the finest scenery in the Northeast. Along the way you can visit some spectacular waterfalls, a crafts community, a restored 19th-century village, and numerous other attractions. For the most part, busy and commercialized roads are avoided. It is an especially nice trip to take during the fall foliage season, and—if you can stay overnight—combines well with the following trips to the Lower Poconos and Jim Thorpe (see pages 140 and 144).

GETTING THERE:

By car, Delaware Water Gap is less than a hundred miles north of downtown Philadelphia. The easiest and quickest (but not the shortest) route there is to take the Pennsylvania Turnpike Northeast Extension (I-476) north to Exit 33, then US-22 east almost to Easton. Head north on PA-33 to Sciota, there picking up US-209 to Stroudsburg, and PA-611 into Delaware Water Gap. The total distance is about 102 miles. A shorter-but-slower route is to take PA-611 all the way, a distance of about 82 miles.

From Delaware Water Gap to the farthest point on this trip, Dingmans Ferry, is about 26 miles, following US-209 to the northeast. Return to Delaware Water Gap via New Jersey.

PRACTICALITIES:

Good weather is essential for this outdoor trip, which is best made between April and November. Be sure to wear comfortable walking shoes, and consider bringing a picnic lunch.

For further information contact the **Delaware Water Gap National Recreation Area**, Bushkill, PA 18324, ☎ 570-588-2451, Internet: www.nps.gov/dewa, or the **Pocono Mountains Vacation Bureau**, 1004 Main St., Stroudsburg, PA 18360, ☎ 570-424-6050 or 800-762-6667, Internet: www.poconos.org.

FOOD AND DRINK:

You'll have wonderful opportunities for a picnic lunch on this daytrip. Bushkill Falls offers full facilities, along with a snack bar. Additionally, the Delaware Water Gap National Recreation Area has picnic facilities at both Dingmans Falls and Kittatinny Point, and at various other scenic spots throughout the entire 35-mile area.

Adequate eateries in this heavily-touristed region can be found at Delaware Water Gap, Stroudsburg, along US-209, and in New Jersey at Peters Valley and Walpack Center.

SUGGESTED TOUR:

Numbers in parentheses correspond to numbers on the map.

Begin your tour at the spectacular *Delaware Water Gap (1) itself where, over countless millennia, the Delaware River carved a path between the Kittatinny Ridge in New Jersey and the Pocono Mountain Plateau in Pennsylvania. The gap, about 900 feet across at river level, widens to span a mile at the crest, making a dramatic cleft in these ancient mountains, which were once as high as the Rockies. There are three marked gap overlooks; one on the site of the old Kittatinny House, a popular resort hotel destroyed by fire in 1931, one at Point of Gap, and one at Arrow Island. Wildlife abounds here; and you can hike along marked trails, including the Maine-to-Georgia Appalachian Trail. If you lack the ambition for that, you might consider riding the **Delaware Water Gap Trolley,** which offers an hour-long narrated tour aboard a bus spiffed up to look like a trolley. *Depot on PA-611,* ☎ *570-476-9766. Operates daily Apr.–Nov., 10–4.*

From the gap head north alongside the river to **Shawnee-on-Delaware** (2), an old resort with some modern attractions. If you happen to have kids in tow, you might want to stop at **Shawnee Place**, a play-and-water park geared to active youngsters from 3 to 12. ☎ *570-421-7231, Internet: www.shawneemt.com. Open early June weekends, then late-June to Labor Day, daily 10–5. Admission $12, adult spectators $8, seniors $6, under 40" tall $6.*

Continue north on a narrow, winding road into the Pennsylvania side of the National Recreation Area. After about nine miles you'll come to US-209, a busy highway lined with commercial establishments. A left turn quickly brings you to the **Pocono Indian Museum** (3), where the history of the Delaware Indians is brought to life through unique displays of artifacts. Here you can walk through a real bark house, and see thousand-year-old pottery as well as a more recent scalp. *PA-209, Bushkill, PA,* ☎ *570-588-9338, Internet: www.poconoindianmuseum.com. Open daily, 9:30–5:30. Adults $4, seniors $2.50, ages 6–16 $2.*

Heading north on PA-209, you'll soon come to the well-marked left turn for a most delightful attraction:

BUSHKILL FALLS (4), Bushkill Falls Rd., Bushkill, PA 18324, 570-588-6682, Internet: www.visitbushkillfalls.com. Open April–Oct., daily 9–dusk. Adults $8, seniors $7, children 4-10 $2, under 4 free. Picnic area and grills,

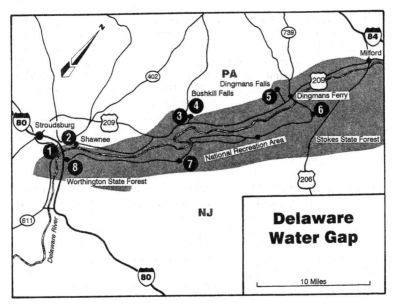

nature trails, Native American exhibit, wildlife exhibit, fishing, paddle boat rentals, miniature golf, shops, snack bar. Partially ♿, but not falls.

Bushkill Falls, the "Niagra of Pennsylvania," has been a classic tourist attraction since 1904, when the Peters family first opened their natural haven to the public. They still own it and have made few changes (other than trail improvements) in the decades since. This is a wonderful escape into an earlier time when a stunning waterfall in a near-primeval setting was all it took to keep folks happy.

From the entrance, there are four trails to and around the falls. The easiest of these goes to a scenic overlook at the top of the 100-foot-high *Main Falls, can easily be done in 15 minutes, and involves no climbing. The **Popular Route** takes you to the bottom of the main falls and up the other side to some upper falls before returning about 45 minutes later. This can be extended by including the **Pennell Falls Trail**. Serious hikers will enjoy the gorgeous **Bridal Veil Falls Trail**, which winds through the boulder-strewn gorge past all eight waterfalls and takes about two hours, including roughly 200 feet of vertical ascent. All of the trails end at the snack bar and old-fashioned pavilion, where you can enjoy lunch or drinks. There are several other attractions, including a Native American exhibit, miniature golf, and paddle boats on a pond.

Continue north on US-209 for about 12 miles to Dingmans Ferry, where you can turn left to **Dingmans Falls (5)**. This is located within the

National Recreation Area and may be visited at any time during daylight hours. There is no admission charge. The **Visitor Center** offers an audiovisual show, nature exhibits, and information. From the parking lot, a half-mile-long nature trail leads through a picturesque gorge dotted with stands of hemlock and rhododendron to the Pocono's highest waterfalls, **Dingmans**, and the aptly-named **Silver Thread Falls.** *Visitor Center open May–Oct., daily 9–5,* ☎ *570-828-7802. Partially* ⅋.

Return to Dingmans Ferry and turn right on PA-739-S, crossing the toll bridge over the Delaware into the New Jersey side of the National Recreation Area. Continue on to the:

PETERS VALLEY CRAFTS CENTER (6), 19 Kuhn Rd., Layton, NJ 07851, ☎ 973-948-5200, Internet: www.pvcrafts.org. *Store and gallery open daily all year, 10–5. Studio visits on weekends, June–Aug., 2–4. Store is* ⅋.

Located on the edge of the National Recreation Area, Peters Valley is a year-round residential community where skilled artisans are invited to live and work in exchange for teaching workshops in their various specialties. Workshops have covered such topics as hand-forged tools, the lost-wax process of ceramic shell casting, contemporary teapots, kiln building, goldsmithing, enameling, electroforming and electroplating, landscape and portrait photography, quilting, collage art, handbound books, knotting and coiling, embroidery, silk painting, rustic furniture, and joinery. The gallery and store feature work by resident craftspeople and other nationally-known artists.

A road through the National Recreation Area leads south for about 12 miles to:

MILLBROOK VILLAGE (7), Old Mine Rd., ☎ 908-841-9531. *Grounds open daily, village open spring to late Oct., Thurs.–Sun. 9–5. Free.*

A small hamlet that developed around a mill built in 1832, Millbrook flourished during the mid-19th century. By the early 1900s, however, it fell into an irreversible decline. What you see today is a skillful re-creation of a late-19th-century rural community, peopled by guides in period costume who demonstrate the crafts of yesteryear. It is located within the National Recreation Area and is operated by the National Park Service.

Continue south another 12 miles to the **Kittatinny Point Visitor Center** (8), where you can find out about all the other attractions in the Delaware Water Gap National Recreation Area, see the exhibits, and watch the audiovisual program. ☎ *973-496-4458, Internet: www.nps.gov/dewa. Open May–Oct., daily 9–5; rest of year, weekends 9–4:30. Free.* ⅋. From here, Interstate highway I-80 leads across the Delaware River and into Pennsylvania, where you can retrace your route back to Philadelphia.

Trip 24
The Lower Poconos

When you think of the Pocono Mountains, you think of resorts; hardly the place to make a daytrip. Yet there are several attractions within reasonable driving range of Philadelphia that make one-day excursions here highly worthwhile. A few of these were explored on the previous trip to Delaware Water Gap, and others are featured on the following one to Jim Thorpe. On this daytrip to the lower Poconos, you can experience a wonderful Colonial farm where the 18th century comes back to life, a friendly country winery that's more than a bit off the beaten path, and a ski resort with many summer attractions including a fun-filled alpine slide, water slides, and more. At Hickory Run you can climb across a strange geological formation created some 20,000 years ago, and enjoy the amenities that Pennsylvania's state parks are noted for.

For those able to stay overnight, this trip can easily be combined with both the previous and the following one to create a real mini-vacation.

GETTING THERE:

By car, the lower Poconos are about a hundred miles north of downtown Philadelphia. Take the Pennsylvania Turnpike Northeast Extension (I-476) north to Exit 33, then US-22 east almost to Easton. Turn north on PA-33 to the Snydersville exit, then turn right on Manor Drive and follow signs for Quiet Valley.

For the Cherry Valley Vineyards, return to PA-33 and go south a few miles to the Saylorsburg exit. The winery is on Lower Cherry Valley Road.

For Camelback, head north on PA-33, turning left (north) on PA-611 to Tannersville. From there follow local signs.

To Hickory Run, go west on I-80 to Exit 40, then south on PA-534 to the park entrance.

Return to I-80 and go east a short distance to Exit 42. From here the Pennsylvania Turnpike Northeast Extension (I-476) will take you back to Philadelphia.

PRACTICALITIES:

Quiet Valley, the main attraction of this trip, is open daily except Mondays from about mid-June through Labor Day; and also on special occasions in May, October, and December. Plan your trip then, and wear comfortable walking shoes.

For further information contact the **Pocono Mountains Vacation**

Bureau, 1004 Main St., Stroudsburg, PA 18360, ☎ 570-424-6050 or 800-762-6667, Internet: www.poconos.org.

FOOD AND DRINK:

This is another great trip for picnicking as facilities are available at Quiet Valley, Camelback, and Hickory Run State Park. If you'd rather eat at a restaurant, here are some suggestions:

Brittania Country Inn (Upper Swiftwater Rd. in Swiftwater, near I-80 Exit 44, north on PA-611, then west on PA-314, and left onto Upper Swiftwater Rd.) British cuisine in a casual setting. ☎ 570-839-7243. X: lunches on Mon., Tues., & Wed. $$

Peppe's Ristorante (Eagle Valley Mall in East Stroudsburg, at the junction of PA-Bus-209 and PA-447) An attractive place for Italian cuisine. ☎ 570-421-4460. X: weekend lunches. $$

Sarah Street Grill (Quaker Plaza, between 5th & 6th streets, in Stroudsburg) Steaks, burgers, pizza, veggies, and the like. ☎ 570-424-9120. $ and $$

LOCAL ATTRACTIONS:

Numbers in parentheses correspond to numbers on the map.

*QUIET VALLEY LIVING HISTORICAL FARM (1), 1000 Turkey Hill Rd., Stroudsburg, PA 18360, ☎ 570-992-6161, Internet: www.past connect.com/quietvalley. *Open June 20 to Labor Day, Tues.–Sat. 10–5:30, Sun. 1–5:30. Last tour at 4. Adults $7, seniors $6, children 3-12 $4. Annual Farm Animal Frolic in May, Harvest Festival in Oct., and Old Time Christmas in Dec. Continuous guided tours. Picnic area. No pets, no videotaping.* ⬤ *can be accommodated, call in advance.*

Quiet Valley is a journey back in time to a self-sufficient Colonial farm run much as it was in 1765 when a hardworking Pennsylvania Dutch family first settled here. The costumed staff members are more than tour guides; they are actors playing the roles of family members going about their daily chores of spinning, weaving, meat smoking, gardening, and tending the animals. As they take you through the farm's 14 buildings, some original, they describe their lives as colonists and demonstrate such skills as forging, wool dyeing, candle dipping, and broom making. In an age of mass production, these activities may come as a revelation to the kids, who will also enjoy petting the animals and trying the ***hay jump** in the barn.

CHERRY VALLEY VINEYARDS (2), RD #5, Box 5100, Saylorsburg, PA 18353, ☎ 570-992-2255. *Open daily 11-5. Free tours on weekends only at 1 & 5.*

Founded in 1986, this small and friendly family winery produces some very good wines from vinifera, hybrid, and native grape varieties; and also

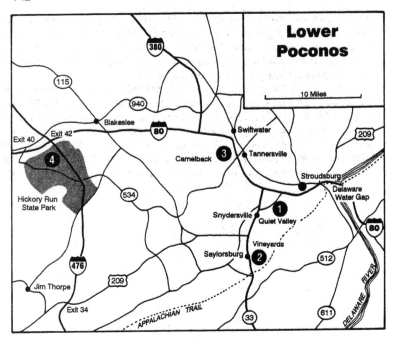

from fruits. Some of these, especially the Chardonnay, are dry, while most retain the fruity taste of grapes without being foxy. Try some; you may wish to purchase a few bottles.

CAMELBEACH WATERPARK (3), Tannersville, PA 18372, ☎ 570-629-1661, Internet: www.camelbeach.com. *Open mid-June through Labor Day, daily 11–6; mid-May to mid-June, weekends 11–6; day after Labor Day to late Oct., weekends 11–5. Alpine slide $5, water slide $5, combination ticket for most attractions $21.95, seniors 65+ and children 6–11 $17.95, spectators $10.95. Go-carts extra.*

Camelback is one of the leading ski resorts in the Poconos, but during the summer it throbs with another kind of energy. Day visitors here can have fun at any of the 12 attractions, including a 3,200-foot-long alpine slide, two water slides, go karts, bumper boats, kiddie cars, miniature golf, a play park, a carousel, a swimming pool, and a scenic chairlift. There's also a mountaintop restaurant overlooking it all.

HICKORY RUN STATE PARK (4), RD #1, Box 81, White Haven, PA 18661, ☎ 570-443-0400, Internet: www.dcnr.state.pa.us/stateparks/parks/hickory.

Open daily all year. No entry fee. Picnicking, playgrounds and fields, nature center, hiking trails, swimming beach (Memorial Day to Labor Day), fishing, camping (fee), snack bar (Memorial Day to Labor Day), ice fishing, sledding, snowmobiling, cross-country skiing. Leashed pets in day-use area, no pets on beach or campsites. Partially &.

Here are 15,500 acres of wooded hills threaded with clear streams and waterfalls. The park's special feature is a lake 1,800 feet long and 400 feet wide, with scenically contoured shores and trees stretching down to where the water should be—but there's no water. Instead, boulders: pinkish, rounded, and piled up like heaps of jellybeans. This is the glacial *Boulder Field, a National Natural Landmark. One of the more startling views is of energetic "swimmers" clambering across the lake to the opposite shore.

Jim Thorpe

Jim Thorpe, as the historic town of Mauch Chunk is now known, lies within easy daytrip range of Philadelphia and is a unique place well worth the journey. It takes its name from the great Native American athlete who astonished the world with an unprecedented record-breaking performance at the 1912 Olympics. Jim Thorpe was not born here, nor did he ever pass through here while he was alive. The story of how the town came to be named for him is a story of hard times: hard times for the man, who was unfairly stripped of his Olympic medals (since restored) on a technicality, and hard times for Mauch Chunk (the Indian name for "Bear Mountain") and East Mauch Chunk, booming coal and railroad towns in the 19th century, declining and economically strapped in the 20th. In 1953 Jim Thorpe died in poverty after a long, painful illness, and his wife sought to have him buried with a public memorial in his home state, Oklahoma. Oklahoma said no. Hearing of the plight of the Mauch Chunks, Mrs. Thorpe proposed to lend the towns her husband's name in return for their assistance in memorializing him. Though the towns had been squabbling for years, their citizens were inspired by this idea, transcended their differences, and merged to become Jim Thorpe, Pennsylvania.

The town of Jim Thorpe lies at the bottom of a gorge on the Lehigh River, flanked by sheer mountainsides, in a region sometimes known as the "Switzerland of America." The town's appearance is as fascinating as the story of its name. In its heyday it spawned a slew of self-made millionaires who built the palatial residences and impressive public buildings you'll see on your walk. They were also responsible for Mauch Chunk's once being a popular summer resort, and for the railroading heritage that is still so much alive today.

If time permits, you can also visit a fabulous model railroad setup in nearby Lehighton. Those able to stay overnight might consider combining this trip with the previous two, or with the one to the Allentown area.

GETTING THERE:

By car, Jim Thorpe lies about 81 miles northwest of downtown Philadelphia. Take the Pennsylvania Turnpike Northeast Extension (I-476) north to Exit 34, then US-209 west through Lehighton into Jim Thorpe. Park by the train station for your walking tour of the town.

PRACTICALITIES:

Most of the attractions are open daily from Memorial Day through

September or October, but check the individual listings to be sure. For further information contact the **Carbon County Tourist Promotion Agency**, Railroad Station, PO Box 90, Jim Thorpe, PA 18229, ☎ 570-325-3673 or 888-JIM-THORPE, Internet: www.jtasd.k12.pa.us/carbon_county.

FOOD AND DRINK:

Emerald Restaurant & Molly Maguires Pub (24 Broadway) Irish-American and Continental cuisine in an authentic setting. ☎ 570-325-8995. $$

Hotel Switzerland (5 Hazard Sq.) This old Victorian establishment features American cuisine. ☎ 570-325-4563. $ and $$

Black Bread Cafe (47 Race St.) Sandwiches and vegetarian fare for a healthy lunch. ☎ 570-325-8957. $

SUGGESTED TOUR:

Numbers in parentheses correspond to numbers on the map.

Downtown Jim Thorpe, a.k.a. **Old Mauch Chunk**, is best explored on foot. Begin your walk at the **Jersey Central Railroad Station** (1), a splendidly Victorian structure of 1888 that once welcomed hordes of tourists to the "Switzerland of America." Although regular passenger service ceased in 1954, **vintage train rides** are still offered on weekends and holidays from May through December. *Rail Tours, Inc.,* ☎ *570-325-4606, Internet: www.railtours-inc.com.* The former Men's Waiting Room (there was another one for the ladies!) is now the local **Tourist Office**, which you should visit.

Follow the map up Packer Hill to the nearby:

*ASA PACKER MANSION (2), Packer Hill, Jim Thorpe, PA 18229, ☎ *570-325-3229. Open day after Memorial Day through Oct., daily 11–4:15; April to late May, Nov. and early Dec., weekends 11–5. Last tour at 4:15. Adults $5, children 7–12 $3.*

Asa Packer (1805–79) came to Mauch Chunk in 1833 and soon grew rich producing coal boats for the Lehigh Canal (see page 119). By mid-century he had switched to railroading by raising the necessary funds to build the Lehigh Valley Railroad, a line running from Mauch Chunk to Easton that eventually stretched from the Canadian border to New York City, carrying much coal as well as passengers. One of the wealthiest men in the country at that time, Packer was as much a philanthropist as a tycoon. He founded Lehigh University in Bethlehem, served two terms as a U.S. Congressman, served in the state legislature and as a county judge, and once ran for governor.

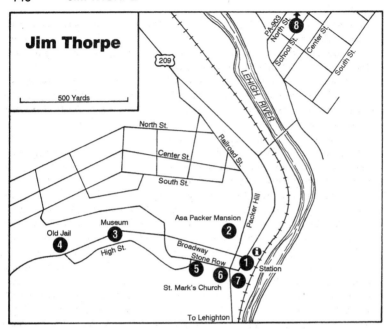

Asa Packer built this magnificent Italianate mansion overlooking Old Mauch Chunk (and his beloved railroad) in 1861, living there for the rest of his life. His daughter, Mary Packer Cummings, continued to live in it until her death in 1912, bequeathing the house and its furnishings to the Borough of Mauch Chunk and its successors. What you see today is not a restoration; it is the real thing, existing just as it was when the Packers lived there.

Among the highlights you'll see on the tour are the office with a desk that supposedly once belonged to Robert E. Lee, a parlor of true Victorian splendor, a main hallway filled with Gothic art, a sitting room with fabulously handcarved woodwork, and a dining room with stained-glass windows.

Head downhill and turn right onto **Broadway**, soon passing what was once Mauch Chunk's "Millionaires Row." Although few of the people who built these houses were actually millionaires, they were wealthy by the standards of the late 19th century, having gained social and economic prominence from their roles in the coal, lumber, and transportation industries. The Mauch Chunk Opera House, built in 1882, is still used as a theater and for various civic events. A bit farther along, the **Mauch Chunk Museum** (3), housed in the county's oldest church, traces local history with working models of canal locks and the gravity railroad, along with other displays. *41 West Broadway, ☎ 570-325-9190, Internet: www.mauchchunkmuseum.org. Open in spring, summer and fall, Tues.–Sun. 10–4. Adults $3, children under 8 $1.*

Continue up to the **Old Jail** (4), an 1871 penal facility that remained in use until 1995. It was here that the "Molly Maguires," a violent gang of terrorists and labor organizers, were hanged in 1877 and 1878. Today, it's open to tourists, who are free to leave after their visit. Be sure to see the mysterious "handprint-on-the-wall" that supposedly proves the innocence of the last man to be hanged here. At one time the jail boasted two gallows, one indoor and one outdoor, so bad weather was never an obstacle to justice. *128 West Broadway, ☎ 570-325-5259.*

Return on Broadway and turn right to Race Street, known for its **Stone Row** (5). This group of 16 row houses was built by Asa Packer for the engineers and foremen of the Lehigh Valley Railroad. Individualized with bay windows, balconies, and door styles, the houses were built of stone for fire prevention purposes. Today they are occupied by artisans, serving as studio, display, and residential space. Below this stands **St. Mark's Episcopal Church** (6), a Gothic Revival structure of 1869. Built into the hillside, this remarkable stone church contains some real art treasures, including early stained-glass windows by Louis C. Tiffany. There is also an ornate baptismal font with great gas standards representing the flames of the Holy Spirit, replicas of the altar and reredos in Windsor Castle, England, and a gold-and-silver alms basin set with jewelry. *Open for tours late May through Oct., daily 1–3:30. Donation. ☎ 570-325-2241.*

Back near the train station is the **Old Mauch Chunk H.O.- Scale Model Train Display** (7), featuring over a dozen trains racing along some 1,100 feet of track lined with some 200 tiny buildings and crossing a hundred bridges. *41 Susquehanna St., ☎ 570-386-2297. Open July–Oct., Mon.–Fri. noon–5 and weekends 10–5; rest of year, weekends noon–5. Closed holidays. Adults $3, seniors $2, children 6–14, $1.*

NEARBY ATTRACTIONS:

Across the river on Route PA-903 (North Street) stands the **Jim Thorpe Mausoleum** (8), the final resting place of the renowned athlete. It is inscribed with the words spoken by Sweden's King Gustav as he presented Jim Thorpe with the gold medals at Stockholm's 1912 Olympics: "Sir, you are the greatest athlete in the world."

The **Lehigh River** offers some terrific whitewater rafting. If you want to shoot the rapids, try **Jim Thorpe River Adventures** (☎ 570-325-2570 or 800-424-RAFT, Internet: www.jtraft.com) or **Pocono Whitewater Rafting** (☎ 570-325-3656 or 800-944-8392, Internet: www.whitewaterrafting.com). There's also recreation at man-made **Mauch Chunk Lake** three miles west of town, and a great view from **Flagstaff Mountain Park**, some 1,400 feet above it.

Railfans and hikers might also explore the bed of the historic **Switchback Gravity Railroad**, completed in 1827 as the first of its kind in America.

On the way home, you'll soon pass through the town of **Lehighton**, home of the **Pocono Museum Unlimited**. Here's another great model train display, this time in the larger "O" scale, with 16 trains traveling along over 2,000 feet of track. The set is realistically laid out with over a hundred buildings, moving vehicles, an operating amusement park, waterfalls, a lake with live fish, and much more. Drama is added with a simulated thunderstorm, rain, and natural sounds, and day changes into night as almost 4,000 lights come on. *Located on PA-443, 4 miles west of town,* ☎ *570-386-3117. Open June through Labor Day, Wed.–Mon. 10–5; day after Labor Day through Dec., Wed.–Mon. noon–5; rest of year Fri.–Sun. 10–5. Closed New Year's, Easter, Thanksgiving, Christmas. Adults $4, seniors $3, children 5–12 $2.* ♿.

*Princeton

F ounded in 1696 by Quakers who called it "Prince's Town," Princeton is one of the most pleasant towns anywhere for casual strolling. Its streets are lined with well-preserved 18th- and 19th-century houses recalling a major battle of the Revolutionary War, the brief times when this was the nation's capital, and the many famous people who lived here over the years. Its major attraction is, of course, the University, which can easily take hours to explore.

GETTING THERE:

By car, Princeton is about 44 miles northeast of downtown Philadelphia. Take the Interstate I-95 north past Trenton, then US-206 northeast into Princeton. Park as close to Nassau Street (NJ-27) as possible; there are several commercial lots just north of this.

By train: SEPTA provides hourly service on their Route R7 to Trenton. There you board a New Jersey Transit train (marked for New York) for Princeton Junction, where you change to a shuttle train that goes directly to the station on campus within walking distance of most sights. The total trip takes about 90 minutes. Bargain round-trip tickets are available. *SEPTA* ☎ *215-580-7800, Internet: www.septa.org, NJT* ☎ *973-762-5100, Internet: www.njtransit.state.nj.us.*

Amtrak offers limited service to Princeton Junction on their Northeast Corridor line, with NJT connections to campus, as above. ☎ *800-USA-RAIL, Internet: www.amtrak.com.*

PRACTICALITIES:

Avoid making this trip on a Monday or major holiday, when the most interesting sights are closed. Operating hours are reduced on Sundays. Some of the minor out-of-town attractions have more limited hours; check the individual listings if you're interested in seeing them.

For further information contact the **Chamber of Commerce of the Princeton Area**, 216 Rockingham Rd., Princeton, NJ 08540, ☎ 609-520-1776, fax 609-520-9107, Internet: www.princetonchamber.org.

FOOD AND DRINK:

Princeton has a wide selection of eateries in every price range; with an emphasis on eclectic cuisines and student budgets. A few choices are:

Le Plumet Royal (20 Bayard Ln, NJ-206 near Nassau St.) Contemporary French cuisine in a Colonial-era inn. Sunday brunch. Dress nicely and reserve, ☎ 609-924-1707. $$$

Lahiere's (11 Witherspoon St. at Nassau St.) A local favorite since 1919, serving French, Continental, and American cuisine. Dress well and reserve, ☎ 609-921-2798. X: Sun. $$ and $$$

Triumph Brewing Company (138 Nassau St.) A micro-brewery serving six varieties of suds along with some wildly creative dishes. ☎ 609-924-7855. $$

Teresa's Pizzetta Caffe (19 Palmer Square East) Modern Italian cuisine, including creative pizzas, in an attractive, casual trattoria. ☎ 609-921-1974. $ and $$

Hoagie Heaven (242 Nassau St.) All sorts of sandwiches. ☎ 609-921-7723. $

LOCAL ATTRACTIONS:

Numbers in parentheses correspond to numbers on the map.

PRINCETON UNIVERSITY (1–7), Princeton, NJ 08544, ☎ 609-258-3603, Internet: www.princeton.edu. *The Orange Key Guide Service conducts free campus tours lasting about an hour. They depart from the rear of Maclean House (1), to the right of the main gates of the University (see map); Mon.–Sat. at 10, 11, 1:30, and 3:30; Sun. at 1:30 and 3:30. Groups should make advance reservations. No tours on Sat. afternoons during home football games, or from mid-Dec. to early Jan. Summer hours may vary, check first. Most of the campus is ♿.*

Tours, led by undergraduates, include visits to Nassau Hall, the University Chapel, and Prospect Gardens. You can also take self-guided tours, first stopping at the **Tour Office** (1) for a map and guide pamphlets. Among the attractions are:

Nassau Hall (2). *Usually open on Sun.–Fri. afternoons until 5, and on Sat. 9–5.* Built in 1756 and twice rebuilt after fires, this was the original home of what was then called the College of New Jersey. The college was founded in 1746 under a royal charter from King George II and first located in Elizabeth, then in Newark. In 1756 it moved to Princeton when the town offered £1,000 and a tract of land, but it did not officially adopt its present name until 1896. In addition to housing the entire college at that time, Nassau Hall also served as a barracks for both Continental and British troops during the Revolution, as a meeting place for the first legislature of the State of New Jersey, and as the capitol of the United States from June through November of 1783. It was named in honor of King William III of the House of Orange-Nassau, which also explains Princeton's colors. The Faculty Room, which you may visit, contains Charles Willson Peale's famous painting of *Washington at the Battle of Princeton* along with portraits of King George II, King William III, and those of a number of illustrious graduates including presidents James Madison and Woodrow Wilson.

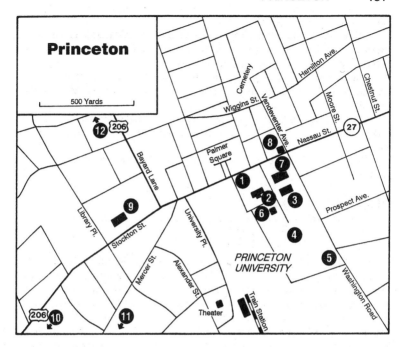

University Chapel (3) was completed in 1928 to replace an earlier one that had burned down. Services are held in a variety of faiths, including Protestant, Catholic, Orthodox, and Jewish. Modeled after the chapel of King's College in Cambridge, England, it has four great stained-glass windows representing Love, Truth, Endurance, and Hope. Among the figures depicted are John Witherspoon, the University's sixth president and the only clergyman to sign the Declaration of Independence.

Prospect Garden (4) surrounds the Florentine-style Prospect House, a mansion of 1849 that became the residence of the University's presidents in 1878 and is now a dining and social facility for the faculty. After its gardens were demolished by a rampaging football crowd in 1904, Princeton's then-president Woodrow Wilson had an iron fence erected to enclose the five acres, and Mrs. Wilson laid out the flower garden in approximately its present form. It contains a vast array of trees, bushes, plants, and flowers; from common domestic varieties to the most exotic. Some of the trees predate the house, and at least one example of each variety is labeled with its botanical and common name.

The **Natural History Museum** (5), Guyot Hall, contains archaeological, biological, and geological specimens. Among its treasures are skeletons of a saber-toothed tiger, a giant pig, a three-toed horse, and a baby dinosaur. The building's exterior is decorated with some 200 carvings of flora and fauna, both those extinct and those still with us. ☎ *609-258-4101. Open*

Mon.–Fri. 9–5. Free. &.

*The Art Museum (6), McCormick Hall. ☎ *609-258-3787, Internet: http://webware.Princeton.EDU/artmus. Open Tues.–Sat. 10–5, Sun. 1–5. Closed Mon. and major holidays. Admission $3.* &. Picasso's 1971 sculpture, *Head of a Woman*, stands in front of this modern museum building. Inside, the absolutely first-rate collections range all the way from Egyptian, Greek, and Roman antiquities to contemporary American painting and sculpture. Between these are medieval works of art including a stained-glass window from Chartres, Renaissance paintings, Oriental art, some major works of the French Impressionists, and fine photography. If you like art, you'll love this museum.

The Putnam Sculptures, a collection of some 22 modern sculptures, is scattered all over the campus, both indoors and out. It includes works by Calder, Epstein, Lipchitz, Moore, Nevelson, Noguchi, Picasso, and Segal among other 20th-century masters.

Firestone Library (7), the home of more than four million books, is the central research library for the University. Its holdings are especially rich in materials relating to the American Revolution. You might want to visit its Exhibition Gallery, to the right of the main entrance.

Princeton Town, whose historic core lies just north of the campus, has a number of attractions of its own, including:

BAINBRIDGE HOUSE (8), 158 Nassau St., Princeton, NJ 08542, ☎ 609-921-6748, Internet: www.princetonol.com/groups/histsoc. *Open Tues.–Sun., noon–4. Donation. Guided tours of Princeton Sun. 2 p.m. or by appointment.* &.

Built in 1766, this was the birthplace of Commodore William "Old Ironsides" Bainbridge, who commanded the USS *Constitution* during the War of 1812. Now the headquarters of the **Historical Society of Princeton**, the house features a museum with changing exhibitions, a library, photo archives, and a museum shop. Maps and other information for self-guided tours of the town are available here.

Just a few blocks west of this is **Morven** (9). Once the home of Richard Stockton, a signer of the Declaration of Independence, this brick house of 1755 reportedly served as headquarters for British General Cornwallis in 1777, was visited by Washington, and from 1953 until 1981 was the official residence of New Jersey's governors. *55 Stockton St.,* ☎ *609-683-4495. Tours on Wed. 11–2 or by appointment. Closed July and Aug.* The present governor lives down the road at **Drumthwacket** (10), a restored 1835 mansion that may be visited. *354 Stockton St.,* ☎ *609-683-0057. Tours on Wed., noon–2, call ahead to confirm. Closed Jan., Feb., Aug.*

About a mile or so out of town, on Mercer Street, is the **Princeton**

Battlefield State Park (11), where George Washington won a decisive victory over the British on January 3, 1777. Princeton, of course, was loyal to the Crown, and as a result got itself looted after the hostilities. On the property is the **Thomas Clarke House**, a Quaker farmhouse of 1770. Furnished as it would have been during the Revolutionary War, it also exhibits artifacts of the battle. *500 Mercer Rd.,* ☎ *609-921-0074. House open Wed.–Sat. 10–noon and 1–4, Sun. 1–4. Free.*

Five miles north of Princeton via US-206 (Bayard Lane) stands **Rockingham** (12). While waiting for the signing of the peace treaty with England, the Continental Congress convened at Princeton. General Washington was invited to attend and made his headquarters at nearby Rockingham, using the Blue Room as his study. Here, in November 1783, he wrote his "Farewell Address to the Armies." You can visit his study and step out as he must have on the balcony, but you won't see the same terrain he saw, for the restored building has been moved from its original site. *108 Route 518 at River Rd., Rocky Hill, NJ 08540,* ☎ *609-921-8835. Open Wed.–Sat. 10–noon and 1–4, Sun. 1–4. Free.*

Flemington

B argains, fun, and a strong sense of America's past go together in Flemington, New Jersey's factory outlet town *par excellence*. First settled in 1756 by Samuel Fleming on land originally owned by William Penn, this friendly small town has a remarkably well-preserved core with historic buildings dating as far back as the mid-18th century. In fact, some 60% of its structures are on the National Register of Historic Places. In the late 1800s Flemington became a center for the production of fine pottery and glassware, as it still is, and a hub of railroad activity with some 54 trains a day by 1889. Today, its lovely old center is surrounded by a formidable array of factory outlets, shops, and restaurants. The railroad still runs on steam; only now it carries tourists and shoppers out for a few hours of nostalgic fun. A recent addition to Flemington's attractions is the utterly fantastic Northlandz—surely worth the trip in itself, especially if you have kids in tow or are still one at heart.

GETTING THERE:

By car, the best (but not shortest) route from Philadelphia is to take I-95 northeast for about 34 miles to Exit 4, then NJ-31 11 miles north to Ringoes. Here connect with US-202, driving 6 miles north to the Flemington Circle. Take NJ-31 another mile north, then East Main Street southwest into the town. There are free parking lots for visitors both downtown and around the outlet stores.

The shorter route via PA-611 and connecting roads is much slower.

PRACTICALITIES:

Most of the shops, and Northlandz, are open daily all year round. The railroad operates on weekends and holidays from Easter through December, and also on Thursdays and Fridays in July and August. For further information contact the **Flemington Information Center**, Ramada Inn on US-202, P.O. Box 903, Flemington, NJ 08822, ☎ 908-806-8165. Some Internet sites are: www.flemington-nj.com and www.flemington.net.

FOOD AND DRINK:

There are plenty of places to eat in Flemington, including the usual fast-food suspects near the 202/31 traffic circle. Among the better choices are:

Rattlesnake Southwestern Grill (208 Rte. 202/31, 1.5 miles south of the traffic circle) Southwestern American cuisine for lunch or dinner. ☎ 908-788-7772. $$

Upper Crust Tea Room (146 Main St.) Light meals, luncheons, and teas in a Victorian setting. ☎ 908-788-9750. X: Sun. $ and $$

Linda's Eatery (Liberty Village) A cafeteria with comfort food, especially turkey dishes. Indoor/outdoor seating. ☎ 908-284-9100. $

LOCAL ATTRACTIONS:

Numbers in parentheses correspond to numbers on the map.

Historic Flemington is centered on Main Street around the imposing **Union Hotel** (1) of 1877, a four-story brick structure with a mansard roof and gingerbread porches. Many famous media people stayed there during the notorious 1935 "Trial of the Century" that took place across the street in the former **Hunterdon County Courthouse** (2), a Greek Revival building of 1828. It was here that Bruno Hauptmann was convicted and sentenced to death for the kidnapping and murder of Charles Lindbergh Jr., the infant son of the pioneer aviator.

Nearby, at 114 Main Street, is the **Doric House** (3), a Greek Revival structure dating from 1846. Built as a home, it has been restored. Turn right on Mine Street and right again on Park Avenue. A left on Bonnell Street takes you past **Fleming's Castle** (4) at number 5, a simple Colonial home that must have seemed like a palace in those primitive days. Built in 1756 by the town's founder as an inn, it is the oldest house in Flemington and has been preserved by the Daughters of the American Revolution. Across the street, between numbers 56 and 60, is the small **Case Cemetery** (5), where the area's first settlers are buried along with their friend, Indian Chief Tuccamirgan.

Factory outlets in town tend to be located up and down Main Street and along the nearby side streets. Large color-coded directories with maps will guide you to the stores. Some of the most famous of these are in the **Flemington Cut Glass Complex** (6) beginning at Main and Church streets. The first and largest factory outlet in the U.S. for crystal and glass, this series of stores also offers a wide assortment of cookware, gifts, home decorations, and fixtures. Another pioneer in this kind of retailing is the **Flemington Fur Company** (7) on Spring Street, a block east of the Union Hotel, which has been serving customers from all over the country since 1921.

Liberty Village (8) and **Turntable Junction** (9) are two adjacent shopping "villages" of reproduction Colonial-style buildings attractively arranged around open commons. Located two blocks west of Masin Street on either side of Church Street, they contain some 80 factory outlet shops

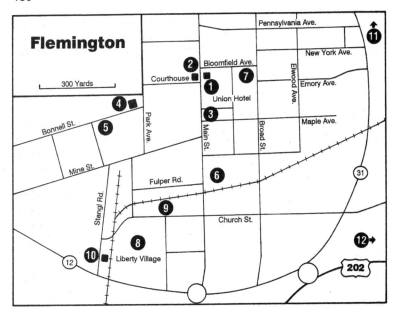

featuring all kinds of famous-brand merchandise at discount prices, cafés, and restaurants. Like the shops in town, those in Liberty Village and Turntable Junction are open every day except Easter, Thanksgiving, Christmas, and New Year's; usually from 10–6 or 9; and are largely wheelchair-accessible.

Nearby is the:

BLACK RIVER & WESTERN RAILROAD (10), P.O. Box 200, Ringoes, NJ 08551, ☎ 908-782-9600, Internet: www.geocities.com/Colosseum/Bleachers/ 5398brw. *Vintage steam or diesel trains operate Sat., Sun., and holidays from Easter through Dec., running one-hour round trips between Flemington and Ringoes. During July and August they also run on Thurs. and Fri. There are also occasional trips between Ringoes and Lambertville. Call for current schedules. Adults $8, children 3–11 $4, under 3 free.*

Visit the Ringoes Station, built in 1854 by the Flemington Transportation Company and restored by the Black River & Western. Ringoes Station has a souvenir car, snack bar, and picnic grove.

The **Flemington Fair and Speedway** (11), on NJ-31 just north of the town, offers the chance to experience a typical small country fair with all of its agricultural roots intact. Begun in 1856, the **Fair** runs from the

Tuesday before Labor Day through Labor Day. Its **Speedway**, one of the best motor racing tracks in the northeast, has auto racing events on Saturdays from May through Oct. *For information on either,* ☎ *908-782-2413.* &.

Heading north about two miles on US-202 brings you to:

*NORTHLANDZ (12), 495 Rte. 202 South, Flemington, NJ 08822, ☎ 908-782-4022, fax 908-782-5131, Internet: www.northlandz.com. *Open daily except Christmas: Sat.–Sun. 10–6, Mon.–Fri. 10:30–4 Indoor tour: Adults $13.75, seniors 62+ $12.50, children 2-12 $9.75. Snack bar. Gift shop. Outdoor miniature steam train rides.* &.

More than just the largest model train layout on Earth, this is really a fantasy world of almost surrealist proportions. Surely the result of a very, very fertile imagination—or a mad model railroader—Northlandz is superficially realistic but actually quite weird. It simply has to be seen to be believed. Mountains tower three stories high as trains—as many as 125 of them—speed across improbable bridges up to 40 feet long, then plunge into tunnels, emerging in wildly narrow canyons. The entire walk through its many scenes and levels is a full mile in length, opening occasionally into exhibitions of rare dolls, art, and even an impressive theater with a 2,000-pipe organ that is played several times a day. Outside, there is an operating one-third scale steam railway that takes visitors on journeys through the woodland site. You'll have fun at Northlandz, and so will the kids!

Trip 28

Southeastern Monmouth County

A restored 19th-century industrial village, a preserved narrow-gauge steam railroad, a Victorian retreat on the sea, and a Revolutionary War battlefield are your options on this excursion into the past. With perfect timing you could probably "do" all four in a day, but a more relaxed approach would be to settle for two or three, according to your interests.

For those staying overnight, this trip combines beautifully with the following ones to the Jersey Shore.

GETTING THERE:

By car, Allaire State Park and the Pine Creek Railroad are about 68 miles northeast of downtown Philadelphia. Take I-95 north to its intersection with US-1 and follow that east into Trenton. There pick up NJ-29 and continue east to I-195. Take this east to Exit 31 (Squankum). Go north on Route 574 a very short distance, then east on Route 524 (under the interstate) and into the park.

For Ocean Grove, get back on I-195 and go east a few miles to its end. From there take the Garden State Parkway (toll) north to Exit 100, then NJ-33 east to Ocean Grove, just north of Bradley Beach.

For Monmouth Battlefield, go west on NJ-33 to Freehold, then take Route 522 west into the park. The easiest (not the shortest) return from here is via US-9 south from Freehold to I-195, then retrace your route back to Philadelphia.

PRACTICALITIES:

This is really a summer trip, to be taken between early May and late September. Go on a weekend if you can, because that's when the Historic Allaire Village opens its buildings to visitors, and when the Pine Creek Railroad runs its steam trains. Please check before you go, however, as schedules are flexible and some attractions *are* open at other times. Although the trip goes right to the sea, you probably won't have time for a dip.

For further information contact the **Monmouth County Department of Public Information & Tourism**, 6 West Main St., Freehold, NJ 07728, ☎ 800-523-2587. For information about Ocean Grove, contact the **Ocean Grove**

Tourism Bureau, Box 277, Ocean Grove, NJ 07756, ☎ 732-774-4736 (mid-May through mid-October).

FOOD AND DRINK:

Allaire State Park and the Monmouth Battlefield have both picnic facilities and snack bars offering light meals (in season). For restaurants, you'll have to go to Ocean Grove or other nearby communities. Some good choices are:

Old Mill Inn (Old Mill Rd., Spring Lake Heights, at Ocean Rd. between NJ-35 and NJ-71) Steaks and regional American cuisine with a view, overlooking the old mill pond. Sunday brunch. ☎ 732-449-1800. $$

La Nonna Piancones (804 Main St. in Bradley Beach) A casual place for contemporary Italian cuisine. ☎ 732-775-0906. X: Sun. lunch. $$

Raspberry Café (58 Main St. in Ocean Grove) Soups, sandwiches and light meals in an attractive, simple café. ☎ 732-988-0833. $

Sampler Inn (28 Main St. in Ocean Grove) A cafeteria with wholesome home cooking; an Ocean Grove landmark since 1917. ☎ 732-775-1905. X: Nov.–Apr. $

LOCAL ATTRACTIONS:

Numbers in parentheses correspond to numbers on the map.

ALLAIRE STATE PARK (1), P.O. Box 220, Rt. 524, Farmingdale, NJ 07727, ☎ 732-938-2371. *Open daily all year, 8 to dusk. Visitor Center open Memorial Day–Labor Day, Wed.–Sun. 10–5; day after Labor Day to end of Oct., weekends 10–4. Buildings open May–Oct., weekends only, 10–4. Building tours $1.50. Parking fee (Memorial Day–Labor Day only), weekends and holidays $3 per car. Picnic facilities, canoeing, nature center, fishing, riding and hiking trails, camping, winter sports, snack bar. Leashed pets only in park, no pets in campsites. Some facilities are ở.*

In 1941 the family of newspaperman Arthur Brisbane deeded 800 acres of land to the people of New Jersey for use as a "historical center and forest park reservation." Since then the park has grown to cover some 3,000 acres of the New Jersey coastal plain. Its attractions include the fascinating **Historic Allaire Village**, whose buildings are open on weekends from May through October and are often the scene of special events. In the late 1700 Allaire was the site of a furnace and forge where iron was smelted from the "bog ore" produced by decaying vegetation. In 1822 James P. Allaire purchased the ironworks to supply his foundry in New York City and built a bustling industrial community of over 400 people. With the discovery of higher-grade Pennsylvania ore and the increasing use of coal, Allaire declined, and the ironworks shut down in 1848. Today, the village has been beautifully restored; and you can visit a furnace, a carpenter's shop, a blacksmith's, a bakery, a general store, and other

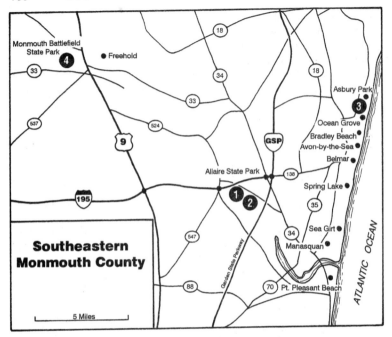

original buildings where staff dressed in the work clothes of the 1830s demonstrate the old trades. This is a fascinating experience for young and old alike.

The ***Pine Creek Railroad** (2) is a must for just about every visitor. *All aboard!* for a trip back in time on New Jersey's only live steam narrow-gauge railroad. You'll ride in antique cars pulled by a coal-burning loco-motive (veteran diesel engine sometimes employed) of the kind that was used to push back the frontiers of the American West. Adjacent to the sta-tion is an open work area where many old locomotives and cars are being painstakingly restored by volunteers. *Allaire State Park,* ☎ *732-938-5524. Operates daily in July and Aug., noon–4:30; weekends noon–4:30 in May–June and Sept.–Oct. Fare $2.50 per person.*

OCEAN GROVE (3). *Tourist season Memorial Day to weekend after Labor Day. Beach fees $4.50. Beach picnics, swimming, fishing, boardwalk activi-ties. No pets on beaches.* **Ocean Grove Tourism Bureau**, *Box 277, Ocean Grove, NJ 07756,* ☎ *732-774-4736 (mid-May–through mid–Oct.), or* **Chamber of Commerce**, ☎ *800-388-4768. An Internet site to check is:* www.oceangrovenj.com. *Boardwalk is ⅊.*

This attractive small town, noted for its Victorian architecture, serves as a setting for religious and cultural programs, Bible meetings, evangelical talks, and recitals. A National and State Historic Site, it was founded in 1869 for Methodist camp meetings. The **Ocean Grove Auditorium**, built in 1894, seats 6,500 persons and is the focal point of the town. Preachers and evangelists use its big stage on Sundays, while famous entertainers and musicians perform on other days. The **Centennial Cottage**, an authentic Ocean Grove seashore vacation home, has been completely restored to its 1870s appearance and is operated as a period museum. *Corner of Central Ave. and McClintock Street,* ☎ *732-774-1869. Open July–Aug., Mon.–Sat., 11–3.*

MONMOUTH BATTLEFIELD STATE PARK (4), 347 Freehold-Englishtown Road, Freehold, NJ 07726, ☎ 732-462-9616. *Park open daily 8–dusk, Visitor Center daily 9–4. Picnicking facilities, playground, refreshments, hiking and riding trails, nature center. Admission free. Partially ᶜ.*

The largest single battle of the Revolutionary War was fought here on June 28, 1778, with an indecisive outcome. In the midst of the carnage there appeared a heroine, one Mary Ludwig Hays, who carried pitchers of water to the stricken soldiers and became forever known as "Molly Pitcher." Her story, and that of the battle, is re-created with an audio-visual show and an electric relief map in the Visitor Center near the entrance. While there, you can pick up a map and explore the 1,500-acre battlefield itself, perhaps stopping at the **Craig House** of 1710, and at a reproduction of what is thought to be Molly's Well.

Trip 29
The Jersey Shore: Barnegat Peninsula

Other folks may go to the seaside; Philadelphians go "down the shore." The Jersey Shore, that is. At its closest only a 60-mile drive from downtown, the Jersey Shore has long held a magnetic attraction for the people of southeastern Pennsylvania, who usually stay for at least several days, if not weeks. Making a daytrip here allows you to sample the various beaches and decide which appeal to you most for a real vacation later on. The three beaches covered on this excursion each have their own personality, from bustling amusement parks to isolated sand dunes. Toms River, on the return route, has some interesting museums and a nearby nature center that are worth a visit.

For those able to stay overnight, this trip combines well with both the previous and the following ones.

GETTING THERE:

By car, Point Pleasant Beach is about 76 miles east of downtown Philadelphia. Take I-95 north to its intersection with US-1, then follow US-1 east to Trenton and get on NJ-29 to I-195. Follow I-195 east to NJ-34, taking that and NJ-35 south into Point Pleasant Beach.

Continue south on NJ-35 through Bay Head, Seaside Heights, and Seaside Park—a drive of about 12 miles. Island Beach State Park lies just south of this.

Take NJ-37 west from Seaside Heights for about seven miles to Toms River.

The easy-but-not-short route from Toms River back to Philadelphia is to take US-9 north to I-195, then I-195 west to NJ-29. Continue west on this to Trenton, them take US-1 south to I-95, following that into Philadelphia. The total return drive is 77 miles.

Those with good navigational skills can cut a good 20 miles off this by heading south from Toms River on County Route 530. Follow this west to Mount Holly, then take NJ-38 into Camden, and US-30 over the Ben Franklin Bridge into Philadelphia.

PRACTICALITIES:

Although you *could* make this trip at any time, chances are you'll enjoy it more between Memorial Day and Labor Day—when the beaches are open and the many amusements in full swing. Island Beach State Park and the mainland attractions are open all year round.

Come prepared for the beach, and don't forget the sunscreen lotion and sunglasses. All of the towns charge a nominal fee to use their beaches. Parking near the beachfront is metered (quarters only), and there are parking lots. Free parking is usually some distance from the water.

For further information on **Point Pleasant Beach** contact the **Point Pleasant Beach Chamber of Commerce**, 517A Arnold Ave., Point Pleasant Beach, NJ 08742, ☎ 732-899-2424. For **Bay Head** ☎ 800-4-BAYHED. For **Seaside Heights** ☎ 732-793-1510 or 800-SEASHOR, Internet: www.injersey.com/nj/ocean/seasidehts. For the **entire area** contact the **Toms River/Ocean County Chamber of Commerce**, 1200 Hooper Ave., Toms River, NJ 08753, ☎ 732-349-0220.

FOOD AND DRINK:

Besides the numerous inexpensive eateries along the boardwalk, and perhaps a beach picnic at Island Beach State Park, these are some of the better places for a good meal:

Grenville by the Sea (345 Main Ave., NJ-35, in Bay Head) Creative cuisine in an historic 1890's hotel. Affiliated with a New Jersey winery, so don't order beer. ☎ 732-892-3100. X: Mon. $$ and $$$

Jack Baker's Wharfside (101 Channel Dr. in Pt. Pleasant Beach, half-mile east of NJ-35) Enjoy seafood overlooking Manasquan Inlet. ☎ 732-892-9100. $$

Barmores Shrimp Box (75 Inlet Dr., Pt. Pleasant Beach, half-mile east of NJ-35 via Broadway) A relaxed, casual place for freshly-caught fish, dinner only. ☎ 732-899-1637. $$

Old Time Tavern (Dove Mall, north of jct. of NJ-37 and NJ-166, in Toms River) Steak, seafood, pasta, pizza, and the like in a casual family restaurant. ☎ 732-505-5307. $ and $$

King's Wok (1226 NJ-166, just south of NJ-37 in Toms River) Szechuan, Hunan, and Cantonese specialties. ☎ 732-286-1505. $

LOCAL ATTRACTIONS:

Numbers in parentheses correspond to numbers on the map.

POINT PLEASANT BEACH (1), Point Pleasant Area Chamber of Commerce, 517A Arnold Ave., Point Pleasant Beach, NJ 08742, ☎ 732-899-2424. *Beach season Memorial Day to Labor Day. Nominal beach fees. Swimming, deep-sea fishing, boat rentals, waterskiing, rides, amusements, boardwalk activities, special events. No pets on beaches. Boardwalk is ⅙.*

This Atlantic Ocean bungalow colony has two miles of white sandy beaches and a bustling boardwalk lined with arcades, rides, stores, and restaurants. The town is home port to a fleet of commercial fishing ves-

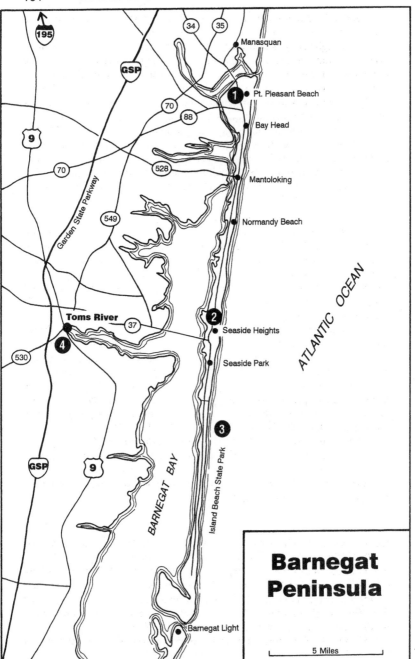

Barnegat Peninsula

5 Miles

sels, but folks out for pleasure rather than business will find plenty of action in these waters, either on their own or in numerous fishing tournaments throughout the season. The Off-Shore Grand Prix, one of the major powerboat races in the United States, attracts large crowds every July, and in September the Seafood Festival offers delicacies from the deep as well as an art show.

Don't miss **Jenkinson's Aquarium**, a state-of-the-art facility with all sorts of exotic life forms that swim, crawl, walk, or fly. There's a petting tank, a live coral reef, a fossil room, and more. *Boardwalk and Parkway,* ☎ *732-899-1212. Open June–Aug. daily 10–10, rest of year daily 10–5. Closed Christmas and New Year's. Adults $6.50, seniors and ages 3–12 $4.*

Head south through the popular summer resort communities of Bay Head, Mantoloking, Normandy Beach,, Lavallette, and Ortley Beach to:

SEASIDE HEIGHTS (2), Seaside Business Association, P.O. Box 98, Seaside Heights, NJ 08751, ☎ 732-793-1510 or 800-SEASHOR, Internet: www.in jersey.com/nj/ocean/seasidehts. *Tourist season late May to mid-Sept. Beach fees. Some free parking on west side of town. Swimming, fishing, crabbing, surfboat rental, water skiing, jet skiing. Free entry to amusement park, fees per activity. No pets on beach. Beach access & available free,* ☎ *732-793-9100 in advance.*

Fun and games for the whole family abound on this beautiful three-mile beachfront and mile-long boardwalk, crammed with some of the best rides, games of chance, snack bars, restaurants, and shops to be found along the Jersey Shore. The **Ferris Wheel** offers great views of it all. One of the nation's finest hand-carved wooden merry-go-rounds, the ***Historic Dentzel/Looff Carousel***, has been charming people for over 80 years. **Water Works**, a water park with slides, rides, and a pool offers plenty of fun. *Open daily, Memorial Day to Labor Day,* ☎ *732-793-6488.*

There are fireworks on July 4 and every Wednesday night, and numerous special events throughout the season. Call in advance to get this year's schedule.

Continue south through the more sedate **Seaside Park**, which has its own boardwalk and amusement pier, to:

ISLAND BEACH STATE PARK (3), P.O. Box 37, Seaside Park, NJ 08752, ☎ 732-793-0506. *Open daily all year, daylight hours; summer hours 8–8. Parking fee. Guided nature tours, swimming, surf fishing (by permit), picnicking (no facilities provided), surfing, beach strolling, scuba diving: all permitted in designated areas only. Life guards, bathhouses, storage lockers, snack bars from mid-June through Labor Day. No pets in swimming areas, leashed pets only elsewhere. Some facilities are &.*

One of the few remaining natural barrier beaches and by far the best along the Jersey Shore, this narrow 10-mile strip of land is a lovely spot to picnic and enjoy the sights and sounds of the ocean. Two nature areas offer acres of dunes dotted with holly clumps and briar thickets, and there's a recreation area for more active pursuits along with a self-guided nature trail. The southern tip of the park is just a stone's throw from Barnegat Light on Long Beach Island, subject of the next daytrip. Please remember that the dunes and beach grass are crucial to the island's fragile environment; walk and drive only in designated areas.

Toms River (4), back on the mainland, makes a convenient stop before heading back to Philadelphia. This thriving community, rich in memories of the Revolutionary War, is home to the **Ocean County Museum**. Housed in a 19th-century Victorian structure, it features displays of early industries, county history, and memorabilia of the dirigibles that once operated from nearby Lakehurst Naval Air Station until the famous Hindenburg disaster occurred there in 1937. *26 Hadley Ave., Toms River, NJ 08754,* ☎ *732-341-1880. Open Tues. and Thurs., 1–3, and Sat. 10–3. Donation $2.*

Also nearby is the **Cattus Island Park** with its scenic bay views, abundant bird life, nature center, and some 14 miles of hiking trails. *1170 Cattus Island Blvd. (via Fischer Blvd. off NJ-37, follow signs), Toms River, NJ 08753,* ☎ *732-270-6960. Park open daily dawn to dusk, environmental center daily 10–4. Free. Partially ♿.*

The Jersey Shore: Long Beach Island

Continuing your sampling of the Jersey Shore, this daytrip gets away from the crowds and explores an 18-mile-long barrier isle that features New Jersey's most picturesque lighthouse, several quiet villages reminiscent of Cape Cod, and a small-but-highly-enjoyable amusement park. If you can stay overnight, why not consider combining this with the previous trip to the Barnegat Peninsula, or with the following one to the Pine Barrens?

GETTING THERE:

By car, you basically have a choice of an easy-to-follow-but-long route, or a much shorter one requiring some navigation. Both take about the same time. Via the **long route**, Long Beach Island is 88 miles east of downtown Philadelphia. Take US-30 across the Ben Franklin Bridge, then I-676 south to NJ-42. Follow that onto the Atlantic City Expressway (toll), getting off at Exit 7, the Garden State Parkway (toll). Head north on the parkway to Exit 63 and go east on NJ-72 into Ship Bottom on Long Beach Island.

The much **shorter route**, about 61 miles, again takes you across the Ben Franklin Bridge on US-30, then east on NJ-70 to its intersection with NJ-72 and into Ship Bottom. From there it's only eight miles north to Barnegat Light, and about eight miles south to Beach Haven.

PRACTICALITIES:

Again, don't leave home without the sunscreen lotion and sunglasses, and expect to pay a nominal fee to use the beaches. This is really a summer trip, to be made on a fine day between Memorial Day and Labor Day.

For further information contact the **Southern Ocean County Chamber of Commerce**, 265 W. 9th St., Ship Bottom, NJ 08008, ☎ 609-494-7211 or 800-292-6372, e-mail: sochamber@aol.com.

FOOD AND DRINK:

Picnic tables are available at the Barnegat Lighthouse State Park, and there's a snack bar nearby. There's also a snack bar at Fantasy Island. Few restaurants line these quiet streets, but you might try:

The Dutchman's Brauhaus (Long Beach Island Causeway, on the mainland near Manahawkin, overlooking the bay) German, Continental, and American specialties, served indoors or out. ☎ 609-494-6910. $$

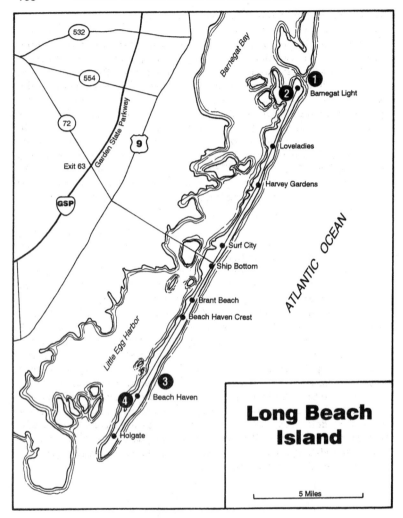

Long Beach Island

5 Miles

LOCAL ATTRACTIONS:

Numbers in parentheses correspond to numbers on the map.

*BARNEGAT LIGHTHOUSE STATE PARK (1), P.O. Box 167, Barnegat Light, NJ 08006, ☎ 609-494-2016. *Park open daily all year from dawn to dusk; light-house Memorial Day to Labor Day, daily 9–4:30; May 1 to day before Memorial Day and day after Labor Day through Sept., Wed.–Sun. 9–4:30; rest of year Sat.–Sun. 9–3:30. Park free, lighthouse $1 (under 12 free).*

Fishing, picnic tables, snack bar nearby. Partially ♿.

Located at the northern tip of the island, this small, 31-acre state park features "***Old Barney**," a classic red-and-white lighthouse from the mid-19th century. You can climb all 217 steps of its spiral staircase for a spectacular ***view**, or just admire the scene from sea level. The waters around here were always dangerous, with many a sailing ship breaking up on the shoals when their captains hugged the coast too closely. Legend has it that pirates, including Captain Kidd (1645–1701), practiced their trade here; as did the notorious scavengers who lured boats into shallow waters with deceptive lights on shore—and then robbed them. To reduce the carnage, the first lighthouse on this site was built in 1834. The present structure was completed in 1858 by General George Meade of Civil War fame. Its light served as a beacon until being extinguished in 1944. The open seas off Barnegat are still rough, making them popular with surfers.

Just a few blocks south of the lighthouse is an old one-room schoolhouse that now houses the **Barnegat Light Museum** (2), where artifacts of local history are displayed along with Old Barney's original Fresnel lens. *Central Ave. at 5th St., Barnegat Light, NJ 08006, ☎ 609-494-8578. Open daily in summer, 2–5, or by appointment. Donation.*

Beach Haven (3), reached after driving south through affluent beachfront villages (with some surprisingly modern architecture) for about 15 miles, is the only really commercialized town on the island. Its **historic district** has a number of well restored Victorian buildings, and there are some excellent **shopping areas** along Bay Avenue between 3rd and 9th streets. Use of the **beach** requires a tag, obtainable at the beach entrance.

While in Beach Haven, be sure to visit **Fantasy Island** (4), an unusually good family-oriented amusement park with a Victorian ambiance, offering adult and kiddie rides, midway games, a family casino arcade, food stands, and an ice-cream parlor. *West 7th St. at Bay Ave., ☎ 609-492-4000, Internet: www.fantasyislandpark.com. Open daily in summer and partially on weekends at other times. Admission is free.*

Trip 31
From the Pine Barrens to the Sea

Heading southeast across New Jersey towards the ocean takes you through a strangely remote and rustic region known as the Pine Barrens, home of the legendary Jersey Devil. According to local folklore, this demonic being was the 13th child born to a Mrs. Leeds in 1735, and had bat wings, red eyes, and a forked tail. Although supposedly exorcised after eating its family in 1740, its spirit still haunts the Pine Barrens.

In the heart of this region lies the restored 19th-century village of Batsto, where visitors can explore the nation's early industrial heritage, surrounded by New Jersey's largest wilderness area. Following country roads along the Mullica River and then turning south soon leads you to one of America's oldest wineries—a fine place to sample the juice and perhaps have lunch.

You are now only a few miles from Atlantic City, but about to enter a completely different world. Southern New Jersey's only real fine-arts museum, The Noyes, is beautifully sited next to a fabulous wildlife refuge on the edge of the sea. This can be thoroughly experienced on a self-guided eight-mile auto tour of the coastal habitat. And, if that's not enough, there are quaint shops at Smithville and a different kind of wilderness at the Bass River State Forest.

If you can stay overnight or longer, this trip combines nicely with the previous ones to the Jersey Shore.

GETTING THERE:

By car, Batsto, the first stop, is about 44 miles southeast of downtown Philadelphia. Take US-30 across the Benjamin Franklin Bridge and head south on I-676. Continue on NJ-42 and the Atlantic City Expressway (toll) to Exit 28, Hammonton. From there go north on NJ-54 to County Route 542 (Pleasant Mills Road), and follow it east into Batsto.

From Batsto to Egg Harbor is about 12 miles. Take County Route 542 (Pleasant Mills Road) east for about five miles, then County Route 563 (Green Bank Road) seven miles south, followed by County Route 561A (East Moss Mill Road) to the Renault Winery on North Bremen Avenue.

Continue on County Route 561A (Moss Mill Road) for 10 miles to US-

9 (New York Road) at Smithville, then go two miles south to Oceanville, home of the Noyes Museum and the Forsythe National Wildlife Refuge.

To reach Bass River, head north on US-9 to the Garden State Parkway. Continue north on this a short distance to Exit 52, then follow local roads for a mile to the state park.

The fastest and easiest route back to Philadelphia is via the Atlantic City Expressway, a drive of 61 miles from Oceanville.

PRACTICALITIES:

Although at its best between Memorial Day and Labor Day, this area can be enjoyed at any time—weather permitting. Bear in mind that the buildings at Batsto are closed off season, and that the Noyes Museum is closed on Mondays and Tuesdays.

Be sure to pack insect repellant if you're coming between late spring and early fall, lest New Jersey's State Bird, the mosquito, eats you. You'll also want appropriate footwear if you plan on hiking any of the nature trails.

For further information contact the sites directly, or the **New Jersey Division of Travel & Tourism**, ☎ 609-292-2470 or 800-537-7397, Internet: www.visitnj.org.

FOOD AND DRINK:

Renault Winery (72 N. Bremen Ave., Egg Harbor City, US-30 at NJ-50, 2.5 miles north on Bremen Ave.) Lunch from a creative menu is served daily in the Garden Café, while the Gourmet Restaurant offers exquisite, elaborate evening dinners. Reservations required for dinner, ☎ 609-965-2111. Sunday brunch. $$ and $$$

Ram's Head Inn (9 W. White Horse Pike, US-30, in Absecon) Elegant dining in an old mansion; traditional American cuisine. Dress well and reserve, ☎ 609-652-1700. $$ and $$$

Little Brat's Haus (615 E. Moss Mill Rd., US-9, in Smithville) Good German food with a view. ☎ 609-652-9377. $$

Shore Diner (6710 Tilton Rd., near Exit 36 of the Garden State Pkwy. in Pleasantville) A pleasant, family place with generous portions. ☎ 609-641-3669. $ and $$

LOCAL ATTRACTIONS:

Numbers in parentheses correspond to numbers on the map.

*BATSTO HISTORIC VILLAGE (1), Wharton State Forest, Route 542, Hammonton, NJ 08037, ☎ 609-561-3262, Internet: www.state.nj.us/dep/forestry/histsite. *Grounds open daily, dawn to dusk.*

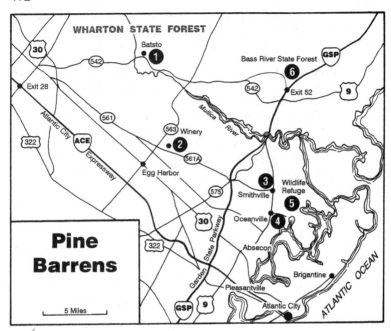

Buildings open Memorial Day to Labor Day, daily 10–4, and at various other times of the year on varied schedule. Guided tours: Adults $2, ages 6–11 $1. Parking on weekends and holidays from Memorial Day to Labor Day $3, otherwise free. Free self-guided tour and nature trail. Visitor Center is ♿.

Located near abundant bog-iron deposits, the historic village of Batsto played an important role in the industrial development of the region. Its iron works, founded in 1766, was a major supplier of munitions and other wartime products to George Washington's Continental Army. During the mid-19th century it turned to the manufacture of glass after cheaper sources of iron developed elsewhere; and later to lumbering, cranberry farming, and livestock breeding. From a population of nearly a thousand at its peak, the village declined severely toward the end of the century, becoming part of the vast Wharton Estate that was sold to the State of New Jersey in 1954 as a nature preserve.

Many of the original buildings survived, and others have been restored. The **Batsto Mansion** with its Victorian tower, the perfect picture of a haunted house, may be visited on guided tours that begin at the Visitor Center. While there, you can pick up a map for a self-guided exploration of the entire village, which includes the village store, gristmill, blacksmith's shop, barns, workers' homes, and other attractions.

Batsto Village lies at the southern edge of the **Wharton State Forest**, an 111,000-acre tract of Pine Barrens offering picnicking, primitive camping, hiking, canoeing, and some winter sports. The Nature Trail and Nature Center offer exhibits and programs on Pine Barrens wildlife. ☎ 609-501-00234, Internet: www.state.nj.us/dep/forestry/parks/wharton.

RENAULT WINERY (2), 72 North Bremen Ave., Egg Harbor City, NJ 08215, ☎ 609-965-2111. *Open Mon.–Sat. 10–4, Sun. 11–4. Closed Christmas and New Year's. Tours $2, under 18 free.* ♿.

Established in 1864, this is among the oldest vineyards in the land. It survived Prohibition by cleverly producing a legal, popular "medicinal tonic" that was actually 22% alcohol! Highly enjoyable tours of the premises are offered, ending with wine tastings. There is both a garden café and a gourmet restaurant, both offering appropriate wine dishes, plus a gift shop and a museum.

The route now takes you through **Smithville** (3), a quaint collection of specialty shops in restored buildings, restaurants, and the like that bills itself as the "Towne of Historic Smithville & The Village Green." Rides on a miniature train are offered, and there are various amusements such as a carousel, miniature golf, and paddle boats. *US-9 at Moss Mill Rd., Route 561A,* ☎ *609-652-7777.* ♿. Just south of here is Oceanville, home of:

THE NOYES MUSEUM OF ART (4), Lily Lake Rd., Oceanville, NJ 08231, ☎ 609-652-8848, Internet: www.jerseycape.com/users/thenoyes. *Open Wed.–Sun. 11–4. Closed holidays. Adults $3, seniors (65+) and students with ID $2, under 12 free. Free on Fri. Gift shop.* ♿.

Southern New Jersey's only fine-arts museum features a collection of 19th- and 20th-century American fine and folk art from the Mid-Atlantic region, along with a renowned collection of vintage bird decoys. Located on the edge of picturesque Lily Lake, adjacent to the wildlife refuge (below), its gorgeous exhibitions and terraced galleries provide a pleasant experience in a tranquil setting.

EDWIN B. FORSYTHE NATIONAL WILDLIFE REFUGE, BRIGANTINE DIVISION (5), Great Creek Rd., Oceanville, NJ 08231, ☎ 609-652-1665, Internet: www.fws.gov/r5fws/nj/ebf. *Open all year during daylight hours, weather permitting; office hours 8–4 weekdays. Admission $4 per private vehicle. Pets must be kept on a short leash. Interpretive nature trails, self-guided auto tour. Insect repellant recommended mid-May through Sept.* ♿.

In 1984, the Brigantine and Barnegat National Wildlife refuges were combined and named after Edwin B. Forsythe, the late conservationist congressman from New Jersey. The refuge consists of 40,000 acres of coastal habitats vital to the protection of migratory water birds. The eight-mile **auto tour** includes 14 stops and takes an hour to complete. Over 250 species of birds have been sighted on the refuge, including the endangered peregrine falcon, piping plover, least tern, and the black skimmer. The spring and fall migrations are spectacular (write or call in advance for a calendar of wildlife events); the birds may nest as far north as the Arctic, and winter as far south as South America, passing seasonally through here via the Atlantic Flyway. Besides these spring and fall transients, tens of thousands of migratory waterfowl may winter here, weather permitting. And all this with the high-rise skyline of Atlantic City as a backdrop across the bay!

BASS RIVER STATE FOREST (6), P.O. Box 118, Stage Rd., New Gretna, NJ 08224, ☎ 609-296-1114, Internet: www.state.nj.us/dep/forestry/parks/bass. *Open daily all year, daylight hours. Parking fee Memorial Day to Labor Day $5 per car weekdays, $7 weekends and holidays, otherwise free. Swimming, bathhouse, picnic area and grills at beach, boating, fishing, hiking and riding trails, camping, playground. No pets at beach or in overnight facilities. Brochure and map available at entrance. Restrooms and beach at Lake Absegami are ♿.*

This large and beautiful 25,434-acre forest has good facilities and a lovely lake, Absegami, which makes a perfect spot for a swim or a picnic. Horses may be rented just outside the park.

Atlantic City

Casino gambling is Atlantic City's major drawing card, with its gaming halls offering the greatest concentration of glitz and glitter this side of Las Vegas. Within its casinos you'll find a total world of escapist fantasy, while on the outside this venerable resort is rapidly recovering from its longtime slump and now has a great deal more to entice visitors than just the games of chance.

What began in the late 1700s as a simple fishing village blossomed into a seaside resort with the development of railroads. Taking full advantage of its proximity to the major metropolitan centers of Philadelphia and New York, Atlantic City was incorporated in 1854 and immediately began drawing thousands of city dwellers intent on escaping the summer heat. Its first boardwalk appeared in 1870, and in time a variety of long amusements piers were added, making the place more attractive than ever. By the 1920s and '30s Atlantic City had indeed evolved into the showplace of the nation.

Alas, it was not to last. Widespread ownership of automobiles, an expanding highway system and, especially, the development of jet airliners offered newly-prosperous Americans a wide range of year-round seaside vacation spots: Miami, the Bahamas, the Caribbean, the Riviera, Tahiti—the list goes on and on. Atlantic City just couldn't compete, and declined rapidly, hitting rock bottom in the 1970s.

A renaissance began around 1977 with the introduction of legalized gambling, seen as the city's last and only hope. It worked, at least as far as the boardwalk area was concerned, although there are still seriously depressed areas only blocks from all the glitter. Millions of people now visit, spending literally billions of dollars, some of which has gone into making this a more attractive destination—one well worth the easy daytrip that it is.

For those able to stay overnight—and there are plenty of hotels to stay in—this trip combines beautifully with the previous one to the Pine Barrens.

GETTING THERE:

By car, Atlantic City is about 65 miles southeast of downtown Philadelphia. Take US-30 across the Ben Franklin Bridge and head south on I-676. Continue on NJ-42 and the Atlantic City Expressway (toll) to its end, bearing right onto Missouri Avenue (a.k.a. Christopher Columbus Avenue). Park at any convenient lot from Atlantic Avenue on. The casinos offer inexpensive parking for patrons of their gaming halls.

By train, New Jersey Transit offers frequent, inexpensive commuter service from Philadelphia's 30th Street Station, stopping at Cherry Hill, Lindenwold, Atco, Hammonton, Egg Harbor, and Absecon en route. The entire ride takes about 90 minutes. There's a free shuttle bus (show your rail ticket) from Atlantic City's station to the Boardwalk and casinos. ☎ 800-AC-TRAIN for schedules. Taking the train can be much cheaper than driving, but you won't be able to visit the few out-of-town "Nearby Attractions."

Casino buses operated by numerous companies offer inexpensive rides from just about anywhere in eastern Pennsylvania, New Jersey, Delaware, and New York City to specific casinos in Atlantic City. Check the Yellow Pages under "Bus Lines."

GETTING AROUND:

You can walk just about anywhere on and around the Boardwalk, but should you get tired there are public buses (New Jersey Transit) along Atlantic Avenue ($1 fare), and jitneys along Pacific Avenue ($1.50 fare). Two taxi companies are: City, ☎ 609-345-3244, and Yellow, ☎ 609-344-1221.

PRACTICALITIES:

You can visit Atlantic City at any time, but summer is certainly best for all of the non-casino attractions. For further information contact the Atlantic City Convention & Visitors Authority, 2314 Pacific Avenue, Atlantic City, NJ 08401, ☎ 609-348-7100 or 800-BOARDWK, Internet: www.atlantic citynj.com.

FOOD AND DRINK:

Most fancy restaurants are open for dinner only and usually have dress codes, so they're not of much use for daytrippers. The casinos offer bargain buffet restaurants, and there's a food court at the Shops on Ocean One. Here are a few choice eateries that are open for lunch:

Gary's Little Rock (5212 Atlantic Ave. in Ventnor, between Little Rock and Weymouth Aves.) Fabulous, innovative, eclectic menu in a striking setting. Dress well and reserve, ☎ 609-823-2233. $$$

Planet Hollywood (Caesar's Hotel Casino, Boardwalk at Arkansas Ave.) For that special Hollywood experience, if not for the food. ☎ 609-347-7827. $$

Café 21 (1523 Boardwalk near New York Ave.) A wide range of ethnic dishes from around the world is offered at this casual eatery. ☎ 609-347-3300. $ and $$

Inn of the Irish Pub (164 St. James' Place) Soups, sandwiches, stews, and other light fare in an authentic Irish pub that's open round the clock. ☎ 609-345-9613. $

Tony's Baltimore Grill (2800 Atlantic Ave. at Iowa Ave.) Good Italian food at prices hard to beat. ☎ 609-345-5766. $

White House Sub Shop (2301 Arctic Ave. at Mississippi Ave.) Tens of millions of subs have been sold at this world-famous institution. ☎ 609-345-1564. $

LOCAL ATTRACTIONS:

Numbers in parentheses correspond to numbers on the map.

The old **Convention Center** (1) was built in 1929, seats some 22,000, has the world's largest pipe organ, and hosts the annual **Miss America Pageant** early each September. It has recently been renovated at great expense. Stop by the lobby for some local travel brochures, and try to take a peek into the glorious main hall.

The famous ***Boardwalk** (2) next to the beach was first erected in 1870 to reduce the amount of sand carried by visitors' feet into hotel lobbies. Originally this was just planks laid directly on the sand, but in 1890 it was rebuilt into something resembling the present structure. The name apparently does not derive from the boards that it's made of, but from a Mr. Alexander Boardman, whose idea it was. In any case, this is reputedly the first structure of its type in the world. About 60 feet wide by some five miles long, the Boardwalk is perhaps best experienced by riding one of those unique attendant-pushed **rolling wicker chairs** that have been used here since 1884. The fares are clearly posted on each chair; about $10 for up to 13 blocks, $20 for 14 to 26 blocks, and so on, plus tip.

Along the Boardwalk you'll soon come to the original **Park Place** (3) of "Monopoly" fame, which is decorated with a statue of the game's inventor. In fact, street names all over town will remind you that this most popular of board games was based on the acquisition of wealth through Atlantic City real estate. Don't look for "Marvin Gardens" though—that's in nearby Margate.

Jutting out from the Boardwalk are several piers that date from earlier times. The westernmost of these, built in 1906 and once known as the "Million Dollar Pier" after its cost, has been reworked to resemble an ocean liner (more or less), and now houses a snazzy indoor mall called **The Shops on Ocean One** (4). Besides some 100 boutiques and specialty stores, it features an amusement area and over 20 places to eat anything from a hot dog to a luxury meal. The upper outdoor decks offer a nice, free view of the ocean and skyline. ☎ *609-347-8082.* ♿.

Farther along, the **Central Pier** (5), begun in 1884, has shops and a small amusement area that operates in summer. On the Boardwalk near it is **Ripley's Believe-It-or-Not Museum**, with all sorts of strange and unusual exhibits, as well as an "interactive funhouse." The Steeplechase Pier and **Steel Pier** (6) both date from the turn of the century; the latter—recently renovated—now being an extension of the Trump Taj Mahal and housing various rides, entertainments, and a food court.

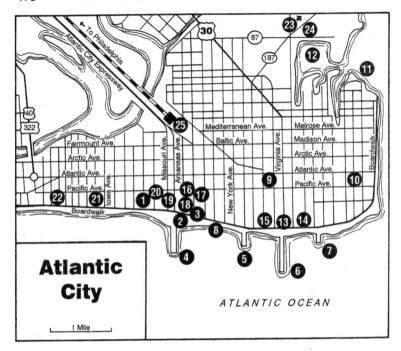

At the eastern end, the city-owned **Garden Pier** (7) is home to the **Florence Valore Miller Art Center** with its three galleries featuring changing exhibitions, and the **Atlantic City Historical Museum**, which celebrates the city's unique history. ☎ *609-347-5837. Open daily 10–4, closed major holidays. Free.* ♿.

The Beach (8) has much to recommend it, especially as it's free and open to all. While there are no public bath houses for changing, there are several free public rest rooms along the Boardwalk. Life guards are on duty throughout the summer. Even if you don't go in the water, this is a fine beach for sunbathing or just frolicking in the sand. The facilities opposite South Carolina Avenue (between the Central and Steel piers) are ♿.

Gordon's Alley (9), between Pacific and Atlantic avenues by North Carolina Avenue, was New Jersey's first pedestrian mall and houses a number of quality shops. Not far from it is the attractive **Absecon Lighthouse** (10) of 1857, recently restored and once again open to the public. ☎ *609-927-5218.* **Gardner's Basin** (11), on the Inlet side of the island, has a small collection of historic boats, a popular restaurant, and an honest nautical atmosphere that contrasts sharply with the casinos' glitter. ☎ *609-348-2880.* Close to this is the **Farley State Marina** (12), a modern sheltered harbor with a wide range of facilities. ☎ *609-441-3604.*

Casino hotels are, of course, the lifeblood of Atlantic City and the lure that brings tens of thousands of visitors there daily. Among them, the most utterly fantastic is the **Trump Taj Mahal** (13), which has to be seen to be believed. Surely one of the most expensive buildings on Earth, or at least in New Jersey, it is also the state's tallest. Its ludicrous façade facing the Boardwalk is like a scene out of a 1930s Hollywood adventure epic set in an imagined Orient. Inside, it gets even better, so be sure to pop in for a peep. The **Showboat** (14), practically next door, is less outrageous but still worth a visit.

Stroll west on the Boardwalk to Atlantic City's first casino hotel, now known as **Resorts** (15). Passing rows of fast-food places and souvenir shops brings you to the **Sands** (16) and **Claridge** (17) casino hotels, both set back from Park Place and reached from the Boardwalk by a people mover. Next to this duo is **Bally's Park Place** (18), noted for its monumental escalator connecting the casino and dining levels.

At the corner of Arkansas Avenue, just across the Boardwalk from the Ocean One Pier, a statue of a Roman gladiator lets you know that you've arrived at **Caesars Atlantic City** (19), home of Planet Hollywood and one of the glitziest casino hotels in town. Be sure to explore its grandiose interior to gain a new understanding of the word decadence.

Trump Plaza (20), by contrast, is almost tasteful and caters to a high-rolling clientele with its mix of luxury suites, superb cuisine, and ice-cold elegance. Passing the Convention Center (1), the next big casino is the **Tropicana** (21).

The last casino on the Boardwalk, the **Atlantic City Hilton** (22), is among the smallest in town but by no means the least glitzy. Atlantic City has two other casino hotels (and more in the works), both out by the Absecon Inlet. More relaxed and tasteful than the Boardwalk establishments, these are **Harrah's** (23) and the **Trump Castle** (24).

Back in town, the new **Atlantic City Convention Center** (25), a 500,000-square-foot facility with the latest in technology, sits atop the train station.

NEARBY ATTRACTIONS:

Should you tire of Atlantic City, there are several other sights nearby that can easily be reached by car. The closest, just south of town on Atlantic Avenue, is **Lucy the Margate Elephant**, a six-story, 90-ton pachyderm made of wood and tin. This National Historic Landmark was built in 1881 as a real estate promotion, then operated as a tourist attraction into the early 1960s. Facing demolition, the sadly deteriorated Lucy was donated to the City of Margate and rescued by the Save Lucy Committee, a volunteer civic group that began restoring her in 1973. Today, you can tour this Victorian architectural folly, beginning at the hind legs and climbing up the spiral staircase to Lucy's "howdah" for a nice view of the surrounding seascape. *9200 Atlantic Ave., Margate,* ☎ *609-823-6473. Open daily 10–8* *from mid-June to Labor Day, and weekends in spring and fall. Adults $3, under 12 $1.*

Just north of Atlantic City, on NJ-87 in Brigantine, is the private, non-profit **Marine Mammal Stranding Center and Sea Life Museum**. This organization has rescued over a thousand stranded whales, dolphins, seals, and sea turtles since its founding in 1978. You can observe their activities and examine the replicas of various marine mammals in the museum. There are also displays on related environmental problems. *3625 Brigantine Blvd., NJ-87,* ☎ *609-266-0538. Open daily, Memorial Day to Labor Day, 11–5; rest of year, weekends noon–4. Donation.* ♿.

Small children will enjoy a visit to **Storybook Land**, where they can play in fairytale structures, pet the animals, and ride in a miniature train. *1671 Black Horse Pike, Cardiff, NJ, 10 miles west of Atlantic City via US-322,* ☎ *609-641-7847. Open daily mid-June to mid-Sept., 10–5:30; variable schedule from March to mid-June and mid-Sept. through Dec. Closed Dec. 24–25, Jan, & Feb. Admission $10.95, over 64 $8.50, infants under 1 free.*

Several of the attractions on the previous trip to the Pine Barrens are also close enough to be included on this daytrip. These include the **Renault Winery**, the **Towne of Historic Smithville**, the **Noyes Museum of Art**, and the **Edwin B. Forsythe National Wildlife Refuge**.

Delaware's Brandywine Valley

Extending north from Wilmington to the Pennsylvania border, Delaware's Brandywine Valley was one of the major birthplaces of America's industrial wealth. The Brandywine River provided ample waterpower for the mills while the lovely countryside made an ideal locale for the fabulous mansions that resulted from the profits.

This is the land of the du Ponts, an aristocratic French family who fled that country's revolution in the late 18th century and began the great DuPont chemical empire by opening a gunpowder mill on the banks of the Brandywine in 1802. Eventually they became extremely rich and established vast estates in the surrounding hills, filling them with exquisite treasures, magnificent homes, and beautiful gardens. Among those open to the public and included in the trip are Winterthur, noted for its period American antiques and natural landscaping; Hagley, the original du Pont home in America, adjacent to the company's first mills; and Nemours, a Louis XVI château that looks like a scene right out of France. For variety the trip also includes the picturesque little town of Centerville, the Delaware Museum of Natural History, and a toy museum.

The Brandywine Valley continues north into nearby Pennsylvania, where it offers some equally intriguing sights, described on pages 76-80 and 81-83. You might want to make a weekend of this by staying overnight and combining both trips.

GETTING THERE:

By car, Winterthur is about 35 miles southwest of Philadelphia. Take Route I-95 to Wilmington, getting off at Exit 7 (Delaware Avenue) and heading a few miles northwest on **DE-52.** Centerville and the Museum of Natural History are also along this road, while the Toy Museum, Hagley, and Nemours lie slightly to the east on **DE-141** (see map).

Trains operated by **Amtrak** provide frequent, fast service between Philadelphia's 30th Street Union Station and Wilmington—where you'll need to rent a car for the remaining few miles of the trip. **Commuter trains** (Route R-2) operated by **SEPTA** cover the same route; these are slower but considerably cheaper.

PRACTICALITIES:

Most of the attractions on this daytrip are at their best during late spring and early fall, and can be crowded on summer weekends. Winterthur, the Museum of Natural History, and Hagley are open daily except for a few holidays. The Toy Museum closes on Mondays and some holidays. Nemours closes completely from December through April, and is always closed on Mondays. Reservations are suggested for the latter.

For additional information, phone the sites directly or contact the **Greater Wilmington Convention & Visitor Bureau**, 100 W. 10th St., Wilmington DE 19801, ☎ 302-652-4088 or 800-422-1181, Internet: www.wilmcvb.org.

FOOD AND DRINK:

Some good places for lunch are:

Buckley's Tavern (5812 Kennett Pike, DE-52, in Centerville) Relaxed indoor-and-outdoor dining in a delightful little town; innovative American cuisine. ☎ 302-656-9776. $$

Garden Restaurant (Winterthur Museum) Winterthur's full-service restaurant offers lunch on weekdays, teas on weekends, and champagne brunches on Sundays. Reservations required, ☎ 302-888-4826. $$

Brandywine Brewing Company (3801 Kennett Pike, DE-52, at DE-141, Greenville) Steaks, chowders, burgers, sandwiches, pastas, and salads at a microbrewery. ☎ 302-655-8000. $ and $$

Crossroads Café (Winterthur Museum) A cafeteria with a difference, Crossroads features themed "food stations" instead of the usual line. A wide variety of dishes is available. ☎ 302-888-4600. $

Cappuccino Café (Winterthur Museum) Sandwiches, salads, desserts, and beverages right next to the museum. ☎ 302-888-4600. $

LOCAL ATTRACTIONS:

Trying to see all of these attractions in the same day is practically impossible, so pick and choose carefully—allowing enough time to thoroughly enjoy those you do visit. You can always come back another time, or stay overnight! *Numbers in parentheses correspond to numbers on the map.*

*WINTERTHUR MUSEUM, GARDEN & LIBRARY (1), Route 52, Winterthur, DE 19735, ☎ 302-888-4600 or 800-448-3883; TDD 302-888-4907, Internet: www.winterthur.org. *Open Mon.–Sat. 9–5, Sun. noon–5. Last ticket sale at 3:45. Closed New Year's, Thanksgiving, and Christmas. General admission: Adults $8, seniors and students (12–18) $6, children (5–11) $4, children under 5 free. General admission includes Galleries, gardens, garden tram, and the Children's Touch-It Room. No reservations needed. Introduction Tour through selected period rooms, add $5, reservations advised. Decorative Arts tours of 1 or 2 hours for guests over 12, add $9 or $13*

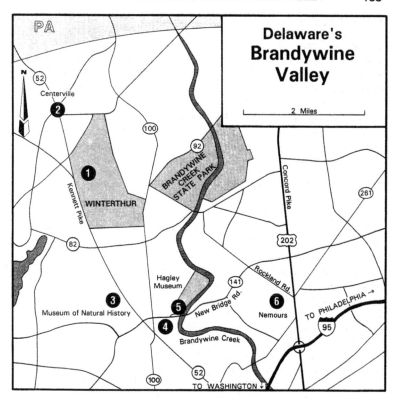

respectively, reservations needed. Special events. Gift shops. Café, cafeteria, full-service restaurant. ⬧.

Admirers of the decorative arts come from all over the world to visit Winterthur, a vast estate whose nine-story **mansion** contains some 175 period rooms furnished with 89,000 objects made or used in America between 1640 and 1860. Included are outstanding pieces of furniture, textiles, clocks, silver, needlework, porcelains, Oriental rugs, paintings, and anything else of quality that once decorated the finest American homes. This is indeed the foremost collection of its type on Earth, but you needn't take the full tour to appreciate it. Even a general admission visit of perhaps two hours or so will prove rewarding.

Adjoining the mansion (and beautifully spanning a creek) are the **Galleries**, where many of the choicest items now reside in museum settings. There is also a theater with an introductory video show, and the **Touch-It Room** where children and their parents can pretend to be living in the past. A new addition is the renowned **Campbell Collection of Soup Tureens.**

Nearly a thousand acres of "naturalistic" *gardens and woodlands cover the gently rolling hills surrounding the mansion. These offer magnificent vistas and intimate little glens, and can be seen on foot or by riding the garden tram.

The estate was begun in 1837 by James Antoine Bidermann of Winterthur, Switzerland, who had married Evelina Gabrielle du Pont in 1816 and moved to America. Their heir preferred to remain in Europe, and so in 1867 the du Pont family bought the property. A descendant, Henry Francis du Pont (1880–1969), was born here and pretty much created what you see today—both the collections and the gardens. In 1951 he turned it all over to the nonprofit Winterthur Corporation, which opened it to the public.

A General Admission ticket allows you to explore the Galleries at leisure, stroll the gardens or ride the tram, and visit the Touch-It Room, all without reservations. For an additional fee you can take one of three different guided tours through selected period rooms in the mansion, ranging from one to two hours in length. Advance reservations are strongly advised for these special tours, although same-day arrangements are possible if space permits. Winterthur is exceptionally barrier-free, and makes exemplary efforts to accommodate handicapped visitors.

Just up the road is the delightful little village of **Centerville** (2), noted for its antique dealers, boutiques, and galleries. If you're shopping, remember that Delaware (Oh, happy state!) has no sales tax.

Turn around and return south on DE-52, again passing Winterthur, to the:

DELAWARE MUSEUM OF NATURAL HISTORY (3), Route 52, Greenville, DE, ☎ 302-658-9111, Internet: www.delmnh.org. *Open Mon.–Sat. 9:30–4:30, Sun. noon–5, closed New Year's, Easter, July 4, Thanksgiving, Christmas. Adults $5, seniors $4, children (3–17) $3, children under 3 free. Gift shop. Nature films.* ♿.

Would you like to examine the world's largest bird egg? How about a 500-pound clam, an African watering hole, or a walk over the Great Barrier Reef? And how about wild dinosaurs? All of this and much, much more can be seen in this modern museum. Children of all ages have hands-on experiences in the Discovery Room, while stuffed animals await your visit in reproductions of their natural habitats.

Continue south and turn east on DE-141 to the:

DELAWARE TOY & MINIATURE MUSEUM (4), 3 Old Barley Mill Rd., DE-141, Wilmington, DE 19807, ☎ 302-427-8697, Internet: http://thomes.net/toys. *Open Tues.–Sat. 10–4, Sun. noon–4. Closed major holidays. Adults $5, seniors $4, under 12 $3.*

Toys, games, trains, boats, planes, dolls and their houses, miniatures, and other reminders of childhood—from the 18th century to today, from America to Europe—it's all here, and it's fun to see.

Practically next door is the:

*HAGLEY MUSEUM (5), P.O. Box 3630, Wilmington, DE 19807, ☎ 302-658-2400. *Open mid-March through Dec., daily 9:30–4:30; Jan. through mid-March, weekends 9:30–4:30, weekdays one tour only at 1:30. Closed Thanksgiving, Christmas, Dec. 31. Adults $9.75; seniors and students with ID $7.50, children (6–14) $3.50, under 6 free. Family rate $26.50. Bus to sites. Gift shop. Picnic facilities. ♿ most sites, some are difficult, inquire first.*

This is where it all began. E.I. du Pont de Nemours built his first black powder works on these 230 acres of riverside land along the Brandywine in 1802, harnessing abundant waterpower to drive the machinery that ground and mixed the ingredients of a superior gunpowder. Not only were the mills built here, but also the first du Pont mansion, situated dangerously close to the highly explosive works, where E.I. could keep his eye on things.

Many of the original mills and other early industrial buildings, some 19th-century workers' homes, the company's first office, and the original du Pont estate have been restored and are now operated as an historical museum, ready to be explored on foot or by bus. What is missing, understandably, is the gritty atmosphere of an early industrial site—you'll have to imagine for yourself the dirt, sweat, stench, and heat that must have made this a nasty place at the time. Well, you can't have everything.

Begin your visit at the **Henry Clay Mill** near the parking lot. Built in 1814 as a cotton-spinning mill, it was converted by the DuPont Company in 1884 for the manufacture of powder containers. Today it houses the visitor reception and a **museum** on the history of the site. Be sure to see the introductory video and the three-dimensional model of the valley with its interesting sound-and-light show.

From here you can either walk or take the little jitney bus to **Hagley Yard**, where skilled machinists demonstrate the use of old-time lathes, drill presses, and other devices in the ***Millwright Shop**. A walk-through exhibit explains the steps in manufacturing gunpowder, and you can take a guided tour to the waterside **Eagle Roll Mill** of 1839 to watch waterpower at work mixing the ingredients of black powder. Don't worry—the stuff isn't real, so it won't blow up.

Many of the workers lived on **Blacksmith Hill**, one of several communities built by the DuPont Company to provide decent housing. Most of the buildings are gone, but you can visit the well-preserved ***Gibbons-Stewart House** of 1846, where a foreman once lived. Workers' children learned their ABCs at the **Sunday School** of 1817, now restored to its original condition.

Farther along the river are the *Birkenhead Mills, where a recon-structed waterwheel still operates, and the Engine House, where you can watch a live demonstration of an 1870's stationary steam engine.

You'll have to take the bus to reach *Eleutherian Mills, located upstream beyond a public road. This is where the first mills were built in 1802, and where the founder, Éleuthère Irénée du Pont (1771–1834), lived. Although only foundations of the mills survive, the *du Pont Family Home of 1803 remained in the family until 1958, when it was restored as a muse-um. A guide will take you through lovely interiors that reflect the tastes of five generations of du Pont wealth. You'll also get to see the First Office of the DuPont Company, the Workshop where 19th- century experiments in chemistry were made, the French Garden of 1803, and the original Barn. The latter houses a Conestoga wagon and other 19th-century vehicles, along with early automobiles including a massive du Pont Auto from the 1920s, built in Wilmington.

For another glimpse of du Pont wealth, continue east on DE-141, turn-ing right at Rockland Road and following signs to:

NEMOURS MANSION AND GARDENS (6), P.O. Box 109, Wilmington, DE 19899, ☎ 302-651-6912. *Open May through November, tours Tues.–Sat. at 9, 11, 1, and 3; Sun. at 11, 1, and 3. Reservations strongly urged. Visitors must be over 16 years of age. Visit by tour only, $10. Many steps to climb. Allow at least 2 hours for the tour and arrive at least 15 minutes ahead of time.*

The du Pont's patriarch, Pierre Samuel du Pont de Nemours (1739–1817), was a French aristocrat closely associated with King Louis XVI, so it's no wonder that he fled to America in the aftermath of the French Revolution. It was against this background that his great-great-grandson, Alfred Irénée du Pont, built the fabulous *château of Nemours in 1909–10, and named it after the ancestral family home about 45 miles south of Paris. Some of the furnishings in its 102 rooms belonged to the king or his wife, Marie Antoinette. Others, equally valuable, date from as far back as 15th-century Europe.

The tour includes a bus ride through the formal *gardens, extending for a third of a mile from the mansion. Along the way you'll pass gates con-structed in 1488 for Henry VII's Wimbeldon Manor in England, and others that once graced the palace of Catherine the Great in St. Petersburg, Russia. Finally, there's the garage with its rare automobiles built for the du Ponts from 1912 to 1951.

Wilmington

You probably wouldn't think of Wilmington as a tourist destination; few people do. Yet, this bustling corporate headquarters city has several attractions that make the trip worthwhile. On top of that, it is only minutes from the world-class lures of the Brandywine Valley (pages 76-83 and 181-186). Visitors can easily combine elements of this daytrip with some of those for a custom itinerary.

First settled by Swedish fur traders in 1638, the tiny colony of New Sweden was captured by the Dutch in 1655. A mere nine years later the English took over, and the town grew under William Penn's Quaker influence. Having an ideal port location, Wilmington was also blessed with abundant water power along its Brandywine River. This attracted early industrialists, especially the aristocratic du Ponts who fled revolutionary France and founded the mighty chemical empire that dominates the area today.

If you're considering an overnight stay, this trip combines very well with those to Delaware's Brandywine Valley, Chadds Ford or Kennett Square in Pennsylvania, or New Castle and Odessa.

GETTING THERE:

By car, Wilmington is about 30 miles southwest of Philadelphia via Route I-95. Get off at Exit 6 for the downtown sites, Exit 7 for the art museum and zoo, or Exit 9 for Rockwood.

Trains operated by **Amtrak** provide frequent service between Wilmington and Philadelphia. **Commuter trains** (Route R-2) operated by **SEPTA** follow the same route; they're not as fast but much cheaper. Downtown sites are within possible walking distance of the station, but you'll need to take a bus (or car) to the others.

PRACTICALITIES:

Avoid Wilmington on a Monday or major holiday, when many of the attractions are closed. The History Museum is also closed on Sundays, as is Rockwood. Tours of the Grand Opera House are held on Thursdays only. The Wilmington and Western Tourist Railroad operates on summer weekends and some other times, but call first.

Shoppers will be delighted to know that Delaware has no sales tax.

Public transportation throughout the Wilmington area is operated by DART, ☎ 302-652-DART or 800-652-DART, Internet: www.dtcc.edu/dart for routes and schedules.

For further information, contact the **Greater Wilmington Convention & Visitors Bureau**, 100 West 10th St., Wilmington, DE 19801, ☎ 302-652-4088 or 800-422-1181, Internet: www.wilmcvb.org.

FOOD AND DRINK:

Some good choices for lunch are:

Tavola Toscana (1412 DuPont St., between Pennsylvania and Delaware avenues, a mile south of the art museum) A great place for inspired Northern Italian cuisine. ☎ 302-654-8001. X: weekend lunches. $$$

Waterworks Café (16th and French streets, 6 blocks northeast of the Grand Opera) Continental cuisine in a former waterworks on the river; indoor and outdoor dining. ☎ 302-652-6022. X: Sat. lunch, Sun., Mon., holidays. $$

DiNardo's (405 Lincoln St. at 4th St., 2 miles west of the opera house) This boisterous, popular crab house serves great seafood in the most casual setting. ☎ 302-656-3685. $$

Shipley Grill (913 Shipley St., near Willington Sq. in the heart of downtown) Steak and seafood with an imaginative touch. ☎ 302-652-7797. X: Sun. lunch. $$

LOCAL ATTRACTIONS:

Numbers in parentheses correspond to numbers on the map.

DELAWARE HISTORY MUSEUM (1), 504 Market St. Mall, ☎ 302-656-0637, Internet: www.hsd.org. *Open Tues.–Fri., noon–4; and Sat. 10–4. Closed Sun., Mon., and major holidays. Admission charged.* &.

Delaware's history comes alive in this restored five-and-dime from the 1940s. Exhibitions change, but focus on such subjects as business, maritime history, agriculture, and the ethnic background of the state's population.

Close by is **Willington Square** (2), a lovely group of 18th-century houses moved to this site in the 1970s.

Three blocks to the north stands the **Grand Opera House** (3), a highly-decorated cast-iron structure of 1871. Recently restored, it is now Delaware's Center for the Performing Arts, where opera and symphonies are regularly performed. *818 Market St. Mall, ☎ 302-658-7898, Internet: www.grandopera.org. Call for tour information.* &.

A few blocks to the south is one of America's oldest train depots, **Amtrak Station** (4). Fully restored to its Victorian splendor, it remains in constant use today.

About a mile east of Market Street are two reminders of Wilmington's earliest days. **Old Swedes Church** (5), now known as Holy Trinity, was built in 1698 and is possibly the oldest house of worship in America to remain in use today. Originally Lutheran, it has been Episcopalian since 1791 but still contains some of the original furnishings, including the pulpit. Nearby, a small Swedish farmhouse of 1690 now contains a museum of 17th- and 18th-century artifacts. *606 Church St.* ☎ *302-652-5629. Open Mon.–Sat. 10–4. Admission $2.* The **Fort Christina Monument**, a short stroll to the east, marks the spot where the Swedes first stepped ashore in 1638. Nearby is an old log cabin of the type that the earliest settlers used.

The **Kalmar Nyckel Foundation** (6), on the shores of the Christina River just to the east, celebrates the first permanent European settlement in the Delaware Valley in 1638. Here you can see a replica of the ship, the *Kalmar Nyckel*, that brought those first Swedes here, along with a museum and a re-created 17th-century shipyard. Ten stories high and 139 feet long, the *Kalmar Nyckel* is Delaware's seagoing ambassador of good will and is sometimes out on a cruise. Check first to make sure it's in port. *1124 East 7th St.,* ☎ *302-429-7447, Internet: www.kalnyc.org. Open Mon.–Sat. 10–4, Sun. noon–4, closed major holidays. Adults $8, seniors $6, children 7–12 $4.*

Another recent addition to Wilmington's cultural scene is the **First USA Riverfront Arts Center** (7), an enormous former ship assembly plant that was beautifully transformed into an exhibition venue featuring world-class temporary exhibitions. *800 S. Madison St.,* ☎ *302-777-1600 or 888-395-0005. Check ahead for current offerings.* Adjacent to it is the **Shipyard Shops** complex of upscale catalog outlets, **Frawley Stadium**—home of the Wilmington Blue Rocks Class A minor league baseball team ☎ *302-888-2015, Internet: www.bluerocks.com*—and the lovely **Tubman—Garrett Riverfront Park**.

Outside the central city are several other attractions, starting with the:

BRANDYWINE ZOO (8), 1001 N. Park Drive, ☎ 302-571-7747. *Open daily 10–4. Admission charged Apr.–Oct.; Adults $3, seniors and children 3–11 $1.50. Free from Nov.–March.* &.

Although it's been a local landmark since 1905, the Brandywine Zoo takes a modern, enlightened approach to animal care. There are exotic species, of course, but the emphasis is on animals native to North and South America, and especially on presenting those native to Delaware in their natural habitat.

DELAWARE ART MUSEUM (9), 2301 Kentmere Parkway, ☎ 302-571-9590, Internet: www.udel.edu/delart. *Open Tues.–Sat. 9–4., Sun. 10–4, remaining open until 9 on Wed. Closed Mon., Thanksgiving, Christmas, New Year's Day. Adults $5, seniors $3, students $2.50. Gift shop.* &.

The greatest treasures in this modern museum are the works of Howard Pyle (1853–1911), a native of Wilmington who was virtually the father of American illustration and a founder of the Brandywine school. His students—N.C. Wyeth, Maxfield Parrish, Frank Schoonover and others—are also very well represented, as are other famous American artists such as Thomas Eakins, Winslow Homer, Andrew Wyeth, and a host of contemporary painters. The museum is also renowned for its vast collection of English Pre-Raphaelite paintings and decorative arts, displayed in Victorian settings.

ROCKWOOD MUSEUM (10), 610 Shipley Road, ☎ 302-761-4340, Internet: www.rockwood.org. *Open Tues.–Sat. 11–4. Adults $5, seniors $4, children 5–16 $2. Tours. Gift shop.* &.

Located in the eastern part of town, near Exit 9 of Route I-95, Rockwood is a gorgeous 19th-century country estate with a Rural Gothic manor house and lovely gardens. Its interior features English, European, and American decorative arts of the 17th, 18th, and 19th centuries. There is also a conservatory filled with period flora.

WILMINGTON & WESTERN TOURIST RAILROAD (11), Greenback Station on DE-41, 3 blocks north of the junction with DE-2, just west of Wilmington. ☎ 302-998-1930, Internet: www.wwrr.com. *Operates every Sun., May–Dec.; every Sat. June–Aug., and at other times. Adults $7, seniors $6, children 2–12 $4. Gift shop.* &.

Ride behind an old steam or antique diesel locomotive as you chug your way through Red Clay Valley, stopping at a picnic grove before returning. What a nice way to end the day!

Trip 35
New Castle and Odessa

Most of America's Colonial heritage is British in nature, but here in northern Delaware you'll find much evidence of the Dutch and the Swedes, who arrived earlier. That's why their flags still fly from the Old Court House in New Castle, alongside the Union Jack and the Stars and Stripes. New Castle, once the state capital, has an exceptionally well-preserved historic district with houses and public buildings dating from as far back as the 1600s. Several of these can be visited as you stroll along the cobblestone lanes near the water's edge.

Civil War buffs—and anyone who likes boat rides—will enjoy a visit to Fort Delaware, a defensive bastion on Pea Patch Island in the middle of the Delaware River.

Finally, you can finish off the day at the Historic Houses of Odessa, a group of 18th- and 19th-century homes maintained and operated by the Winterthur Museum (see page 182) in the tiny village of Odessa.

GETTING THERE:

By car, New Castle is about 35 miles southwest of Philadelphia. Take I-95 south to Exit 11, then I-495 south to Exit 2. From here, DE-9 leads south directly into New Castle. Turn left on Delaware Street, following it to the Old Court House.

If you plan to visit Fort Delaware, take DE-9 ten miles south to Delaware City and follow signs east to the state park. Continue south another ten miles on DE-9 to Odessa, turning north on DE-299 to the historic houses.

For a faster route from New Castle directly to Odessa, take DE-273 west to US-13, US-301 and follow it south to the historic houses. The distance is 18 miles.

PRACTICALITIES:

Avoid taking this trip on a Monday, when everything is closed. Most of the sites also close completely during January and February, and on certain holidays. Fort Delaware is closed from October until the last weekend in April, and also on many weekdays, so call ahead. The famous **Yuletide in Odessa** festival is held in early December.

For further information, contact the sites directly.

FOOD AND DRINK:

You'll find the best selection of restaurants to be in and around New Castle, including:

Air Transport Command (143 N. DuPont Hwy., US-13, by the airport at New Castle) Continental American cuisine served in a replica World War II European farmhouse overlooking the runway. ☎ 302-328-3527. $$

Lynnhaven Inn (154 N. DuPont Hwy., US-13, near the airport) A long-time favorite for steak and seafood in a Colonial setting. ☎ 302-328-2041. X: weekend lunch. $$

Arsenal on the Green (30 Market St., near the Old Court House in New Castle) Classic American cuisine in an historic 1809 building. ☎ 302-328-1290. X: Sun. lunch. $$

Cellar Gourmet (208 Delaware St., near the Old Court House in New Castle) Casual light dining in the cellar of an 1802 house, featuring sandwiches, quiche, soup, and the like. ☎ 302-323-0999. $

Another good idea is to bring a **picnic lunch** with you to Fort Delaware State Park, where tables and grills are provided free. Fast-food places abound along Route 13 in the vicinity of New Castle.

SUGGESTED TOUR:

Numbers in parentheses correspond to numbers on the map.

Begin your tour in the historic town of **New Castle** (1–6), founded in 1651 by Peter Stuyvesant, the dictatorial Dutch administrator of the New Netherlands in America. Then known as Fort Casimir, the town held a strategic location commanding all traffic on the Delaware River. In 1654 it fell to the Swedes but was soon recaptured by the Dutch, who lost it to the British in 1664. William Penn first stepped foot in the New World here in 1682.

Park your car and start with the:

OLD COURT HOUSE (1), 2nd and Delaware streets, New Castle, DE 19720, ☎ 302-323-4453. *Open Tues.–Sat. 10–3:30, Sun. 1:30–4:30, closed Mon. and holidays. Free. ♿, first floor only.*

Look at a map of Delaware and notice the peculiar circular line dividing it from Pennsylvania, a result of the Mason-Dixon survey of 1763-68. The exact center of this 12-mile radius is the handsome cupola atop the Old Court House. From the balcony beneath it fly the flags of the United States, Great Britain, Sweden, and Holland—the countries to which New Castle belonged to at one time or another.

Built in 1732, the Old Court House was used by the Colonial Assembly until Dover became Delaware's capital in 1777. The exterior has been restored to match an 1804 drawing, and the interior furnished as it

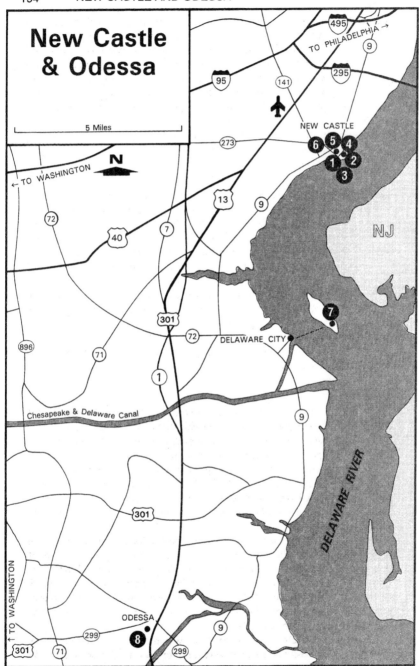

was under British rule. Step inside and take the free guided tour, beginning in the **courtroom** with its prisoner's dock, witness stand, and judges'
bench. Upstairs is the meeting room of Delaware's **Colonial Assembly**, and
some other chambers lined with portraits of prominent figures in the
state's history, including that of Thomas West (1577–1618), the 12th Baron
de la Warre, after whom the river (and consequently the state) is named.
He was the governor of Virginia and apparently never ventured this far
north.

Leave the courthouse and continue down Delaware Street, turning
left into The Strand to visit the:

GEORGE READ II HOUSE AND GARDEN (2), 42 The Strand, New Castle, DE
19720, ☎ 302-322-8411, Internet: www.hsd.org. *Open Mar. through Dec.,
Tues.–Sat. 10–4, Sun. noon–4; closed Mon. and major holidays. Adults $4,
students 13–21 $3.50, children 6–12 $2. Special events in May and Dec.* &.

Undoubtedly the most elegant residence in New Castle, the George
Read II house was built between 1797 and 1804 by a prominent lawyer and
son of a signer of the Declaration of Independence. Much of it is furnished in the style of the 1820s, while three contrasting rooms reflect the
Colonial Revival tastes of a century later when the house was acquired by
the Philip Lairds in 1920. Of particular note are the gilded fanlights, the silver hardware, and the elaborately carved woodwork. The house is surrounded on three sides by **landscaped gardens** laid out in the 1840's style of
Andrew Jackson Downing.

Return along the other side of The Strand, taking a look down **Packet
Alley**. A historical marker here informs you that this is where stage coaches bound for Maryland once met the packet boat from Philadelphia, making it a vital link in communications between North and South.

Continue on to a marker commemorating the spot where, on
October 27, 1682, William Penn (1644–1718) first stepped foot on American
soil. Originally a part of Pennsylvania, this area became unhappy with
Penn's rule and in 1704 set up its own government as the colony, and later
state, of Delaware.

Stroll through a riverside park called **The Battery** (3), with its sweeping
views of the busy waterway and the Delaware Memorial Bridge to New
Jersey. At the end of Delaware Street you'll see the curious little ticket
office of the former **New Castle and Frenchtown Railroad**, the second-oldest rail line in the country. Built in 1832 and now restored, the office stands
next to a rebuilt section of the original wooden tracks topped with iron
strapping, attached to stone ties.

Return along Delaware Street and turn right onto Second Street,
passing the Dutch-inspired **Town Hall**. Behind it is **The Green**, laid out by

Peter Stuyvesant in 1655. Always a busy place, weekly markets and great fairs were held here from the earliest times. This was also the site of the town jail and gallows. To the right is the **Presbyterian Church** of 1707.

Turn left to visit **Immanuel Church** (4), founded as the first parish of the Church of England in Delaware in 1689 and completed in 1708. It was expanded and modified several times, and devastated by fire in 1980. A rebuilding in 1982 closely followed the design of 1820, complete with box pews. An unusual feature of the church is the rare set of change-ringing bells, used on special occasions. Several of Delaware's most illustrious early citizens are buried in the surrounding graveyard. *Open daily 10–5. Free. 100 Harmony St. ☎ 302-328-2413.*

A left turn on Third Street brings you to the **Old Library Museum**, a strange hexagonal structure of 1892 that now houses the New Castle Historical Society and its exhibits on local history. *40 E. 3rd St., ☎ 302-322-2794. Open Sat. 11–4, Sun. 1–4, and Thurs.–Fri. when possible 11–4. Free.* Continue on to the **Old Dutch House** (5), virtually unchanged since it was first built around 1700 and today open to visitors. The furnishings are typical of New Castle's early Dutch settlers, down to the inevitable *klompen* (wooden shoes). *32 E. 3rd St., ☎ 302-322-2794. Open Mar.–Dec., Tues.–Sat. 11–4, Sun. 1–4; weekends only rest of year; adults $2, under 12 $1. ♿.*

A block west on Delaware Street stands the **Amstel House** (6) of 1738, once the home of Delaware's governor. Incorporating sections of an earlier house, it has a complete Colonial kitchen and many fine antiques. *Open at the same times as the Old Dutch House, above, same admission, combined ticket available.*

After enjoying New Castle, you might want to continue south on DE-9 to visit a Civil War fort, or head directly down US-13, US-301 to the Historic Houses of Odessa.

FORT DELAWARE STATE PARK (7), Pea Patch Island, opposite Delaware City, DE 19706, ☎ 302-834-7941, Internet: www.destateparks.com/fdsp.htm. *Open from the last weekend of April through Sept.; Sat., Sun., holidays 10–6; also on some weekdays from mid-June through Labor Day. Call for current schedule. Admission including boat fare: Adults $6, ages 2–12 $4. Picnic facilities. Special events. Gift shop. ♿.*

Park your car at the end of Clinton Street in Delaware City, opposite the old locks of the original **Chesapeake and Delaware Canal** of 1829. The canal has since moved south a mile or so, but there is still an active harbor here. At the adjacent State Park office you can buy your tickets and board the boat for a short cruise to the island. Upon landing, a jitney will take you to the fort.

Pea Patch Island, all 178 acres of it, supposedly acquired its name after a boat loaded with peas ran aground there, and the peas sprouted. Today it is mostly a **nature preserve** whose remote marshes provide habitat for herons, egrets, ibis, and other wading birds. An **observation tower** allows visitors to watch without disturbing the wildlife.

Fort Delaware, on the eastern end of the island, was built in 1859 on the site of earlier fortresses. It guarded the sea approaches to Wilmington, Philadelphia, and the Delaware Valley. Surrounded by a 30-foot moat and reached via a drawbridge, the massive bastion has 32-foot-high granite-and-brick walls that are up to 30 feet thick. During the Civil War it held as many as 12,500 Confederate prisoners of war at a time, of whom some 2,700 perished of diseases. The fort was modernized for the Spanish-American War, and again garrisoned during World War I. In World War II it was maintained by German POWs. Strangely, throughout its entire history, Fort Delaware never fired a shot in anger.

Visitors can explore nearly all of the fort, see period rooms and armaments, climb up to the ramparts, and even venture into the spooky dungeons. This is a great destination for kids!

Continuing ten miles farther south brings you to the:

HISTORIC HOUSES OF ODESSA (8), P.O. Box 507, Odessa, DE 19730, ☎ 302-378-4069. *Open March through Dec., Tues.–Sat. 10–4, Sun. 1–4. Last combination tour at 3. Closed Mon., Easter, July 4, Thanksgiving, Dec 24–25, Jan., Feb. Adults $4 for one house, $6 for two, $7 for three. Seniors over 59 and students 12–17 $3 for one house, $5 for two, $6 for three. Children 5–11 $1 per house. Gift shop. Special events prior to Christmas.*

Then known as Cantwell's Bridge, tiny Odessa was once a prosperous little grain-shipping port on Appoquinimink Creek, an estuary of Delaware Bay. As business declined in the mid-19th century, however, it attempted to glorify its port facilities by renaming the town after the great Ukrainian seaport that was in the news then as a result of the Crimean War. It also made the fatal mistake of forcing the newfangled Delaware Railroad to bypass the town. The disastrous peach blight of the late 19th century didn't help matters, either. After that, Odessa just fell asleep until the 1950s, by which time its magnificent houses had become a tourist asset.

The Winterthur Museum of the Brandywine Valley (see page 182) now operates four historic properties in Odessa. These include the **Corbit-Sharp House** of 1774, a Georgian mansion built for the town's leading citizen. It is authentically furnished in the style of the late 18th century. Nearby is the **Wilson-Warner House**, a wealthy merchant's mansion of 1769 now furnished as it would have been in 1829, when an inventory was made during a bankruptcy sale. No longer an inn, the 19th-century Federal-style **Brick Hotel** has been renovated as an exhibition gallery of exceptionally ornate Victorian furniture in the manner of John Henry Belter (1804–63), the master of the Rococo Revival. Finally, there is the early-18th-century log-and-frame-built **Collins-Sharp House** presently used for educational programs such as hands-on hearth cooking for children.

Trip 36
Kent County

Dover became Delaware's capital in 1777, when invading British troops chased the Colonial Assembly out of New Castle (see page 192). The politicians apparently liked their new home as they've stayed there ever since. Founded in 1683 by William Penn, this relaxed and rather quaint little town hardly looks like a state capital, but then again Delaware is a very small state.

There are enough attractions in and around Dover to keep you busy all day, however if you skip a few of these you might want to head north to the historic town of Smyrna, which has some off-the-beaten-track sites. In Dover you can visit the Old State House of 1792, browse through off-beat museums, and experience local agricultural life from Colonial days to the early 20th century. Just south of the capital is the immense Dover Air Force Base and its fine museum of vintage aircraft, and beyond that the John Dickinson Plantation of 1740, a reconstructed farm complex with its grand mansion and humble slave quarters. Smyrna offers several 18th-and 19th-century houses, including a Queen Anne country house of 1753 that you can visit on weekends.

GETTING THERE:

By car, Dover is about 82 miles southwest of Philadelphia. Take I-95 south to Exit 11, then I-495 south to Exit 1. From here continue south on US-13/301 (DuPont Highway) to Odessa, then US-13 past Smyrna and into Dover. Turn right on Loockerman Street, then left on Federal Street to the Visitor Center, near which you can park.

PRACTICALITIES:

Most of the attractions are closed on Mondays, and some on Sundays as well. Check the individual listings in this chapter. The **Old Dover Days** celebration, when private historic houses and gardens are open to the public, is held on the first Saturday in May.

For further information, contact the **Delaware State Visitor Center**, Federal Street at Duke of York Street, Dover, DE 19903, ☎ 302-739-4266. Another source is the **Kent County Convention & Visitors Bureau**, 9 East Loockerman St., Dover, DE 19901, ☎ 302-734-1736 or 800-233-KENT, Internet: www.visitdover.com.

FOOD AND DRINK:

Some dining choices are:

Blue Coat Inn (800 N. State St., near the north end of town) Early American specialties and seafood in a Colonial setting by a lake. ☎ 302-674-1776. X: Mon. $$ and $$$

W.T. Smithers (140 S. State St., north of The Green) Creative American cuisine in an early-19th-century house. ☎ 302-674-8875. $$ and $$$

Tango's Bistro (Sheraton Hotel, 1570 N. DuPont Hwy., US-13, Dover) Contemporary American cuisine in a bright, upscale setting. ☎ 302-678-8500. $$

Captain John's (518 Bay Rd., near junction of US-13 and US-113, just east of town) This relaxed family eatery offers familiar American dishes and a salad bar, but no liquor. ☎ 302-678-8166. $ and $$

In addition, you'll find a few decent luncheonettes in the vicinity of State and Loockerman streets in the historic district of Dover, and the usual fast-food emporiums along US-13.

LOCAL ATTRACTIONS:

Park at (or as close as possible to) the Visitor Center, from which you can easily walk to sites (1) through (6). You'll need a car to reach sites (7) through (11). *Numbers in parentheses correspond to numbers on the map.*

DELAWARE STATE VISITOR CENTER (1), Federal and Duke of York streets, ☎ 302-739-4266. *Open Mon.–Sat. 8:30–4:30, Sun. 1:30–4:30. Free.* &.

Besides the wealth of free (and current!) information you can get here about Dover, Kent County, and all of Delaware, there are also changing exhibitions on related subjects, and a slide show on the historic sites. Upstairs is the new ***Sewell C. Biggs Museum of American Art**, a collection spanning some two centuries of fine art, furniture, and silver. Among the artists represented are Albert Bierstadt, Charles Wilson Peale, George Inness, and Gilbert Stuart. ☎ *302-674-2111. Museum open Wed.–Sat. 10–4, Sun. 1:30–4:30, closed major holidays. Free.*

OLD STATE HOUSE (2), South State Street at The Green, ☎ 302-739-4266, Internet: www.destatemuseums.org/Statehs.htm. *Open Tues.–Sat. 10–4:30, Sun. 1:30–4:30, closed Mon. and State holidays. Free. Tours.* &.

Built in 1792, this is the nation's second-oldest State House in continuous use. Although the General Assembly moved to nearby Legislative Hall in 1934, the State House still remains Delaware's symbolic capitol. It contains an 18th-century courtroom, a ceremonial Governor's Office, legislative chambers, and county offices including a levy courtroom. Don't miss the larger-than-life portrait of George Washington in the Senate chamber, commissioned by the legislature in 1802.

Stretching out in front of the State House is **The Green**, a park-like meeting ground since the town's earliest days. A painting of King George

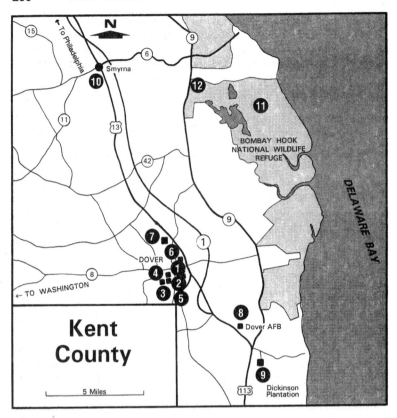

III was burned here when the Declaration of Independence was read to the public in 1776, and it was on this site that Delaware's Continental Regiment was mustered for service in the Revolution. On the north side of the square is the former **Golden Fleece Tavern**, now private offices, where delegates met on December 7, 1787, to be the first to ratify the Constitution of the United States. This is why Delaware calls itself the "First State."

MEETING HOUSE GALLERIES (3), 316 South Governors Ave., ☎ 302-739-4266, Internet: www.destatemuseums.org/Gallery. *Open Tues.–Sat. 10–3:30, closed Sun., Mon., and state holidays. Free.* ⑤.

Two old church buildings now house parts of the Delaware State Museum Complex on Dover's Meeting House Square, laid out by William Penn in 1717. The first of these is the **Old Presbyterian Church** of 1790, where the Delaware State Constitution was drafted in 1792, and the State Constitutional Convention convened in 1831. It is now home to a small but interesting museum of **local archaeology** that focuses in Native American life from prehistoric to Colonial times, and later developments.

The adjacent **1880 Gallery** houses reconstructed turn-of-the- century shops including a drugstore, a working printer's shop, a shoemaker's, a blacksmith's, and more.

JOHNSON VICTROLA MUSEUM (4), Bank Lane at New St., ☎ 302-739-4266, Internet: www.destatemuseums.org/Victrola. *Open Tues.–Sat. 10–3:30, closed Sun., Mon., and State holidays. Free.* 占.

The golden age of the American phonograph lives again when you visit this fabulous museum of Victrolas, where ghostly sounds from the past are played on wind-up machines. Eldridge Reeves Johnson, a local businessman, founded the Victor Talking Machine Company, which he sold to RCA in 1929. Ranging from early Edison cylinders to the beginnings of electronic radio-phonographs in the late 1920s, the amazingly complete displays here cover the pioneer days of recorded sound in a setting that re-creates a Victrola dealer's store of the period.

Another site in the neighborhood is the **Christ Episcopal Church** (5) of 1734, located at South State and Water streets. During the Revolutionary War it was repeatedly attacked by vandals, who unjustly considered all members of the Church of England to be Tories. Actually, one of the Revolution's great heroes (and a signer of the Declaration of Independence), Caesar Rodney (1728–84), is buried in the churchyard along with other famous Delawareans. ☎ *302-734-5731. Church open weekdays.*

A few blocks to the north stands the **Governor's House, "Woodburn,"** (6) at 151 Kings Highway. Erected in 1791, this Georgian residence has been the official Governor's mansion since 1966, and was once a station on the legendary Underground Railroad. ☎ *302-739-5656. Grounds open daily, house open Sat. 2:30–4:30.*

At the northern end of town, along Route US-13, is the:

DELAWARE AGRICULTURAL MUSEUM AND VILLAGE (7), 866 N. DuPont Hwy. (US-13), ☎ 302-734-1618, Internet: www.agriculturalmuseum.org. *Open Jan.–Mar., Mon.–Fri. 10–4; Apr.–Dec., Tues.–Sat. 10–4 and Sun. 1–4. Adults $3, seniors (60+) and children (6–17) $2, under 6 free. Additional charge for special events. Gift shop.* 占.

Farm life on the Delmarva Peninsula from Colonial times to the mid-20th century is brought back to life in this museum village, where you'll see exhibits ranging from milk bottles to a crop duster, an 18th-century log house to a Model T Ford. The re-created village on the banks of Silver Lake has a gristmill, a blacksmith's, a schoolhouse, a store, a train station, various farm buildings, and more.

Head south on US-13, soon bearing left onto US-113, which takes you to the:

AIR MOBILITY COMMAND MUSEUM (8), Dover Air Force Base, DE 19902-8001, ☎ 302-677-5938, Internet: http://amcmuseum.org, also check www.dover.af.mil. *Open Mon.–Sun. 9–4, closed federal holidays. At the Main Gate of the Air Force Base get in the right-hand lane, and park at the Visitor Center. Go inside with your drivers' license, registration, and proof of insurance. Ask for a museum pass, then proceed by car through the gate and follow road signs to the museum. Free. Gift shop. ㅊ.*

The displays of historic military aircraft here include one of the few surviving B-17G bombers of World War II, a C-47 "Gooney Bird," a C-54 transport, an O-2A forward air control plane from the Vietnam conflict, and other former warplanes dating from the 1940s to the recent past. There is also a WWII Link Trainer, a F-106 flight simulator, and similar items.

Immediately south of the air base is the:

JOHN DICKINSON PLANTATION (9), Kitts Hummock Rd., near the junction of US-113 and DE-9, ☎ 302-739-3277, Internet: www.destatemuse ums.org/Dicknsn.htm. *Open Tues.–Sat. 10–3:30, Sun. 1:30–4:30 from Mar.–Dec., closed Mon. and State holidays. Closed Sun. in Jan. & Feb. Free. Tours. Partially ㅊ.*

John Dickinson (1737–1808), often called the "Penman of the American Revolution," was an influential writer, lawyer, and politician who served in the Continental Congress and helped draft the Articles of Confederation. His boyhood home, a plantation built by his father in 1740, has been restored to its late-18th-century condition and may be seen on guided tours. In contrast to the mansion are the re-created outbuildings, including the "log'd dwelling" that is typical of the mean living quarters used by slaves and poor tenant farmers.

Twelve miles north of Dover, on Route US-13, is the little town of **Smyrna** (10). This was once an important shipping center for local farm produce; today its past is recalled in several historic houses and public buildings. Find out more at the **Smyrna Visitors Center.** *5500 DuPont Highway (US-13),* ☎ *302-653-8910.*

Just east of Smyrna, on Route 9, is the **Bombay Hook National Wildlife Refuge** (11), a haven for migratory and resident waterfowl. A 12-mile auto tour route and various foot trails start at the visitor center. ☎ *302-653-6872. Open daily. Vehicle charge. ㅊ.* Near its entrance is the **Allee House** (12) of 1753, a brick farmhouse in the Queen Anne style that is furnished with local antiques. *Dutch Neck Road off DE-9,* ☎ *302-653-6872. Open weekends in spring.*

Section IV

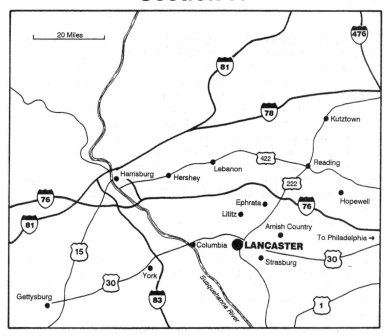

DAYTRIPS IN THE
PENNSYLVANIA
DUTCH COUNTRY

W hat sets this region's lovely, fertile countryside apart from other lovely, fertile countrysides is the culture of the folks who live there. Their collective name, the Pennsylvania Dutch, is a misnomer. Actually, the correct term is *Deutsch*, meaning German. During the early 18th century many non-conformist religious sects from Europe found refuge in William Penn's "Holy Experiment," his tolerant colony of Pennsylvania. Among those who settled in and around Lancaster County are the various orders of "Plain People," who to differing degrees reject much of the modern world and still live more or less as their ancestors did. These include the Amish, the Mennonites, the Hutterites, and the Brethren.

The Old Order Amish are the most conservative of the religious groups, and easily the most unusual. They shun the use of electricity from power lines (but not from private generators), telephones in their homes (but not in barns), ownership of automobiles (but not riding in them), farm tractors, and marriage to non-Amish. The most prevalent symbol of the Amish, at least to outsiders, is their horse-drawn buggies that snarl motor traffic on local roads. Actually, some of the other Plain People also use these slow-moving vehicles, as do several tour operators. Both the Amish and other conservative sects are usually trilingual, speaking German, "Pennsylvania Dutch," and English quite fluently. Far from being a dying breed, the Amish population is growing rapidly; faster than the ability of the land to support them, so that many now operate small businesses or have moved to farmland in other areas. Their amazing ability to come to terms with the modern world without becoming a part of it has made their order prosper to the point where they now number over 130,000 members in the United States and Canada; with some 16,000 in Lancaster County alone.

Other "Pennsylvania Dutch" people, largely of Lutheran and Reformed heritage, have long since embraced the modern world, although they maintain many of their cultural traditions to this day. Known as the "Fancy Dutch" or "Gay Dutch," they live mostly in Berks and Lebanon counties, and are noted for their food, music, and the so-called "hex" signs painted on their barns.

The colorful lifestyles of the various Pennsylvania Dutch people, combined with idyllic scenery, tasty food, and proximity to major urban areas, attracts travelers in droves. That in turn has encouraged more than a few tacky tourist traps to open along the main roads. However, there are still far more genuinely worthwhile attractions than visitors can possibly see in a few days, so you'll have to pick and choose carefully, or plan on coming back another time. Those lucky enough to live in the region can take their time and slowly experience everything on a series of daytrips.

This section is primarily concerned with the heart of the Pennsylvania Dutch Country, namely Lancaster and Berks counties, with forays into nearby Lebanon, Dauphin, York, and Adams counties as well. Some other Pennsylvania Dutch attractions can be found in Lehigh and Northampton counties, both of which are covered in Section III because they are much closer to Philadelphia.

Although most of the Pennsylvania Dutch Country can be seen on daytrips from the Philadelphia area (or from Baltimore or Washington, for that matter), you'll find it far more convenient—and enjoyable—to base yourself in or around Lancaster. Accommodations there are plentiful, and the attractions begin immediately. The regional tourist office (see page 206) will happily supply you with plenty of current information regarding places to stay.

Lancaster

I f Lancaster had remained the capital of the United States, its most famous resident would not have had to travel to Washington when he became President. But, alas, it didn't, so James Buchanan left his grand mansion to take up residence in the White House just before the Civil War. America's largest inland Colonial town has retained much of its historic ambiance, and is still the hub of the prosperous and abundant Pennsylvania Dutch countryside. Its compact downtown is easily explored on foot, whether on a guided tour or on your own.

First settled in 1721, Lancaster became a major manufacturing center, specializing in armaments for the French and Indian War as well as for the Revolution. It was the capital of the United States for just one day, September 27, 1777, when the wandering Congress halted after being chased out of Philadelphia by the British. The next day Congress moved safely across the Susquehanna River to York; an unnecessary precaution as Lancaster was never invaded. The city was also the capital of Pennsylvania from 1799 until 1812.

Lancaster and its surrounding area makes a natural base for exploring the heart of the Pennsylvania Dutch country, sparing you the somewhat tedious drive from Philadelphia. Fortunately, the region has plenty of accommodations ranging from fancy hotels to inexpensive B & Bs. Just ask at the Visitor Center for details.

GETTING THERE:

By car, Lancaster lies some 90 minutes or so west of Philadelphia, with a choice of routes. The fastest is (surprise!) also the longest, at 78 miles. Take Route I-76 (Schuykill Expressway, becoming the Pennsylvania Turnpike) (toll) west to Exit 21, then US-222 south to Lancaster. Enter the city via US-30 west and PA-272 south. A much shorter route, only 65 miles in length but slower and often congested, is via US-30 west to Lancaster, entering town via PA-462.

By train, Lancaster is a less-than-two-hour ride from Philadelphia's 30th Street Station via Amtrak, ☎ 800-USA-RAIL for schedules and fares.

Buses operated by Greyhound provide connections with Philadelphia, a two-hour-plus ride away. ☎ 800-231-2222 for schedules.

PRACTICALITIES:

Many of the attractions are seasonal, usually open from April or May through October, November, or December. Quite a few of them close on

Sundays and/or Mondays, and also on major holidays. Check the individual listings carefully, and play safe by calling ahead. The colorful Central
Market is open on Tuesdays, Fridays, and Saturdays.

For further information, contact the **Lancaster Chamber of Commerce**
at South Queen and Vine streets, ☎ 717-392-1776. Regional information is
available from the **Pennsylvania Dutch Convention & Visitors Bureau,** just
east of the city at 501 Greenfield Road (at US-30), Lancaster, PA 17601, ☎
717-299-8901 or 800-723-8824, fax 717-299-0470, Internet: www.800
padutch.com.

FOOD AND DRINK:

Some choice restaurants in the historic center of downtown
Lancaster are:

Market Fare (Grant & Market streets, by the Central Market) Creative
American cuisine in a traditional dining room resembling a private club.
Reservations suggested. Sunday brunch. Lighter fare in the upstairs café.
☎ 717-299-7090. $$ and $$$

Stockyard Inn (1147 Lititz Pike, PA-501 and US-222, 1.5 miles north of
the Central Market, just east of Amtrak station) American/Continental cuisine in an historic home. ☎ 717-394-7975. X: Sat. lunch, Mon. lunch. $$ and
$$$

The Pressroom (26 W. King St. at Market) American cuisine is served at
this smart bistro in an historic center city building. X: Sun., Mon. ☎ 717-
399-5400. $ and $$

Issac's Restaurant & Deli (Central Market Mall, 44 N. Queen St., by the
market) Wonderful soups, sandwiches, salads, and other light fare. ☎ 717-
394-5544. $

LOCAL ATTRACTIONS:

Numbers in parentheses correspond to numbers on the map.

Begin your daytrip with a stroll through the historic core at
Lancaster's **Downtown Visitor Center**, home of the:

HISTORIC LANCASTER WALKING TOUR (1), 100 South Queen St., ☎ 717-
392-1776. *Operates daily from April through October; tours Sun.–Mon. &
Wed.–Thurs. at 1, Tues. & Fri.–Sat. at 10 and 1. Fee: $7.50.*

Run by a non-profit organization, these 90-minute tours are led by
volunteer guides in period costume. You'll begin with a short audio-visual presentation of the town's history, then take a stroll around its historic
core. Stops are made at whichever sites are open, and the entire tour is
enlivened with colorful stories and anecdotes. Along the nearly-two-mile
route you'll wander through back alleys and visit hidden courtyards, getting a more intimate view of Lancaster than you would on your own.

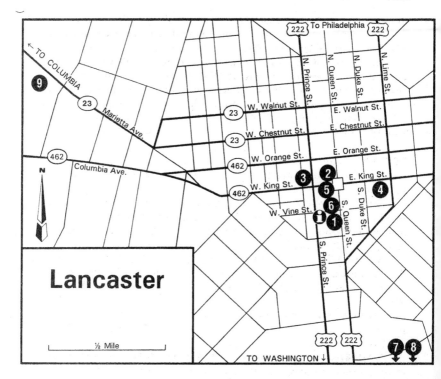

Lancaster

½ Mile

Even if you don't take the walking tour, you can get information about the town at the Visitor Center. Be sure to see the **Central Market** (2), where farmers from around the region sell their fresh produce directly to consumers. Built in 1889 on a site used for the same purpose since the 1730s, this marvelously Victorian red-brick structure is the oldest publicly-owned, continuously-operating farmers' market in America. Some of the local delicacies to try include sweet bologna and shoofly pie, the latter so tasty that you'll have to "shoo" the flies away. *Open Tues. and Fri. 6–4, Sat. 6–2.*

Just a block west of the market stands the **Fulton Opera House** (3) of 1852, built on the foundations of a Colonial jail where the last of the Conestoga Indians were massacred in 1763. Its lush Victorian interior is allegedly haunted by ghosts. Many of the greatest stars of the late 19th and early 20th centuries performed here, including Mark Twain, Buffalo Bill, Wild Bill Hickok, John Phillip Sousa, Ethel Barrymore, W.C. Fields, Sarah Bernhardt, Sophie Tucker, Al Jolson, Alfred Lunt, Irene Dunne, Busby Berkely, and Anna Pavlova. Completely renovated in 1969, the Opera House is now a National Historic Landmark and serves as the community's performing arts center. *12 N. Price St.,* ☎ *717- 397-7425.*

The noted American artist, Charles Demuth (1883–1935), had his studio in the 18th-century **Demuth House and Tobacco Shop** (4), which has been restored. You can visit the studio, art gallery, home, and courtyard garden; as well as the adjacent shop. The latter, still in business, was opened around 1770 and is the oldest tobacco shop in America. *114–120 E. King St. (rear),* ☎ *717-299-9940. Open Tues.–Sat. 10–4, Sun. 1–4. Closed Mon., holidays, Dec. 24, Jan. Free.*

Penn Square, at the intersection of King and Queen streets, is the very heart of historic Lancaster. Near its northwest corner stands the:

HERITAGE CENTER MUSEUM (5), Penn Square, ☎ 717-299-6440. *Open Apr.–Dec., Tues.–Sat. 10–5. Closed Sun., Mon., holidays. Donation. Gift shop.* ♿.

Three centuries of Lancaster County history are explored in this Old City Hall structure from the 1790s. Among the regional fine and decorative arts on display are paintings, furniture, weathervanes, toys, clocks, Pennsylvania long rifles, fraktur, pewter, silver, copperware, quilts, and samplers.

Walk a block south to the:

LANCASTER NEWSPAPERS NEWSEUM (6), 28 S. Queen St., ☎ 717-291-8600. *Always open. Free.* ♿.

Lancaster Newspapers, Inc., has combined the words *newspaper* and *museum* to describe their window displays on the evolution of local newspapers from 1794 to the present. You'll see, directly from the sidewalk, the changing styles of newspapers, early presses, wooden type, a Linotype machine, historical headlines, distribution methods, and their modern presses of today. Explanatory panels tell the whole story.

Return to your car and drive to the next destinations. About a mile and a half to the southeast, in Lancaster County Park, is the:

ROCK FORD PLANTATION & KAUFFMAN MUSEUM (7), 881 Rock Ford Rd., ☎ 717-392-7223. *Open Apr.–Oct., Tues.–Fri. 10–4, Sun. noon–4. Adults $4.50, seniors $3.50, children (6–12) $2. Tours. Gift shop.*

George Washington's adjutant, General Edward Hand, lived in this elegant 18th-century Georgian mansion from 1793 until his death in 1802. Standing on the wooded banks of the Conestoga River, the house is remarkably well-preserved and essentially unchanged. It is furnished with period antiques, some of which once belonged to General Hand. The reconstructed barn now houses the Kauffman Museum of Pennsylvania Folk Arts and Crafts, featuring works of fraktur, pewter, copper, brass, tin, wood carvings, firearms, and furniture from the 18th and 19th centuries.

Five miles south of Lancaster, just off Route US-222, stands the oldest structure in Lancaster County:

HANS HERR HOUSE (8), 1849 Hans Herr Drive, Willow Street, PA 17584, ☎ 717-464-4438. *Open Apr. through Nov., Mon.–Sat. 9–4, closed Sun., Thanksgiving, Dec. to March. Adults $3.50, children (7–12) $1. Picnic facilities. Gift shop.*

America's oldest Mennonite meetinghouse was built by Hans Herr and his family as a wilderness home in 1719. This simple stone structure is considered to be one of the finest examples of medieval Germanic architecture in the country. Today both it, the outbuildings, and the extensive grounds have been restored to their original appearance, and offer a fascinating glimpse into the lives of the early Mennonites.

Return to Lancaster and turn west on PA-23 to:

*WHEATLAND (9), 1120 Marietta Ave., Lancaster, PA 17603, ☎ 717-392-8721. *Open Apr.–Nov., daily, 10–4, closed Easter and Thanksgiving. Special candlelight tours in early Dec. Adults: $5.50, seniors $4.50, students $3.50, children (6–11) $1.75. Tours. Gift shop. ♿, partial access.*

James Buchanan, the 15th President of the United States, purchased this estate in 1848 while he was still Secretary of State, and continued to use it for the rest of his life. He died here in 1868, still defending what most people regarded as a disastrous presidency (1857–61) that failed to prevent the Civil War. Buchanan was the only President to have come from Pennsylvania, and the only one to have remained unmarried. Always politically active, he was a member of the House of Representatives, a U.S. Senator, minister to both Russia and Great Britain, and Secretary of State under President James Polk.

The mansion, built in the Federal style in 1828 by a wealthy lawyer and banker, was named "The Wheatlands" after its then-rural location near fields of wheat. It is furnished much as it would have been during Buchanan's life, with many of his own treasures gathered from around the world. His niece, Harriet Lane, also lived here and added an elegant domestic touch to the decor. She served as First Lady during Buchanan's stay in the White House.

A visit to Wheatland begins with a video show in the carriage house, and continues with a thorough tour of the mansion, led by knowledgeable guides in period costume.

*Heart of the Amish Countryside

F rom the sublimely bucolic to the ridiculously tacky, this drive covers a wide, wide range of Pennsylvania Dutch Country experiences—all within a short distance of Lancaster, and completely feasible as a daytrip from Philadelphia. Along the way you'll encounter some of the most gorgeous rural scenery in the world, which more than compensates for the patches of shameless tourist traps near the beginning and end. Even scattered among these lurk some real gems that are just too good to miss.

Relax, take it easy, and drive slow. There are quite a few attractions along the way, but none as important as the setting itself. Why not pull over to the side of the road and take a walk along country lanes, drinking in the delicious sights and exchanging greetings with the friendly folk you'll meet? And for that matter, why stick to the suggested route? Driving down some of the side roads may lead to serendipitous discoveries— especially north of Route PA-340. For the physically ambitious, this trip makes a wonderful bicycle excursion. The terrain is rolling, with a few moderate hills, and for the most part traffic is light.

GETTING THERE:

The starting point of this 25-mile-long scenic drive is about 11 miles southeast of **Lancaster**, along US-30 just east of Paradise. From **Philadelphia**, take US-30 west for about 58 miles, expecting congestion in the last few miles around Gap and Kinzers.

PRACTICALITIES:

Good weather is absolutely essential for this largely outdoor trip. Weekdays are preferred, as you'll encounter less traffic in the tourist areas. Several of the best attractions are closed on Sundays, and many in the off-season. Check the individual listings, remembering that the drive itself is the main attraction.

You may well encounter more horse-drawn buggies and farm vehicles than cars, so drive slowly and very, very carefully. Passing on the narrow roads should be done with great caution, being careful not to "spook" the horses by blowing your horn.

Taking photographs of Amish people in which they can be recognized is a violation of their religious beliefs concerning graven images, and is highly offensive. Please respect their privacy and avoid trespassing on their land.

For local information, contact the **Intercourse Tourist Information Center**, 3614 Old Philadelphia Pike, Intercourse, PA 17534, ☎ 717-768-3882. Regional information is available from the **Pennsylvania Dutch Convention & Visitors Bureau**, just east of the city at 501 Greenfield Road (at US-30), Lancaster, PA 17601, ☎ 717-299-8901 or 800-723-8824, fax 717-299-0470, Internet: www.800padutch.com.

FOOD AND DRINK:

Pennsylvania Dutch cuisine means hearty servings of "comfort" foods like great-grandmother used to make, often in large restaurants with communal seating and frequently no menus. This "family style" dining is just that—you sit with strangers, pass around the overflowing dishes, take all you want of whatever you want, and generally have a good time. Some establishments offer buffet or à la carte service at private tables instead. Be sure to try the shoofly pie—just this once. Most restaurants do not serve liquor, and some are closed on Sundays. Among the better choices are:

Plain & Fancy Farm (PA-340, 2 miles east of Bird-in-Hand) Fixed-price PA-Dutch meals served family-style in a large barn. Special meals for children. No menu. ☎ 717-768-4400. $$

Good 'N Plenty (PA-896, a half-mile south of PA 340, at Smoketown) An enormous family-style restaurant with copious servings of PA-Dutch favorites. ☎ 717-394-7111. X: Sun. $$

Miller's Smorgasbord (US-30, east of the intersection with N. Ronks Rd.) A fixed-price buffet with all you can eat. Special price for children. In business since 1929. ☎ 717-687-6621. $$

Amish Barn Restaurant (PA-340, a mile east of Bird-in-Hand) Abundant PA-Dutch dishes are offered either à la carte or family-style. ☎ 717-768-8886. X: Jan.–Mar. $ and $$

Bird-in-Hand Family Restaurant (PA-340 near Ronks Rd., Bird-in-Hand) PA-Dutch home cooking, served à la carte or from a buffet. X: Sun. ☎ 717-768-8266. $ and $$

For something different, you might try the restaurants listed for the nearby Strasburg daytrip (see page 218).

SUGGESTED TOUR:

Numbers in parentheses correspond to numbers on the map.

Where better to begin your trip than in **Paradise** (1)? Head about a mile east along US-30 from this small town, and turn north on Belmont Road. Suddenly, in just yards, all of the traffic and tourist traps disappear and you're out in the real countryside. Soon you'll come to **Paradise Bridge** (2), a delightful covered bridge built in 1893, also known as the Leaman Place or Eshelman's Mill Bridge. Before crossing it, pull over to the side of the road, get out, and wait for the first horse-drawn buggy to come along. You won't have to wait long. What an idyllic scene!

Ahead lies the village of **Intercourse** (3), whose curious name raises a few eyebrows—especially as the road from it leads to Paradise. Actually, its name probably refers to its location at the junction of what in the early 19th century were two main highways. Once a delightful Amish settlement, Intercourse is today overrun with quainte gifte shoppes and olde countrie stores, but it does have one compelling sight that will help you understand the rest of the area's attractions, namely:

THE PEOPLE'S PLACE, Route 340, Intercourse, PA 17534, ☎ 717-768-7171. *Open Mon.–Sat., 9:30 a.m.–8 p.m., closing at 5 after Labor Day and before Memorial Day. Closed Sun., New Year's, Thanksgiving, Christmas. Show: Adults $4, children (5–11) $2. Museum: Adults $4, children $2. Combination tickets available. Bookstore. Craft shop.*

The world of the Plain People is skillfully explained in this cultural interpretation center created by Merle and Phyllis Good, two Mennonites who set out to promote a better understanding of the Amish, Mennonite, and Hutterite ways of life. They do this through a 25-minute audio-visual presentation entitled *Who Are the Amish?* (shown continuously from 9:30 to 6:45, 4:30 in winter), a hands-on museum called **Twenty Questions** that you can experience at your own pace, and exhibits of local arts and crafts.

Poke around the shops of Intercourse, then head north on PA-772 (Newport Road), following the map and occasionally making diversions from it as the mood strikes you. Continue north on Hess Road, turning left on East Eby Road. Here, on the right, you'll come to an old **Amish Cemetery** (4), whose gravestones can be read by peering over the fence. Turn left (south) on Stumptown Road, which soon brings you to the utterly delight- ful little hamlet of **Mascot** (5). Right at the intersection, a dam backs up the water of Mill Creek to provide water power for the local mill, as Amish lads fish in the stream. There's even a free place to park here, and not a com- mercial establishment in sight. But there are two marvelous free attrac- tions:

*MASCOT ROLLER MILLS, Ronks, PA. *Open May–Oct. Free.*

Almost too picturesque to believe, the old Mascot Mill was built of stone in 1760 and continued operations until 1977. It was owned by three generations of the Ressler family from 1864 until the retirement of W.

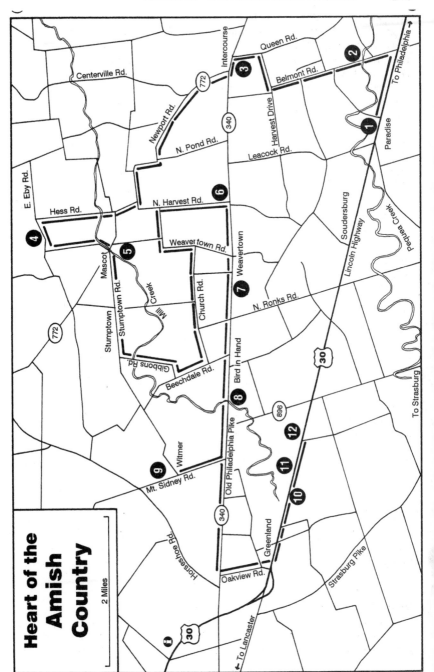

Franklin Ressler, who with his sister created the Ressler Mill Foundation to preserve this rural heritage for all time. A large enough endowment was left to pay for restoration, maintenance, and guides—which is why everything here is free. Stop in, watch the video, enjoy a demonstration of the working machinery, and examine the colorful old Mascot Post Office, unchanged since 1934.

The ***Ressler Family House**, next door to the mill, is equally intriguing, and is also open to visitors as part of the same foundation. It, too, is miraculously free. Everything here is as it was; simple, practical, and well-loved by many generations of the same family. Be sure to take the tour as this is the kind of place that's all too seldom encountered.

Continue west on Stumptown Road, making a left onto Gibbons Road at an especially attractive farm, and another left onto Beechdale Road. In about a half-mile, turn left again on Church Road, and left yet again on Weavertown Road. Finally, a right onto North Harvest Road brings you to the Old Philadelphia Pike, PA-340. To the left is the:

AMISH EXPERIENCE THEATER & AMISH COUNTRY HOMESTEAD (6), 3121 Old Philadelphia Pike, Bird-in-Hand, PA 17505, ☎ 717-768-3600. *Open daily Apr.–Nov., weekends Dec.–Mar., closed Thanksgiving and Christmas; theater daily all year. Homestead: Adults $5, children (4–11) $3.25. Theater: Adults $6.50, children (4–11) $3.75.*

Here visitors can discover how the Old Order Amish live today, without electricity but with surprising adaptations to contemporary life. The replica **Homestead** is authentically furnished, and affords a glimpse into a world you could hardly penetrate otherwise. The adjacent **Amish Experience Theater** tells the story of these remarkable people through the medium of a 30-minute multimedia production, intermingled with the drama of a modern Amish teenager's quest to discover himself.

Head west on PA-340, the old "King's Highway" of the early 18th century, possibly stopping at the **Weavertown One-Room Schoolhouse** (7). This was a real country schoolhouse from 1877 until 1969, after which the teacher and students were replaced with realistic animated figures who put on an entertaining show. ☎ 717-768-3976, *Internet: www.800padutch.com/wvrtown.html. Open Apr.–Oct. daily 10–5, 9–5 from Memorial Day to Labor Day, and weekends 10–5 in Mar. and Nov. Adults $2.95, seniors $2.50, children (5-11) $2.*

Bird-in-Hand, which got its name from the sign of an early inn, is the next village. Just west of it is **Abe's Buggy Rides** (8), a concession that has been offering short two-mile rides in Amish horse-drawn buggies for over 28 years. ☎ 717-392-1794, *Internet: www.800padutch.com/abes.html. Open Mon.–Sat., 8:30–dusk. Adults $10, children (3–12) $5.*

A short diversion north on Mount Sidney Road brings you to the:

*FOLK CRAFT CENTER & MUSEUM (9), 445 Mt. Sidney Rd., Witmer, PA 17585, ☎ 717-397-3609. *Open Apr. to mid-Nov., Mon.–Sat. 9:30–5, Sun. noon–4. Adults $5, seniors $4, children under 12 $2.*

A skillfully re-created early-18th-century structure, along with an authentic old log cabin, houses a fabulous collection of tools and household objects integral to Pennsylvania Dutch life in times past. Visits begin with an introductory film show in an auditorium patterned after an Old Order Mennonite meetinghouse and proceed up the female staircase from an early Lutheran meetinghouse; opposite this is the staircase reserved for males. Don't miss the early copy of the Declaration of Independence printed in German, one of only two copies known to exist. There's also a fine gallery of local folk art, antique quilts, a herb garden, a woodcrafter's shop, and more.

Return to PA-340 and continue west, turning south on Oakview Road. Make a left onto US-30, a congested highway lined with outlet shops, fast-food eateries, strip malls, tourist traps of the worst kind, and—incredibly—a few really worthwhile attractions. The first of these, on the right, is the **Mennonite Information Center** (10), where you can learn more about the Amish and Mennonite ways of life. The center also offers a short film about the Mennonites, and tour guides who can lead you (in your car) to many out-of-the-way places not spoiled by commercialism. Adjacent to the center is the **Hebrew Tabernacle Reproduction**, an actual-size model of the ancient Tabernacle of Jerusalem described in the Bible, including the golden Ark of the Covenant. *2209 Mill Stream Rd., Lancaster, PA 17602, ☎ 717-299-0954, Internet: www.mennoniteinfoctr.com. Open Mon.–Sat., 8–5. Center free, tabernacle tours: Adults $5, seniors $4, children (7–12) $2.50. Tour guides $9.50 per hour plus a flat charge of $7 per car.* ♿.

Down the road, past the **Dutch Wonderland Amusement Park**, is the **Wax Museum of Lancaster County History** (11). The name says it all—an audiovisual presentation of the county's history from the 1600s to the present, including an animated Amish Barn raising. ☎ *717-393-3679. Open daily all year. Adults $5.75, seniors $5.50, children (5-11) $3.50.*

Continuing east on US-30 brings you to a final attraction, the:

AMISH FARM AND HOUSE (12), 2395 Lincoln Hwy. East (US-30), Lancaster, PA 17602, ☎ 717-394-6185, Internet: www.amishfarmandhouse.com. *Open daily all year, 8:30–6 in summer, until 5 in spring and fall, and closing at 4 in winter. Closed Christmas. Adults $5.95, seniors $5.25, children (5–11) $3.25. Gift shop. Snacks.* ♿.

You won't meet any Amish at this commercial attraction, but otherwise it's a quite authentic presentation of their rural ways of life. Visits begin with a lecture and tour of the ten-room **farmhouse**, built around 1805 and simply furnished in the Old-Order Amish tradition. You can then explore the 25-acre **farm** with its barn, windmill, waterwheels, spring house, chicken coop, corn crib, lime kiln, blacksmith shop, and more. Live animals and growing crops add to the interest, as does the small museum.

Strasburg

Railfans (and normal folk, too) will literally be in Paradise when they take this daytrip into America's railroading past. That's the name of the village to which the antique steam train takes you as you ride across the Pennsylvania Dutch countryside, and that's the feeling you'll get as you marvel at the workings of these hissing black beasts.

Strasburg has become quite a center for train enthusiasts ever since the once-defunct Strasburg Rail Road, founded in 1832, came back to life in 1959. No mere tourist attraction, this is a real, standard-gauge working railroad that operates all year round. You've probably already seen its meticulously-restored trains in movies and TV commercials.

Just across the street from the station is the fabulous Railroad Museum of Pennsylvania, one of the largest and most comprehensive of its kind in the world. You can easily spend hours here examining dozens of locomotives and cars dating from the 1820s to the near-present, both inside the museum and out in the yards.

Having two major attractions so close together has naturally brought on other related sights to help make your day even more enjoyable. The village of Strasburg itself is of more than passing historic interest, with houses dating back as far as 1764 and a Main Street that was once part of the first route leading from Philadelphia to the booming West.

GETTING THERE:

By car, Strasburg is about 10 miles southeast of Lancaster via US-222 and PA-741, or 63 miles west of Philadelphia via US-202, US-30, PA-41, and PA-741.

PRACTICALITIES:

The Strasburg Rail Road operates daily from April through September, and on weekends the rest of the year. The Railroad Museum of Pennsylvania is open daily from April through October, and daily except Mondays the rest of the year, closing on some holidays. Most of the other attractions are open on a similar schedule. Strasburg can get quite crowded on summer weekends.

For further information on this region, contact the **Pennsylvania Dutch Convention & Visitors Bureau** at 501 Greenfield Road, Lancaster, PA 17601, ☎ 717-299-8901 or 800-723-8824, fax 717-299-0470, Internet: www.800padutch.com. Another source is the **Strasburg Visitors Information Center** on PA-896, at the Historic Strasburg Inn, ☎ 717-687-7922.

The Strasburg Rail Road runs **special event trains** around Easter, Halloween, and before Christmas. Call them for current details and reservations.

Throughout this area you will encounter many of Lancaster County's "Plain People," especially members of the Amish faith, who choose to reject the trappings of modern life. *Please respect their privacy and religious beliefs by not taking any photographs of them in which faces may be recognizable, a violation of the Biblical command to make no graven images.* Drivers must keep an eye out for slow-moving horse-drawn buggies.

FOOD AND DRINK:

Some good restaurants in and around Strasburg are:

Historic Revere Tavern (3063 Lincoln Highway/US-30, in Paradise, about 5 miles northeast of Strasburg) Steak and seafood in a 1740 inn; lighter fare at lunch. ☎ 717-687-8601. $$ and $$$

Washington House (in the Historic Strasburg Inn on Route 896, in town) Colonial-style dining in a re-created 1793 inn. ☎ 717-687-7691 or 800-872-0201. $$

Red Caboose (312 Paradise Lane/ PA-741, just northeast of the R.R. Museum) Railfans will love having lunch in a dining car surrounded by rolling stock, now part of a motel. Nothing fancy, but it's fun. ☎ 717-687-5001. $ and $$

Isaac's Restaurant & Deli (Route 741 in town, at the Shops of Traintown) Soups, salads, sandwiches, and the like in a friendly atmosphere. ☎ 717-687-7699. X: major holidays. $

Alternatively, you might bring a **picnic lunch** to eat at Groff's Grove, a stop on the steam railroad. Box lunches may be purchased at the station, or you can get the makings of a picnic at the Country Store in Strasburg. The **Dining Car Restaurant** at the station features burgers and other simple dishes ($).

LOCAL ATTRACTIONS:

Numbers in parentheses correspond to numbers on the map.

Since its ticket may be used repeatedly all day long and since it opens first, has a huge parking lot, and is just across the street from the station, you'll probably find it most convenient to start with the Railroad Museum.

*RAILROAD MUSEUM OF PENNSYLVANIA (1), Route 741, Strasburg, PA 17579, ☎ 717-687-8628. *Open Mon.–Sat. 9–5, Sun. noon–5; closed Mondays from Nov.–Apr. and some holidays. Adults $6, seniors $5.50, children $4. Tickets valid for multiple entries throughout the day. Gift shop. Largely ら.*

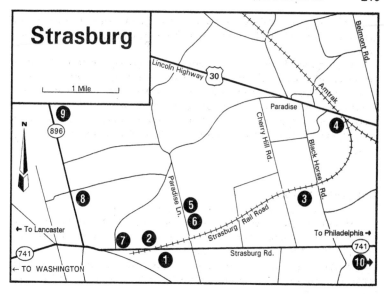

This modern, state-operated museum has one of the very best collections of historic motive power, rolling stock, and railroading artifacts to be found anywhere on Earth. At last count there were over 30 locomotives and about 40 passenger, freight, and service cars on display inside the hall and out in the yards. Two of these are exact replicas of pioneer locomotives from the 1820s, and at least one of the electrics is of recent enough vintage to bear the Amtrak logo. But mostly there is a lot of steam. You can stand in the cab of one engine, climb into the pit beneath another, and peer into all kinds of passenger cars.

Along with the trains are displays on the rich history of Pennsylvania's railroads and a vast collection of old-time memorabilia. Don't miss the 20-minute film shown continuously inside a period station, or the view from the upper balcony. Near the exit is a gift shop with an enticing selection of railroading books, videos, and related matter.

*STRASBURG RAIL ROAD (2), Route 741, Strasburg, PA 17579, ☎ 717-687-7522, Internet www.strasburgrailroad.com. *Open daily Apr.–Sept., weekends the rest of the year. Train schedule varies, usually hourly 10–7 in peak season, hourly noon–3 in off-season. Ride takes 45 minutes round trip. Layover stop may be made at Groff's Grove. Basic fares: Adults $8.25, children (3–11) $4, all day fare with unlimited rides $16.50. $1 extra for reserved seats, premium for parlor and dining cars. Gift shop. Bookstore. Restaurant, snack bar, picnic tables. Partially &, inquire for details.*

America's oldest short-line railroad has been hauling passengers and freight from Strasburg to the Main Line of the Pennsylvania Railroad, a 4.5-mile distance, ever since 1832. Decreasing revenues and destruction caused by violent storms forced it to file for abandonment in 1957, but it was saved and eventually brought back to healthy life by a group of local railfans in 1958. Money for this endeavor was raised by the simple gimmick of making every investor a vice-president! In addition to its considerable tourist trade, the Strasburg Rail Road still carries occasional freight to the main line at Paradise, PA, where it connects with ConRail as Amtrak trains speed by.

A steam locomotive was acquired in 1960 (the line had switched to gasoline power as early as 1926), and some ancient coaches were discovered on a remote siding in New Hampshire, brought here, and restored. Also hauled in pieces to this spot was the Victorian station of 1882, where the tickets are now sold. Over the years since, additional old locomotives and cars were found and refurbished, so that today the railroad boasts one of the finest stables of vintage rolling stock in the nation. In addition to six steam locomotives, these include both open and closed coaches, a fantastic open observation car used in the film *Hello Dolly*, and a parlor car of palatial luxury. On a siding sits the elegant private car built in 1916 for the president of the Reading Railroad, which may be boarded for inspection.

One of the delights of riding the Strasburg Rail Road is the bucolic countryside through which it travels. Small farms, mostly owned by Amish families who still rely on animal power, line the right-of-way. The few small roads that cross the tracks are just as likely to be used by horse-drawn buggies as by automobiles, so you may truly feel that the clock has been turned back nearly a century.

Your ride on the steam train takes you from the **East Strasburg Station** (2) to **Groff's Grove** (3), where you have the option of getting off for a picnic and taking a later train back. While there, you might want to get lost in the **Amazing Maize Maze**, a 10-acre corn field arranged as a challenging maze. In addition, a petting zoo, hay ride, and other treats are featured. *Open July to Labor Day, Tues.–Sat., and mid-Sept. through Oct. on Fri. and Sat.; 10–dusk. Adults $7, children (5–11) $4.* ☎ *717-687-6843, Internet: www.amazingmaze.com.* The end of the line is at **Leaman Place** (4) by the village of **Paradise**, where the tracks join Amtrak's main line and the engine is run around for the return journey.

NATIONAL TOY TRAIN MUSEUM (5), Paradise Lane, Box 248, Strasburg, PA 17579, ☎ 717-687-8976, Internet: www.traincollectors.org. *Open daily 10–5, May–Oct; weekends in April, Nov. to mid-Dec.; plus Good Friday, Easter Mon., Thanksgiving Fri., and Dec. 26–31. Adults $3, seniors $2.75, children (5–12) $1.50. Gift shop.* &.

Not just another commercial enterprise, this is actually the national headquarters of the non-profit Train Collectors Association, an organization devoted to the preservation and history of toy trains. Don't confuse these delights with the more serious model trains that stress authentic detail in scaled miniature. Toy trains are the stuff of childhood dreams, and bear such famous brand names as Lionel and American Flyer.

The vast collections exhibited here include examples dating from 1880 to the present. There are five huge operating layouts in O, S, G, HO, and Standard gauges, all of which respond to the buttons you push. A continuous video show both entertains and educates visitors about the joys that adults (and even children) can have playing with toys.

Almost next door to the Toy Train Museum is the **Red Caboose Motel** (6), ☎ *717-687-5000*, which houses its guests in a yard full of real cabooses! This is the perfect overnight stop for dedicated railfans, who might also want to take on fuel at the motel's Dining Car restaurant.

CHOO CHOO BARN (7), Route 741, Strasburg, PA 17579, ☎ 717-687-7911, Internet: www.choochoobarn.com. *Open daily Apr.–Dec., 10–4:30, closing at 5:30 in summer. Adults $4, children (5–12) $2. Model train shop.* ♿.

Many of Lancaster County's charms have been re-created in O-gauge scale in this 1,700-square-foot model train layout. Thirteen trains whiz around while some 135 animated scenes depict barn-raisings, a circus, a parade, an amusement park, and even a house on fire. Days are compressed, too, as the lights periodically dim and a nightime scene appears.

GAST CLASSIC MOTORCARS EXHIBIT (8), 421 Hartman Bridge Road, Route 896, Strasburg, PA 17579, ☎ 717-687-9500. *Open daily 9–5. Closed Jan 1, Easter, Thanksgiving, Christmas. Adults $8, children (7–12) $4. Gift shop.* ♿.

It's not such a great leap from trains to automobiles, and you'll find plenty of the latter in this exhibition. More than 50 cars are on display at any time, including rare antiques, high-performance sports cars, celebrity specials, and even "wheels" you may have owned yourself at one time.

THE AMISH VILLAGE (9), Route PA-896 a mile south of US-30, Strasburg, PA 17579, ☎ 717-687-8511, Internet: www.800padutch.com/avillage.html. *Open daily 9–6 mid-March to Labor Day, 9–4 day after Labor Day through Oct., 10–4 Nov. and Dec.; and weekends 10–4 the rest of the year. Closed Thanksgiving week, Christmas. Adults $5.50, children 6–12 $1.50. Picnic area. Gift shop.* ♿.

Almost as far removed from railroading as you can get, the nearby Amish Village makes a nice contrast to all those mechanical goings-on. Visitors are treated to a half-hour tour into the world of the Old Order Amish, with stops at an authentically-furnished farm house of 1840, a spring house, an Amish village store, an operating smokehouse, a black-smith's shop, a windmill, and a waterwheel. The schoolhouse was built by Amish craftsmen, and is typical of those in use today. And, of course, there are live farm animals, including pigs, goats, horses, and others.

A visit to a friendly winery can add a pleasant finale to the day's explo-ration. Fortunately, there's a good one just ten miles to the east, on the way to Philadelphia. The **Twin Brook Winery** (10) offers visits to the vineyards, tours of the 18th-century barn now used for wine making, tastings of vinifera and hybrid varietals and blends, and, of course, sales. There are also picnic facilities. *5697 Strasburg Road (PA-741), Gap, PA 17527,* ☎ *717-442-4915. Open Apr.–Dec., Mon.–Sat. 10–6 and Sun. noon–5; Jan.–March, Tues.–Sun. noon–5.*

Columbia

A visit to Columbia is a must for anyone with an interest in timekeeping. If their enthusiasms also extend to fine wines and handcrafted country beers served with lots of atmosphere, so much the better. This trip takes you on a journey through time at one of the world's leading museums of horology, to a winery estate where you can sample the vintages, take a tour, or even bring a picnic lunch, and finally to the only 19th-century brewery in the United States to have survived intact.

Besides these treats, you can also visit an early-18th-century mansion, a still-functioning 19th-century farmers' market, and a centuries-old plantation.

GETTING THERE:

By car, Columbia is about 11 miles due west of **Lancaster** via PA-462. From **Philadelphia**, the quickest—but not the shortest—route is to take the Pennsylvania Turnpike (I-76) west to Exit 21, then US-222 south and US-30 west, a total distance of 88 miles. Otherwise, it's 77 miles via US-30 all the way, but expect heavy traffic and delays along this route.

PRACTICALITIES:

Ideally, you should make this trip on a Saturday between May and October, when everything is open. Otherwise, pick and choose attractions according to their schedules. The Watch & Clock Museum, the winery, and the brewery are open most days, all year round.

If you're visiting the vineyard, or especially the beer garden at Bube's Brewery, remember to have a designated driver or else have soft drinks instead.

For further information, contact the **Susquehanna Heritage Tourist Center**, 445 Linden St., Columbia, PA 17512, ☎ 717-684-5249. Regional information is available from the **Pennsylvania Dutch Convention & Visitors Bureau**, just east of Lancaster at 501 Greenfield Road (at US-30), Lancaster, PA 17601, ☎ 717-299-8901 or 800-723-8824, fax 717-299-0470, Internet: www.800padutch.com.

FOOD AND DRINK:

The Catacombs (102 N. Market St. in Mount Joy, part of Bube's Brewery complex) Gourmet candlelight dining in the old aging cellars of the brewery, 43 feet underground. Medieval feasts on Sundays. Dinner only, reserve. ☎ 717-653-2056. $$$

Alois (102 N. Market St. in Mount Joy, part of Bube's Brewery complex) Elegant Victorian dining; dress nicely and reserve. ☎ 717-653-2057. Dinner only. X: Mon., holidays. $$$

Groff's Farm (650 Pinkerton Rd., a mile southwest of Mt. Joy, off PA-772) Authentic Pennsylvania Dutch cuisine of the highest order, served in a 1757 farmhouse. Reservations advised, ☎ 717-653-2048. $$ and $$$

Railroad House (280 W. Front St., Marietta) American and Continental dishes, with lighter meals in the tavern, and outdoor dining in season. Reservations suggested, ☎ 717-426-4141. X: Mon. $$

Bottling Works (102 N. Market St. in Mt. Joy, part of Bube's Brewery complex) A casual tavern with both light and full meals. There's also an outdoor beer garden. ☎ 717-653-2160. $ and $$

Watering Trough (905 W. Main St. in Mt. Joy, a mile west of town on PA-230) Basic American cuisine in a casual setting. ☎ 717-653-6181. $ and $$

Another option is to bring a picnic lunch to enjoy at the winery.

LOCAL ATTRACTIONS:

Number in parentheses correspond to numbers on the map.

***THE WATCH AND CLOCK MUSEUM** (1), 514 Poplar St., Columbia, PA 17512, ☎ 717-684-8261. *Open May–Sept., Tues.–Sat. 9–4, Sun. noon–4; rest of year Tues.–Sat. 9–4. Closed Mon., holidays. Adults $6, seniors $5, children (6-12) $4.* ♿.

Operated by the National Association of Watch and Clock Collectors, this intriguing museum celebrates the history of timekeeping with over 8,000 items, including clocks dating from the 17th century to the present. Some of them are quite amazing (and even humorous) in the intricate and unexpected ways they have of counting the minutes. Try to be there on the hour, when the whole place comes alive with wondrous sounds.

Five blocks to the southwest is the:

WRIGHT'S FERRY MANSION (2), 38 S. 2nd St., Columbia, PA 17512, ☎ 717-684-4325. *Open May–Oct., Tues., Wed., Fri., Sat. 10–3. Closed Mon., Thurs., Sun., July 4. Adults $5, students (6–18) $2.50.*

Back in 1726, a refined, well-educated Quaker lady left the comforts of Philadelphia to live in what was then a wilderness. Here she set up a thriving silkworm industry and maintained correspondence with some of the leading intellects of Colonial America, including Benjamin Franklin. Successful at business, she had this mansion built in 1738 in a typical English style with Pennsylvania-Dutch overtones. The beautifully restored house now contains one of the best collections of early-18th-century Pennsylvania furnishings to be found anywhere.

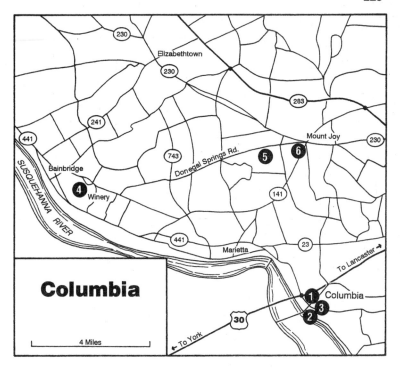

If you happen to be in Columbia on a Friday or Saturday, be sure to visit the **Market House and Dungeon** (3) at Third and Locust streets, just two blocks northeast of the Wright Ferry Mansion. A farmers' market you can understand, and they're always fun to attend. But a dungeon as well? Well, it seems that way back when, the local police used to keep vagrants and felons in a dank lock-up beneath the main floor of the 1869 market house, sending them down there via a chute. You can go down and look at the subterranean pokey yourself, then escape to the fresh produce, meats, cheeses, baked goods, candy, and crafts offered above. ☎ *717-684-0221. Open Fri. 7–4, Sat. 7–noon, or by appointment. Free.*

Several good attractions lie just a few miles north of Columbia. To reach the winery, follow PA-441 along the river for about eight miles and turn right on Wickersham Road. From there follow signs for another 1.5 miles to the:

NISSLEY VINEYARDS & WINERY ESTATE (4), 140 Vintage Drive, Bainbridge, PA 17502, ☎ 717-426-3514 or 800-522-2387. *Open Mon.–Sat. 10–5, Sun. 1–4.*

Closed Thanksgiving, Christmas, New Year's, Easter. Last tour is 45 minutes before closing. No tours during special events. Visitors under age 21 must be accompanied by adult. Free. Wine tastings. Wine sales. Picnic facilities.

Located on a lovely 300-acre estate, the Nissley complex includes some 35 acres of carefully tended vineyards, a stone arch winery, an 18th-century stone mill, meadows, woodlands, and lawns. Nissley wines are made from French-hybrid or native American grapes, or from fruits such as apples, cherries, or black raspberries. They range from very dry to sweet, are labeled as either varietals or proprietaries, and are nearly always vintage dated. Why not bring along a picnic lunch and purchase a chilled bottle to enjoy on the spot?

About seven miles east of the winery, via Donegal Springs Road and Musser Road, is the **Donegal Mills Plantation** (5). This restored 18th- and 19th-century community was first settled in the early 1700s and grew after it was sold to Pennsylvania Germans in 1779. There's a Georgian mansion with Empire and Victorian antiques, an authentically furnished 1760 miller's house, a grist mill of 1830, a bake house, gardens, and wildlife areas. ☎ *717-653-2168. Open mid-March through Dec., weekends, noon–6; or by appointment. Adults $4, children (6–12) $2.*

The perfect place to end the day is in nearby Mount Joy, at:

BUBE'S BREWERY (6), 102 North Market St., Mount Joy, PA 17552, ☎ 717-653-2056, Internet: www.bubesbrewery.com. *Restaurants, bar, and beer garden open daily, see Food and Drink section, above. Free guided tours from mid-June until the day before Labor Day, hourly from 10–5 on Mon.–Sat. and noon–5 Sun. Free short tours for evening patrons all year round. Medieval and Roman feasts. Brewery store.*

Back in 1876, a young German immigrant named Alois Bube bought a small brewery in Mount Joy, made German-style lager beer, expanded the premises, and added a Victorian hotel. Prohibition killed the business, but Mr. Bube's offspring continued to live here until the 1960s, changing nothing. No longer used, the brewery existed in a time warp and eventually became the only one of its era in the United States to have survived intact. Today, after a restoration begun in 1968, it's a complex of restaurants, a bar, a beer garden, a brewing museum, an historic site on the National Register, an art gallery, and a brewery store. Tours take visitors through the old brewery and deep into the earth to visit the catacomb-like aging vaults, once used to hide escaping slaves. A visit here is not only educational, it's lots of fun—and you can eat and drink to your heart's content. Just let someone else drive you home.

Landis Valley
and Lititz

Just north of Lancaster lie some of the area's most intriguing—and least commercialized—attractions. You won't find any tourist traps here, nor many travel amenities, but to make up for that deficiency you'll get to experience the real heartland of Lancaster County.

Reminiscent of Old Sturbridge in Massachusetts, or even Williamsburg in Virginia (but not nearly as large or crowded), the Landis Valley Museum is a friendly living-history village of 18th- and 19th-century farms, houses, and other buildings, all kept alive by craftspeople and guides in period costumes.

For the kids, there's the Hands-On Museum and, later, both a candy wonderland and a place where they can twist their own pretzels. Adults may do it, too.

Lititz, with its beautifully preserved Main Street, is a step back in time to the All-American hometown of legend; quite simply one of the most delightful little towns anywhere. To finish things off, you might consider a side excursion to the Mount Hope Estate and Winery for a tour of the mansion along with a tasting of the wines.

GETTING THERE:

You'll need a car for this trip (or at least a bicycle and strong legs!) From Lancaster, head north on **PA-272** (Oregon Pike) for 5 miles, then turn left on Landis Valley Road to the museum.

Lititz is an additional 7 miles to the north. Head west on Landis Valley Road, then north on **PA-501** (Lititz Pike).

Those going to Mount Hope should head west on **PA-772**, then north on **PA-72**. The estate is just south of Exit 20 of the Pennsylvania Turnpike (I-76), a quick route back to Philadelphia.

PRACTICALITIES:

The Landis Valley Museum is open daily from March through December, but closed on some holidays. Check individual listings for the other attractions, which vary seasonally. Advance arrangements should be made for the Mount Hope Estate. For further information contact the **Pennsylvania Dutch Convention & Visitors Bureau** at 501 Greenfield Road, Lancaster, PA 17601, ☎ 717-299-8901 or 800-732-8824, fax 717-299-0470,

Internet: www.800padutch.com.

FOOD AND DRINK:

Other than the inn mentioned below, there are precious few eateries along this route. Why not pack a picnic lunch to enjoy at the Landis Valley site? From mid-spring to mid-fall, lunch and snacks are also available in the museum complex.

General Sutter Inn (14 East Main St., Lititz) First called the "Zum Anker" and run as an inn since 1764, the General Sutter was rebuilt in 1803 and 1848. It's still the best place in town for a meal. ☎ 717-626-2115. $$

LOCAL ATTRACTIONS:

Numbers in parentheses correspond to numbers on the map.

*LANDIS VALLEY MUSEUM (1), 2451 Kissel Hill Rd., Lancaster, PA 17601, ☎ 717-569-0401. *Open March–Dec., Mon.–Sat. 9–5, Sun. noon–5. Closed holidays except Memorial Day, July 4, and Labor Day. Craft demonstrations Apr.–Oct., guided tours available. Adults $7, seniors (60+) $6.50, youths (6–12) $5, under 6 free. Reduced rates in March, Nov., and Dec. Gift shop. Snacks in summer. Picnic facilities. &, partial access.*

You can really step back into the past in this reconstructed country village of 18th- and 19th-century buildings, where the old ways of life are kept alive by craftspeople and guides in period costumes. The largest outdoor museum of Pennsylvania German rural heritage anywhere, it was begun in the 1920s by George and Henry Landis, two local brothers whose German ancestors came to Lancaster County in the early 1700s. The Commonwealth of Pennsylvania acquired the museum in 1953, and has since added many historic buildings from the area, and re-created others that had been lost. Some of the highlights include a functioning **log farm** of the 1700s, a **Mennonite farmstead** of 1820, an early **tavern**, a **country store** filled with period merchandise, a **firehouse**, and a beautifully-decorated **Victorian house** of the 1870s. About 18 buildings may be visited, several of which feature traditional craft demonstrations from May through October.

Across the street is the:

HANDS-ON HOUSE—CHILDREN'S MUSEUM OF LANCASTER (2), 2380 Kissel Hill Rd., Lancaster, PA 17601, ☎ 717-569-5437. *Open Memorial Day to Labor Day, Mon.–Sat. 10–5, Sun. noon–5; rest of year, Tues.–Fri. 11–4, Sat. 10–5, Sun. noon–5; remains open on Fri. until 8. Admission $4.*

Kids from two to ten will enjoy visiting this Victorian farmhouse from 1902, now filled with all sorts of play and crafts activities geared to different age groups. They can build towns, create art, learn how the body

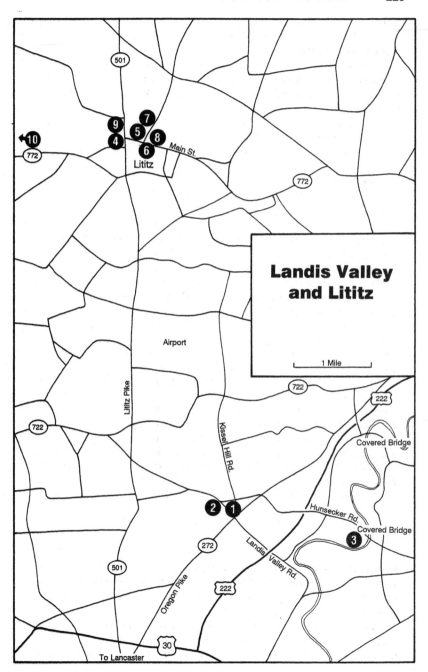

Landis Valley
and Lititz

1 Mile

grows, and even work on an assembly line at the Watcha-Ma-Giggle Company factory. Along with having fun, they'll also learn something.

At this point, covered-bridge mavens might want to make a little side trip to see the longest such span in the county. To do this, return to Route PA-272 and head north just a short distance, making a right on Hunsecker Road. This leads in about two miles to **Hunsecker Bridge** (3), one of the most interesting of Lancaster County's 28 covered bridges (the entire state has over 200!). With real luck, you might just get there as a horse-drawn buggy crosses, evoking a lovely pastoral scene.

Now for another treat! Return to Landis Valley Road and head west, turning north on Route PA-501 (Lititz Pike). This will soon bring you to the delightful village of **Lititz** (4), an as-yet unspoiled survivor in the endless battle against touristy ticky-tack that pervades so much of the county. Named after a village in Bohemia (now the Czech Republic) where the Moravian Church had its origins in 1467, Lititz was founded in 1756 by immigrant Moravians as a refuge from "worldly connections." Their religion, a Protestant denomination that predates the Reformation by some 60 years, stresses simple, honest living, and places great importance on the role of music in daily life. Other Moravian sites in eastern Pennsylvania include Bethlehem (see page 124) and Nazareth (see page 128).

Main Street is lined with a remarkable collection of 18th-century houses, along with a smattering of more "modern" structures from the 1800s. To appreciate the unusual history of this most extraordinary village, head east a few blocks to the **Johannes Mueller House** (5) of 1792, which now houses the Lititz Historical Foundation and its adjacent museum. A rare collection of early artifacts may be seen in the log portion of the house, while the stone section is authentically furnished. There are also items associated with General Johann Augustus Sutter (1803–80), surely the most famous—or infamous—resident of Lititz. Sutter was born in Germany, moved to the West Coast in 1835, founded the colony of Nueva Helvetia at was is now Sacramento, California, became a Mexican citizen, and started his own empire in central California. It was there that gold was discovered in 1848. A womanizer, an adventurer, and a heavy drinker, Sutter was unfortunately not very adept at business, and soon went bankrupt. At the age of 70 he moved to Lititz after hearing rumors of the alleged healing powers of the local spring water. He died there in 1880, and is buried across the street, in the graveyard behind the Moravian Church. *Johannes Mueller House, 137 East Main St., ☎ 717-626-7958. Open May 1 to Memorial Day, Mon.–Sat. 10–4; day after Memorial Day to Dec., Sat.–Mon. 10-4. Adults $3, children (6–18) $1.50. A walking tour map of the village is available.*

Walk across the street to the **Moravian Church Square** (6), most of whose buildings date from the 18th century. The oldest is the Gemeinhaus of 1762, now the parsonage. To its right is the Church of 1787, which has a small museum featuring period musical instruments. *Tours by appointment, Memorial Day through Labor Day.* ☎ *717-626-8515.*

Nearby, in an old factory on North Water Street, is the fascinating **Heritage Map Museum** (7) with its fabulous collection of 15th- through 19th-century maps from around the world. You could spend hours here discovering how man's concept of the world has changed over the centuries as nations came and went, and as new lands were explored. *55 N. Water St.,* ☎ *717-626-5002. Open daily 10–5. Adults $4, children (6–12) $3.*

Maybe by now you're hungry. How about a pretzel? America's first pretzel bakery, the **Sturgis Pretzel House** (8), is just down Main Street, and children from 2 to 100 are invited to come in and twist their own, earning a diploma after mastering the art. You can see the original ovens in action, along with their modern counterparts in the factory. And, of course, there's a pretzel store. *219 East Main St.,* ☎ *717-626-4354, Internet: www.sturgispretzel.com. Open Mon.–Sat. 9:30–4:30, closed New Year's, Easter, Thanksgiving, Christmas. Admission $2.*

Return along Main Street and turn north a block on Broad Street (PA-501). Follow your nose to the **Candy Americana Museum** (9) in the Wilbur Chocolate factory, home of Wilbur Buds. Here you can examine antique confectionery equipment and watch hand-dipped candies being made in the adjoining factory. To the profit of dentists everywhere, the delicious products can be purchased in the outlet store. ☎ *717-626-3249, Internet: www.800padutch.com/wilbur.html. Open Mon.–Sat. 10–5, closed Jan. 1–2, Labor Day, Thanksgiving, and Christmas. Free.*

For some, a marvelous way to end the trip is to drive about 11 miles northwest, following routes PA-772 and PA-72 through Manheim to the **Mount Hope Estate and Winery** (10) for a tour of the mansion and a tasting of the wines. Built in 1800 and later enlarged in the Victorian manner, this opulent ironmaster's palace is also home to various special events, including the annual **Pennsylvania Renaissance Faire** held from August into October. *Call ahead as tour schedules and conditions vary, and reservations may be needed. 83 Mansion House Rd., Manheim.* ☎ *717-665-7021.*

From here you can return south to Lancaster via PA-72, or head north a half-mile to the Pennsylvania Turnpike if you're heading for the Philadelphia area.

Trip 42
Ephrata and Adamstown

An unusual bit of heritage, upscale shopping, superb antiquing, and tasty dining draw visitors north of Lancaster to the area around Exit 21 of the Pennsylvania Turnpike. Here, well removed from the worst of the tourist traps, you'll find the well-preserved structures of an early-18th-century communal society devoted to piety, self-denial, and simplicity. Reminiscent of a medieval monastery, the Ephrata Cloister provides a glimpse into the daily lives of a most remarkable people.

Whether you're shopping for crafts, fashions, antiques, fresh food, or even farm animals, your desires can be satisfied at some of the many off-beat markets that abound between Ephrata and Adamstown. And, to top things off, you can end the day touring a leading country micro-brewery and its Victorian pub.

GETTING THERE:

You'll need a car for this trip. From **Lancaster**, take **PA-272** (Oregon Pike) north for about 14 miles to **US-322**, then go east a few blocks to the Cloister. A longer, but probably faster, route is to take US-222 north to US-322, then west to the Cloister.

For Doneckers and the Farmers' Market, head east on US-322 to North State Road, then turn north.

Rejoin PA-272 and go north a few miles to Adamstown.

If you're coming from **Philadelphia**, take the Pennsylvania Turnpike (I-76) west to Exit 21, a total distance of about 67 miles.

PRACTICALITIES:

The Ephrata Cloister is open daily except some holidays. Doneckers is closed on Wednesdays. You'll need to come on a Friday to witness the Green Dragon Farmers' Market in action, or on a Sunday for the best of the antique markets. Those contemplating serious antique purchases will find the most attractive bargains during the slow season, from January through March.

For further information, contact the **Pennsylvania Dutch Convention & Visitors Bureau** at 501 Greenfield Road, Lancaster, PA 17601, ☎ 717-299-8901 or 800-723-8824, fax 717-299-0470, Internet: www.800padutch.com. Another source is the **Exit 21 Tourist Information Center**, PA-272 at Exit 21 of the PA Turnpike, ☎ 717-484-4801.

FOOD AND DRINK:

The Restaurant at Doneckers (333 N. State St., Ephrata) French and American cuisine, an extensive wine list, and a pleasant country atmosphere make this place a favorite. Reservations advised, ☎ 717-738-9501. X: Sun., Wed., major holidays. $$$

Stoudt's Black Angus (PA-272, Adamstown) Famous for its home-brewed beer, Stoudt's specializes in steak, oysters, and German cuisine in a Victorian setting. Reservations suggested, ☎ 717-484-4385. X: weekday lunches, major holidays. $$ and $$$

The Black Horse (PA-272 a mile north of the PA Turnpike) Excellent American cuisine. Reservations suggested, ☎ 717-336-6555. $$

Issac's Restaurant & Deli (PA-272 just north of PA-322, in the Cloister Shopping Center at Ephrata) A wide variety of creative sandwiches and other light fare. ☎ 717-733-7777. $

Zinn's Diner (PA-272 north of the PA Turnpike) What visitor to these parts can resist a meal at Zinn's? Just look for the statue of Amos, the plastic farmer, and dig into the plain-but-plentiful chow. ☎ 717-336-2210. $

LOCAL ATTRACTIONS:

Numbers in parentheses correspond to numbers on the map.

*EPHRATA CLOISTER (8), 632 W. Main St., Ephrata, PA 17522, ☎ 717-733-6600. *Open Mon.–Sat. 9–5, Sun. noon–5. Closed holidays except Memorial Day, July 4, and Labor Day, also Mon. in Jan. and Feb. Adults $5, seniors (60+) $4.50, youths (6–17) $3. Gift shop. Special events. ↳, partial access.*

One of America's first communal societies, Ephrata was founded in 1732 by Conrad Beissel (1690–1768), a German Pietist who sought spiritual regeneration through an ascetic lifestyle and ancient mystical rites. Preaching among the Mennonites and Dunkards of Lancaster County, this charismatic leader attracted a following to his monastic community, and there developed a substantial economy that thrived until after the Revolutionary War. By that time the celibate orders had died out, and in 1814 the remaining married order formed the Seventh Day Baptist Church. Their descendants continued to use the Cloister until 1934. In 1941 it was taken over by the Pennsylvania Historical and Museum Commission.

The ten surviving buildings of the original Cloister have been restored, and a few others re-created in the distinctive medieval Germanic style that Ephrata is famous for. Visits begin with an audio-visual show, followed by a tour led by a robed guide through rooms of the main structures. After that, you can explore the other buildings, including the print shop, where one of the society's major economic functions was carried out.

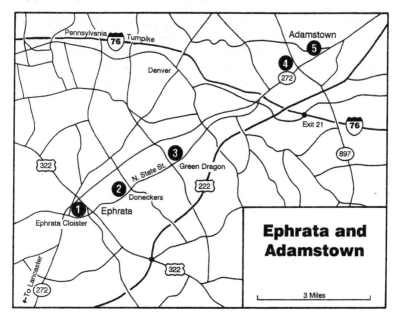

The town of Ephrata is also well-known for its upscale complex of shops, craft boutiques, studios, a farmers' market, a gourmet restaurant, and four inns known collectively as **Doneckers** (2). This community-within-a-community maintains exceptionally high standards, and makes a more-than-worthwhile stop on any day except a Wednesday, when it's all closed. The shops and restaurant are also closed on Sundays. *100-409 N. State St.,* ☎ *717-738-9500.*

If you happen to be in Ephrata on a Friday, don't miss a chance to experience the **Green Dragon Farmers' Market and Auction** (3), where Amish and Mennonite farmers operate hundreds of stalls stocked with local produce and good things to eat. There are also livestock auctions, antique sales, a flea market, and more. *955 N. State St.,* ☎ *717-738-1117. Open Fri., 6 a.m. to 7 p.m.*

Route PA-272 north of the Pennsylvania Turnpike (I-76) is the heart of antique country. Hundreds, even thousands, of dealers offer all manner of stuff, from really valuable furniture to the kind of junk you might throw out when you clean the attic. It's a browser's paradise attracting potential customers from all over the nation; indeed the world. Most of the activity centers around several complexes, including **Renningers** (4), open on Sundays only, from 7:30 a.m. to 5 p.m.

A bit farther up the road is the massive **Stoudtburg** (5) complex *(☎ 717-484-4385),* featuring the enclosed **Antiques Mall** with over 500 quality dealers *(Sun. 8–5)*, the new **Stoudtburg Village**, a pseudo-German *dorf* of the 16th century where the dealers live above their shops *(open weekends)*, a co-op of over 100 dealers *(open Thurs.–Mon.)*, a micro-brewery and pub *(open daily)*, and the Black Angus restaurant *(open daily)*. Truly a self-contained village in itself, Stoudt's makes a wonderful end to your daytrip.

Hopewell Furnace and the French Creek Area

Historic sites and natural beauty comprise this easily-accomplished (and rather inexpensive) daytrip into Berks and Chester counties, equally accessible from either the Lancaster or Philadelphia areas. The 18th-century Hopewell Furnace, one of America's first industrial complexes, is beautifully restored and gives a good insight into both early iron-making and the social conditions it created. More history is seen at the Daniel Boone homestead, where the legendary pioneer was born in 1734. History of another kind, with a lighthearted touch, permeates the nearby Merritt Museums of dolls, childhood, and Pennsylvania Dutch history.

French Creek State Park provides a relaxing escape from more serious matter, while you might end the day at the French Creek Ridge Vineyards sampling the wine, or enjoy great shopping and eating in a romantic Victorian village at St. Peters.

GETTING THERE:

By car, Hopewell Furnace is about 39 miles northeast of **Lancaster** via US-222 and the Pennsylvania Turnpike (I-76) to Exit 22. From there go south a half-mile on PA-10, then east 5 miles on PA-23 and north 3 miles on PA-345. From **Philadelphia**, it's 48 miles via the Pennsylvania Turnpike to Exit 23. From there go 3 miles north on PA-100, 6 miles west on PA-401, and 4 miles north on PA-345.

PRACTICALITIES:

Hopewell Furnace, French Creek State Park, and the Merritt Museums are open daily (except some holidays), while the Daniel Boone Homestead is closed on Mondays and holidays. The vineyard has tours and tastings on weekend afternoons, and also on Thursdays and Fridays in November and December.

For further information, contact the sites directly.

FOOD AND DRINK:

Restaurant choices in this area are very slim, so you might want to bring a **picnic lunch** to enjoy at French Creek State Park. Alternatively, there's a good selection of eateries not too far away near Reading (see page 240), Pottstown (see page 95), and around Adamstown and Ephrata (see page 232) near Exit 21 of the turnpike. One recommendation in the general vicinity of French Creek is:

Windmill Restaurant (on PA-10/23, a half-mile west of turnpike Exit 22, Morgantown) American and Pennsylvania Dutch specialties in a casual setting. ☎ 610-286- 5980. $

LOCAL ATTRACTIONS:

Numbers in parentheses correspond to numbers on the map.

*HOPEWELL FURNACE NATIONAL HISTORIC SITE (1), 2 Mark Bird Lane, Elverson, PA 19520, ☎ 610-582-8773, Internet: www.nps.gov/hofu. *Open daily 9–5, closed Jan. 1, Martin Luther King Jr.'s Birthday, Presidents' Day, Veterans Day, Thanksgiving, and Christmas. Adults $4, under 17 free. Partially &.*

It looks a lot cleaner today than it did in the 18th and 19th centuries, but if your mind can fill in the missing grime, smoke, noise, and stench that were present 24 hours a day, Hopewell will give you a good idea of what one of those early iron-making communities was like. Built in 1771 to satisfy a growing demand for domestic iron goods (imports from Britain were very expensive), Hopewell was located at a spot where water power, timber for charcoal, limestone, and iron ore were readily available. By the 1840s, however, the process was becoming obsolete as new technology allowed the use of cheaper coal instead of charcoal, and a rapidly-expanding iron industry developed around urban transportation centers. Hopewell tried to remain competitive by installing an anthracite furnace in 1853, but all was in vain and the furnace ceased operation in 1883.

While it lasted, Hopewell was a paternalistic society, with the ironmaster living luxuriously in the Big House and the workers in their tenant quarters, buying their goods at the company store. There was a complete village here, parts of which have been restored, and at times during the summer months it comes alive once again with costumed interpreters going about the historic roles.

Begin at the Visitor Center, where you can watch the short, introductory audiovisual show and examine the various artifacts on display. While there, be sure to pick up a free brochure outlining the self-guided walking tour. This will lead you past a 1757 wagon road, charcoal kilns, the waterwheel and blast machinery, the office and company store, the furnace and cast house, the blacksmith shop, surviving tenant houses, a barn, and the master's Big House.

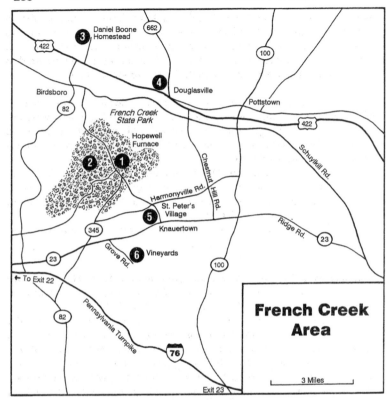

French Creek Area

3 Miles

Hopewell Village is literally surrounded by the next attraction, **French Creek State Park** (2). Here's a great place for a picnic, a swim, a hike, or just to commune with nature. At 11.5 square miles, it's one of the state's larger parks, and also offers playgrounds, a snack bar in season, lakes, boat rentals, fishing, hunting, horseback riding, cross-country skiing, and full camping facilities. *843 Park Rd., Elverson, PA 19520, ☎ 610-582-9680; for general state park info ☎ 800-63-PARKS, Internet: www.dcnr.state.pa.us. Open daily 8 a.m.–sunset. Free, except for some facilities.* ♿.

Continue north on PA-345 to Birdsboro, then north on PA-82 to US-422. Turn right (east) a short distance on this, then make a left onto Daniel Boone Road, leading shortly to the:

DANIEL BOONE HOMESTEAD (3), R.D. #2, Box 162, Birdsboro, PA 19508, ☎ 610-582-4900. *Open Tues.–Sat. 9–5, Sun. noon–5; closed holidays. Adults $4, youths $2.* ♿.

Daniel Boone, that famous frontiersman of Colonial days, was born on this homestead around 1734 and lived here until the age of 16, after which his family moved to North Carolina. It was here, in what was then a virtual wilderness, that he learned the outdoor skills that served him so well in later life. His expeditions into Indian territory led him to establish Boonesboro in Kentucky in 1774, but a lack of business skills resulted in financial ruin and he eventually drifted off to Missouri, where he died in 1820.

The house you see is not the log cabin that Boone was born in; only the foundation of that remains beneath the late-18th-century two-story stone structure that replaced it. This has been fully restored and furnished with primitive period pieces, typical of the time and place although not specific to the Boone family.

Besides the house, the 579-acre homestead includes a blacksmith shop, sawmill, barn, loghouse, and other outbuildings along with a visitor center featuring a video and exhibits relating to Boone's life and times. There are also picnic and hiking areas.

By continuing east on US-422, you'll soon come to Douglassville and the:

MERRITT MUSEUMS (4), Rt. 422, Douglassville, PA 19518, ☎ 610-385-3809 and 610-385-3408. *Open Mon.–Sat. 10–4:30, Sun. 1–5; closed major holidays. Adults $3, seniors $2.50, children 5–12 $1.50. Gift shops.*

Several thousand prize dolls, dating from the early 18th century to the present, are lovingly displayed in **Mary Merritt's Doll Museum**, one of the finest of its type in the nation. To give them a home, there are some 50 doll houses with miniature period furnishings, ranging from a simple barn to a grand French chateau. All sorts of toys are here, too, and there's a re-created Victorian toy shop along with trains, hobbyhorses, wagons, pull toys, and the like. Right next door, and included in the same admission, is **Merritt's Museum of Childhood**, where remembrances of things past are brought to life with a multitude of collectibles from an earlier period of American life.

Continue east on US-422, then head south on PA-100 and west on PA-23. At Knauertown you can turn north on St. Peters Road to **St. Peters Village** (5), a restored Victorian hamlet that was once home to quarry workers. Its delightful location next to the picturesque **French Creek Falls** made it a minor tourist attraction a long time ago, and an inn was established to cater to the visitors. Today, the inn is still there, surrounded by boutiques and other specialty shops. ☎ *610-469-3809 for information.*

Another way to end the day is to continue west on PA-23 for about two miles, and turn left (south) on Grove Road to the **French Creek Ridge Vineyards** (6), a new winery specializing in Chardonnay, Cabernet Sauvignon, and Pinot Noir vintages. Tours and tastings are offered. *200 Grove Rd., Elverson, PA 19520, ☎ 610-286-7754. Open Thurs.–Sun. 11–5; also daily in Nov.–Dec.*

Trip 44
The Reading Area

People come by the thousands to shop in Reading's many outlet stores; the city is in fact promoted as the "Outlet Capital of the World," with bargains galore for all. But there's much more to this area than just crass commercialism, as this daytrip makes abundantly clear.

Reading was founded in 1748 by the sons of William Penn, and named after their ancestral home in England. Like its British counterpart, it is pronounced RED-ding. During the 19th century it prospered mightily as a major industrial center, a heritage that carries on today, especially in apparel manufacturing and the factory outlet stores this spawned. There are now some 300 such outlets in and around the city, attracting about 10 million visitors a year. Many have become rather upscale establishments featuring top-name designer labels, and other luxury merchandise as well. The tourist office will be happy to steer you in the right directions, but while here why not take the time to enjoy some of the genuinely fascinating sights described in this daytrip?

Bargain hunters might prefer to stay overnight, devoting one day to shopping and another to local sights. Those staying over should note that this trip combines well with the previous ones to Hopewell Furnace and the French Creek Area, and the following ones to the Kutztown and Womelsdorf areas.

GETTING THERE:

By car, Reading is about 33 miles northeast of **Lancaster** via US-222. From **Philadelphia** it's about 60 miles to the northwest via I-76 to King of Prussia, then US-422.

From Reading, head northeast a few miles on US-222/US-422 (or take Schuylkill Avenue from downtown) to the intersection with PA-183, which leads north to the Reading Airport. Shortly beyond the terminal buildings, take a left onto Red Bridge Road to the Berks County Heritage Center.

Return to PA-183 and continue north a short distance to Van Reed Road, turning right and following signs to the Mid-Atlantic Air Museum.

Continue north on PA-183 to I-78, turning east on the Interstate a few miles to Exit 8 and Roadside America. On the way back, you might stop along 183 at Bernville, home of Koziar's Christmas Village.

PRACTICALITIES:

The Berks County Heritage Center offers guided tours from May through late October, on Tuesdays through Sundays, but most of the sights may be seen on your own anytime during daylight hours. The Air Museum is open daily, except on major holidays. Roadside America operates every day except Christmas. Koziar's is strictly a winter attraction, open weekends from November 1 until Thanksgiving, then daily until the end of December.

For further information contact the **Reading & Berks County Visitors Bureau**, 352 Penn St., Reading, PA 19602. ☎ 610-375-4085 or 800-443-6610, Internet: www.readingberkspa.com.

FOOD AND DRINK:

Alpenhof (903 Morgantown Rd., PA-10, a mile south of Reading) German cuisine in a Bavarian setting. ☎ 610-373-1624. X: Sat. Lunch. $$

Crab Barn (2613 Hampden Blvd., 3 miles SE of airport, use Spring Valley Rd. exit off 222/422 Bypass) Seafood, chicken, and beef in an old barn. ☎ 610-921-8922. X: weekend lunch. $$

Jimmy Kramer's Peanut Bar & Restaurant ☎ 332 Penn St., downtown Reading) Everything from burgers to gourmet delights in a fun setting. Local beers, free peanuts (throw the shells on the floor!). ☎ 610-376-8500 or 800-515-8500. X: Sun. $$

Shillington Restaurant & Farmers' Market (Lancaster Ave., US-222, at Museum Ave. in Shillington, just southwest of Reading) Pennsylvania Dutch home cooking, a local favorite since 1940. ☎ 610-777-1141. $

Antique Airplane Restaurant (in the Dutch Colony Motor Inn, 4635 Perkiomen Ave., PA-422, just southeast of Reading) A real 1927 airplane hangs from the ceiling in this aviation-themed family restaurant. Homemade comfort food is served. ☎ 610-799-2345. $

Arner's (2101 Howard Blvd., southeast of the Pagoda, downtown Reading) A popular family-style eatery since 1956. Real comfort food and a salad bar. ☎ 610-779-6555. $

LOCAL ATTRACTIONS:

Numbers in parentheses correspond to numbers on the map.

For a panoramic overview, and a surprising sight, follow Penn Street east from routes 222 or 422, crossing the Schuylkill River and heading into downtown Reading. At the end, east of Penn Square, a series of winding roads lead up, up, up to the **Pagoda** (1). Looking like a scene out of old Japan, this seven-story structure was erected in 1908 as a resort, and is now home to the Berks Arts Council. There's an art gallery, and great views. *Skyline Drive,* ☎ *610-655-6374.*

Just north of Reading, between the airport and Tulpehocken Creek (see Getting There, above) is the:

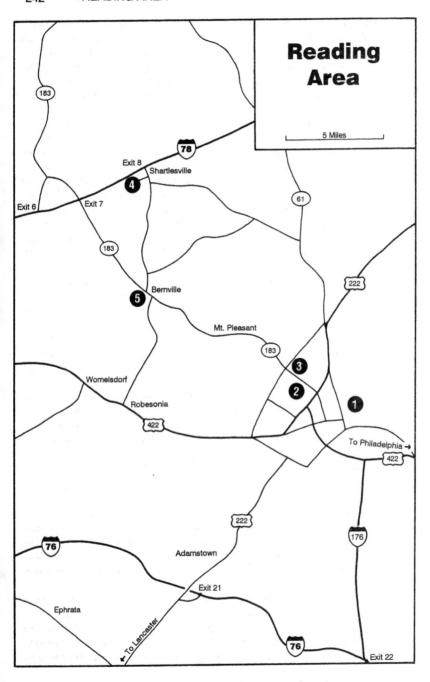

BERKS COUNTY HERITAGE CENTER (2), 2201 Tulpehocken Road, Wyomissing, PA 19610, ☎ 610-374-8839. *Guided tours through interiors offered from May 1 through the last Sun. of Oct., Tues.–Sat. 10–4, Sun. noon–5. Closed Mon. Open Memorial Day, Flag Day, Independence Day, and Labor Day. Each tour: adults $3, seniors $2.50, children 7–18 $2. Outdoor sites are accessible at other times and always free. Gift shop. Snack bar. Hiking & bicycle trail. Partially ⅙.*

Park your car and head directly for the Information Center in the 18th-century **Reeser Farm House**, where you can find out about the various tour offerings and schedules. One of these takes visitors to the **Gruber Wagon Works** of 1882, one of the most complete examples of an integrated rural factory in the nation. Horse-drawn wagons were mass produced here by a team of up to 20 workmen. Another tour visits the **C. Howard Hiester Canal Center**, a large exhibition of artifacts from the former Schuylkill Canal that ran from Philadelphia to Reading in the 19th century. Among the items on display are a houseboat, a toll collection booth, and a pilothouse from a tugboat. Gathered by Mr. Hiester, this is the largest private collection of canal memorabilia in America.

Tulpehocken Creek runs through the property, and alongside it once ran the Union Canal, linking Reading with the Susquehanna River at Middletown. Constructed in 1827, it was never a success due to its narrow channel and locks, and was abandoned in 1884. Some remnants of the canal, including a partially-restored lift lock, can be seen along the 4.5-mile-long **Union Canal Towpath**, a delightful bicycle and walking trail. A free map of the trail and its features is available at the Information Center. Since the Heritage Center is about midway along the trail, you can walk in either direction, remembering that you'll have to return. Fortunately, there are interesting sights within a mile or so, especially to the north.

Crossing the creek right at the Heritage Center is the highly picturesque ***Wertz's Red Bridge** of 1867. This is the longest single-span covered bridge in Pennsylvania, and today carries foot traffic only.

On the other side of PA-183, and slightly to the north, is the:

***MID-ATLANTIC AIR MUSEUM** (3), 11 Museum Drive, Reading, PA 19605, behind the Reading Municipal Airport. ☎ 610-372-7333, Internet: www.maam.org. *Open daily except major holidays, 9:30–4. Adults $5, children 6–12 $2. Rides on second weekend of each month from May to November—call ahead for rates and information. Gift shop. Guided tours. ⅙.*

You never know exactly which aircraft you'll see here, as most of their collection is in flying condition and take to the skies for tours and visits to air shows. Their prize is a B-25 Mitchell bomber from World War II, but there are dozens of other planes both on the apron and in the hangar. Most of them are beautifully restored, and others are undergoing or awaiting restoration. Some may usually be boarded. Civilian aircraft range from airliners such as the Vickers Viscount, the Martin 404, and the DC-3 to a Cessna Commuter, a Beech Super, and the humble, Pennsylvania-built, Piper Cub. There's an extremely rare Kellett Autogiro of 1935, and a fantastic P-61 Black Widow night fighter of World War II. The latter, one of only four still in existence, crashed onto a mountaintop in New Guinea in 1945 and lay covered by jungle until quite recently, when the Indonesian government allowed the museum to recover it. Amazingly, restoration (which you can see) is well under way, and the proud plane is expected to actually fly again!

From here, you can head north on PA-183 for one or two rather unusual sights. When you get to I-78, turn east on the Interstate for about four miles. Get off at Exit 8 (Shartlesville) to visit:

ROADSIDE AMERICA (4), Shartlesville, PA 19554, ☎ 610-488-6241. *Open July through Labor Day, weekdays 9–6:30, weekends 9–7; Labor Day through June, weekdays 10–5, weekends 10–6. Closed Christmas. Adults $4, children 6–11 $1.50. Gift shop.*

They don't make tourist attractions like this anymore. Not only is the miniature world that is so skillfully re-created here a throwback to the 1950s (or even the 30s!), but the place itself—and the ideals it represents—will take you back many decades in time to a simpler, gentler society. The "World's Greatest Indoor Miniature Village," covering some 8,000 square feet on an immense platform encircled by observation platforms, is alive with model trains and other moving vehicles, overhead airplanes in flight, animated figures, flowing streams and waterfalls, tiny factories busy at work, and enough other simulated activities to keep you entranced for a full half-hour. Then comes the grand finale "Night Pageant," when the sky darkens, house lights come on, the Statue of Liberty and the American flag light up, patriotic music sounds, and projections of Jesus and some angels appear in the sky. Finally, a recording of Kate Smith singing "God Bless America" greets the dawning sun and the show is over.

Roadside America had its beginnings around the turn of the century when Laurence Gieringer, age five, became enthralled by the toy-like quality of far-away buildings. By the time he was ten, he and his brother began making models, a hobby continued by Laurence until his death in 1963. Public recognition came in 1935 when a Reading newspaper featured his growing model village in print; by 1938 it had become a public attraction. In the years between then and 1963 it continued to grow to its present size, where it is now maintained as a little slice in the pie of American history.

If you're taking this trip between early November and the end of December, you might want to stop on your way back at Bernville to visit **Koziar's Christmas Village** (5). Open only during the holiday season, and then only in the evenings, Koziar's celebrates Christmas with over half a million tiny colored lights, replicas of storybook characters, a miniature train display, an entire farm converted into a make-believe village, a toy shop, and of course a real live Santa Claus. This is considered to be one of the best displays of its type in the world. Much of it is outdoors, so bundle up! *782 Christmas Village Rd., Bernville, PA 19506, ☎ 610-488-1110. Open Thanksgiving to New Year's Day, Mon.-Fri. 6 p.m.–9 p.m., Sat.–Sun. 5–9:30 p.m.; Nov. 1 to the day before Thanksgiving, Fri.–Sun. 5:30–9:30 p.m. Adults $5.50, seniors and children 5–12 $4.50. Gift shop.*

The Kutztown Area

Nature—on, above and below the earth—is the focus of this stimulating excursion to an experimental organic farm, a rocky mountain top known the world over as a birders' paradise, and a dazzling subterranean cavern. You'll get some good exercise, too, hiking at least two miles over woodland trails; and possibly a good deal more.

If you can stay overnight, why not combine this with other nearby daytrips such as the ones to the Reading Area (see page 240), the Allentown Area (page 131), or Jim Thorpe (page 144)?

GETTING THERE:

By car, the first stop on this trip is about 50 miles northeast of **Lancaster**. Take US-222 all the way to Kutztown, continuing east another 3 miles. Turn left (north) on Kunkle Road for about a mile, then left on Siegfriedale Road to the Rodale Institute.

From **Philadelphia**, it's about 70 miles. Take I-76 (Schuylkill Expressway) northwest to I-476 (the "Blue Route," becoming the Pennsylvania Turnpike Northeast Extension) to Exit 33 (Lehigh Valley). From there head west on US-22, which soon joins I-78, to Exit 13 (New Smithville). Take PA-863 south for a half-mile to a 3-way intersection; then the middle fork (Siegfriedale Road) for 2 miles to the Rodale Institute.

Instructions beyond this are in the text. Following the entire course adds roughly another 50 miles, returning you to Kutztown.

PRACTICALITIES:

The major attraction of this trip, Hawk Mountain, requires sturdy footwear and clothing suitable for hiking. Take along a jacket or sweater—it can be cool at the open lookouts. Some of the trail is on rocky outcroppings with exposure to the sun, so be sure to use sunblock lotion. Binoculars are very helpful, and may be rented at the visitor center. Maximum bird-watching opportunities are from mid-August to mid-December, and peak foliage occurs in October. You'll have the trail more to yourself on weekdays.

The Rodale facility offers tours daily from May through mid-October, while Crystal Cave operates daily from March through November. Avoid making this trip in the dead of winter.

For further information, contact the facilities directly, or the **Reading and Berks County Visitors Bureau**, P.O. Box 6677, Reading, PA 19610, ☎ 610-375-9606 or 800-443-6610, fax 610-375- 9606, Internet: www.reading berkspa.com.

FOOD AND DRINK:

There's a distinct dearth of recommendable restaurants along this route, so you might want to pack a lunch to enjoy along with spectacular views at one of the lookouts on Hawk Mountain. This will be quite primitive—there are no tables or cooking facilities. Be sure to leave nothing behind.

During the tourist season, Crystal Cave offers fast "Pennsylvania Dutch" food at their snack bar. You'll also find the usual fast-food outlets along the highways and in Kutztown.

Those coming from the Lancaster area might stop enroute in Reading (page 241); those coming from the Philadelphia area can find good restaurants in and around Allentown (page 131).

SUGGESTED TOUR:

Numbers in parentheses correspond to numbers on the map. Follow the directions in "Getting There," above, to the:

RODALE INSTITUTE EXPERIMENTAL FARM (1), 611 Siegfriedale Road, Kutztown, PA 19530, ☎ 610-683-1400, Internet: www.rodaleinstitute.org. *Open daily, May 1 through October. Guided tours for individuals and groups of less than 10, Mon.–Sat. at 11. Groups of 10 or more by advance reservation. Guided tours: Adults $6, children $3. Self-guided visits free. Book and gift shop. Picnic area.*

J.I. Rodale began his quest for healthier food back in the 1930s, later promoting his ideas by publishing books and such popular magazines as *Organic Gardening* and *Prevention*. The non-profit Rodale Institute carries on his work, which has become more and more accepted throughout the world as a basis for not only healthy living but also as a viable, sustainable basis for agriculture everywhere. Organic farming actually improves the soil, whereas the use of chemical pesticides and fertilizers tend to deplete it. Organically-grown foods usually cost more at the market, but this is more a matter of distribution systems than of actual cost. As their use increases, prices will surely become more competitive.

Rodale's 333-acre experimental farm, in operation since 1972, is among the world's leading research facilities for organic horticulture and regenerative agriculture. The kind folks here are delighted to tell you all about it and show you around. Begin your visit by the little red schoolhouse of 1909, near which you'll find parking and other facilities.

Head northeast on Siegfriedale Road and PA-863 to I-78, taking that west to Exit 11. From there go north on PA-143 to Kempton, then west on Hawk Mountain Road, passing Eckville, to the:

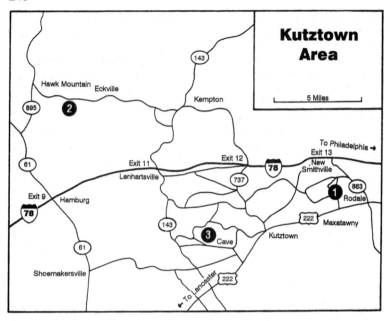

HAWK MOUNTAIN SANCTUARY (2), R.R. 2, Box 191, Kempton, PA 19529, ☎ 610-756-6000, fax 610-756-4468, Internet: www.hawkmountain.org. *Trails open daily dawn to dusk. Visitor Center open daily Dec.–Aug. 9–5, Sept.–Nov. 8–5. Visitor Center free. Trail use: Adults $4, seniors $3, children 6–12 $2, under 6 free. Weekends in Sept.–Nov. and national holidays: Adults $6, seniors $4, children $3.*

Birds of Prey—raptors—of many species can be seen soaring on the warm air currents around this world-famous mountaintop sanctuary from mid-August until mid-December. Spring brings various migrating songbirds. At other times of the year the birds may be gone, but the invigorating hike and spectacular vistas are still there, making for a wonderful day in the great outdoors.

Hawk Mountain Sanctuary was founded in 1934 to protect hawks migrating along an eastern ridge of the Appalachian mountains. It is devoted to the conservation of birds of prey, to education, to research, and to the local environment.

Begin your visit at the Visitor Center, which has a birds-of-prey museum, an art gallery, and a bookstore. You can also rent binoculars there, and obtain the very handy trail map. For the best views, take the **Scenic Lookout Trail** (orange blazes) to the **Hall of the Mountain King**, where in the late 19th century sand was excavated for industrial purposes. From here it went via a gravity railroad called the Slide to a processing plant in the valley below. Only traces of this remain, nature having taken over once again. A trail to

the right leads to the glorious *North Lookout, offering, at 1521 feet eleva-
tion, the best vistas on the mountain. Nearby, there is also a **Sunset
Overlook**, facing in a more westerly direction.

The trek from the Visitor Center to the North Lookout takes about a
half-hour, and although it rises only some 200 feet, it is rocky in parts and
occasionally tricky to follow. A much easier—and shorter—trail leads to
the less exciting **South Lookout**, perhaps a more reasonable choice if
you're out of shape.

For the truly ambitious, there's the very difficult **River of Rocks Trail**,
clambering down over geological formations from the Silurian Period of
over 400 million years ago. From this, or from the North Lookout, it is possible to hike via the Skyline or Golden Eagle trails to the famed
Appalachian Trail that stretches from Maine to Georgia.

Continue west on the same road until you get to PA-895. Turn south
there to PA-61, and continue south on that to I-78 at Hamburg. Head east
on I-78 to Exit 11, then south on PA-143, following signs to:

CRYSTAL CAVE (3), R.D. 3, Kutztown, PA 19530, ☎ 610-683-6765. *Open
March through November, daily 9–5, with extended hours in summer.
Adults $8, children 4–11 $4.75. Miniature golf $2.75. Snack bar, shops, muse-
um, nature trail, tours.*

A classic among tourist attractions, this subterranean wonderland
was discovered in 1871 and soon began drawing visitors. Access was
improved, illumination added, and graded walkways with handrails
installed. By now, millions and millions of people have taken the 45-
minute guided tour, marveling at such sights as the Crystal Ballroom, the
Cathedral Chamber, the Natural Bridge, and many others. As in all good
caves, parts of it remain unexplored, hidden behind crevices too small—
or too scary—to wiggle through, even by the most fearless of spelunkers.

While there, you can pose next to an authentic Amish buggy, which
for some reason has an Indian totem pole behind it. Or you can go for a
walk, have a picnic, play miniature golf, buy rocks, buy souvenirs, or stop
at the snack bar for genuine Pennsylvania Dutch Fast Food. This is a real
old-time travel experience, one that shouldn't be missed.

Continuing southeast on the same Crystal Cave Road soon brings
you to US-222. From here you can go southwest directly to the Lancaster
area via Reading, or east into Kutztown, then north on PA-737 to I-78, taking you via the Northeast Turnpike (I-476) back to the Philadelphia area.

Trip 46

Cornwall, Lebanon, and Womelsdorf

There's a lot of history to be explored on this daytrip; everything from an early iron furnace to a canal tunnel to an 18th-century frontier farmhouse. There are other rewards as well, such as sampling a unique Pennsylvania Dutch delicacy to tasting wines at the vineyard. Although this area is still well within the Pennsylvania Dutch country, it is a bit out of the way and not exactly over-touristed—making this much more of a genuine experience.

For those able to stay overnight, this trip combines well with the ones to Reading, Hershey, and Harrisburg.

GETTING THERE:

By car, the first stop along the way is about 20 miles north of **Lancaster**. Take PA-72 up to Quentin, then turn right on PA-419 a short distance, following signs to the Cornwall Iron Furnace on Rexmont Road at Boyd St.

Return to PA-72 and continue north about seven miles into Lebanon, where you'll find the Stoy Museum, canal tunnel, and the Lebanon Bologna works.

Head east about 15 miles on US-422 to Womelsdorf for the Tulpehocken Settlement Museum and the Conrad Weiser Homestead.

Clover Hill Vineyards are a bit farther east. Take US-422 to Robesonia, turning north on Charming Forge Road and following signs. Return to Lancaster via PA-501.

From **Philadelphia**, Cornwall Furnace is about 80 miles to the west via the Pennsylvania Turnpike (I-76) to Exit 20 at PA-72. Follow the route as above, returning via I-176 to rejoin the turnpike at Exit 22.

PRACTICALITIES:

The Cornwall Iron Furnace is closed on Mondays, and the Conrad Weiser Homestead on both Mondays and Tuesdays. The Stoy Museum closes on Saturdays, and the Tulpehocken Settlement Museum on Wednesdays. All of the sites are closed on most major holidays. In order to see *absolutely everything*, you'll have to come on a Thursday, Friday, or Sunday.

For further information regarding Cornwall or Lebanon, contact the **Lebanon Valley Chamber of Commerce**, 252 North 8th St., P.O. Box 899, Lebanon, PA 17042, ☎ 717-273-3727. For Womelsdorf and the vineyard, contact the **Reading & Berks County Visitors Bureau**, 352 Penn St., Reading, PA 19602, ☎ 610-375-4085 or 800-443-6610, Internet: www.reading berkspa.com.

FOOD AND DRINK:

The Stouch Tavern (138 W. High St. in Womelsdorf) An historical 1785 tavern featuring generous portions of American cooking. ☎ 610-589-4577. X: Tues., Sat. lunch. $$

Lantern Lodge Dining Room (411 N. College St. in Myerstown, just north of US-422 on PA-501) Continental cuisine at a motor inn. ☎ 717-866-6536. $ and $$

Heidelberg Family Restaurant (on US-422 between Womelsdorf and Robesonia) Pennsylvania Dutch specialties and other American dishes; both table and counter service. ☎ 610-693-5060. $

LOCAL ATTRACTIONS:
Numbers in parentheses correspond to numbers on the map.

*CORNWALL IRON FURNACE (1), Rexmont Rd. At Boyd St., P.O. Box 251, Cornwall, PA 17016, ☎ 717-272-9711. *Open Tues.–Sat, 10–4, Sun. noon–5, also on Memorial Day and Labor Day. Closed Mon., New Year's, Thanksgiving, Christmas. Last tour an hour before closing. Adults $3.50, seniors $3, ages 6–12 $2.*

There are other preserved early iron furnaces in America; indeed others in Pennsylvania (see Hopewell, page 236). What makes Cornwall stand out is both its exceptionally early age and its remarkable state of preservation. This is no reconstruction. Built in 1742 to take advantage of the nearby Cornwall Ore Banks, one of the richest sources of iron ore in America, the furnace operated until 1883. By then it was obsolete, a victim to technological progress in both iron-making and transportation. The local ore mines continued to be operated by Bethlehem Steel until 1972, when they, too, were shut down.

Today's visitors begin with an historical overview that offers insight into mining operations, iron-making, and the daily life of the workers, many of whom in the earliest years were slaves. They then tour the 250-year-old site, one of the most perfectly preserved anywhere in the world, and have each step of the process explained. Also on view are the mines, the ironmaster's mansion, and the workers' stone houses.

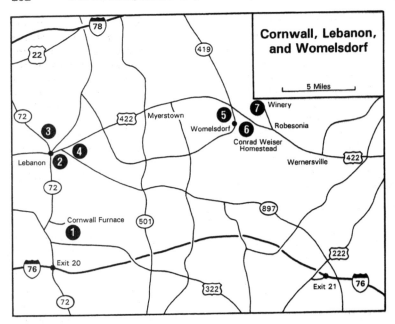

Head north on PA-72 to **Lebanon**, founded in 1756 by German immigrants and today a major food-processing center. Begin your visit with a look at the area's rich history in the **Stoy Museum and Hauck Memorial Library** (2). The building itself, now the headquarters of the Lebanon County Historical Society, has an interesting past. Erected in 1773 as a doctor's residence, it later served as the county's first courthouse. James Buchanan practiced law here in the years before he became President of the United States. Local life since Colonial times is recounted with historical artifacts, period clothing, furniture, and the like. Displays include a one-room schoolhouse, an old-time drug store, a doctor's office, specialty shops, a barbershop, and a general store. There are also exhibits of railroading, firefighting, and World War I memorabilia. *924 Cumberland St., Lebanon, PA 17042,* ☎ *717-272-1473. Open Tues.–Wed. and Fri., 12:30–4:30; Thurs. 10–4:30; Sun. 1–4:30; Mon. 1–8. Closed holidays and holiday weekends. Last tour 90 minutes before closing. Adults $3, seniors $2, ages 5-18 $1.*

Also in Lebanon, in a park off PA-72 just north of town at 25th Street and Union Canal Drive, is the 729-foot-long **Union Canal Tunnel** (3) of 1827. Once part of a 78-mile-long canal linking Reading and Harrisburg, it is now the oldest existing transportation tunnel in America. After enormous financial losses, the Union Canal was finally abandoned in 1885, but the tunnel remains intact as a National Historic Civil Engineering Landmark. There are picnic tables at the site.

You just can't leave Lebanon without sampling some of their world-famous bologna. A great place to do this is at **Weaver's—Baum's Lebanon Bologna** (4). Authentic outdoor smokehouses are still used to cure the delightful mixtures of herbs, spices, and lean beef into wonderful sausages that keep without refrigeration, in a manner that has hardly changed since the 18th century. *15th Ave. at Weavertown Rd., just off US-422, about a mile east of town.* ☎ *717-274-6100 or 800-WEAVERS. Open Mon.–Sat., 9–4. Free.*

Continue east on US-422 to Womelsdorf, home of the **Tulpehocken Settlement Historical Society, Genealogical Society and Museum** (5), where you can explore the fascinating history of the region. *116 N. Front St.,* ☎ *610-589-2527. Open Mon.–Tues. and Thurs.–Sun. 1–4. Closed Wed. and holidays.* Womelsdorf's main attraction, of course, is the:

CONRAD WEISER HOMESTEAD (6), 28 Weiser Rd., on US-422 just east of town, Womelsdorf, PA 19567-9718, ☎ 610-589-2934. *Open Wed.–Sat. 9–5, Sun. noon–5. Closed holidays except Memorial Day, July 4, and Labor Day. Adults $2.50, seniors $2, ages 6–12 $1.*

Conrad Weiser (1696–1760) was a celebrated peacemaker and diplomat, one of the first Americans to have lived among the Indians and learned to appreciate their views on life. He and his family moved here in 1729, building this rustic stone farmhouse and farming the land. His diplomacy with the Iroquois played a pivotal role during the French and Indian War, sparing Pennsylvania much bloodshed. His simple homestead is now a museum of period artifacts that reflect the rustic life on what was then the frontier. There are also picnic facilities in the surrounding park, in case you're looking for a place to enjoy that Lebanon bologna you bought an hour ago.

On the way home, you might want to finish the day off by visiting a nearby vineyard. **Clover Hill Vineyards and Winery** (7) offers such an opportunity, with tastings and a magnificent view. *West Meadow Rd., Robesonia,* ☎ *610-693-8383. Open Mon.–Sat. 11–5:30, Sun. noon–5. Free.*

Trip 47
Hershey

Chocoholics will drool over this trip—and so will your kids. Anyone with a sweet tooth and an appetite for wholesome fun can enjoy the sheer indulgences of a town that exists almost solely for chocolate candy and commercialized amusement. Hershey is nothing if not touristy, but that won't stop you from having a good time.

The chocolate empire started in 1903 by Milton Snavely Hershey resulted in a planned community devoted to humanitarian values, the enjoyment of life, and philanthropy. There are serious things here, and there are refined things as well, but mostly it is the family fun that attracts tourists by the millions. Hersheypark is one of the nation's leading amusement parks, with over 50 rides including some wicked roller coasters. The incredible story of the town's history is told at the Hershey Museum, and there are beautiful gardens and a zoo to explore.

All that sweetness may seem enough, but there's more. Indian Echo Caverns, just southwest of Hershey, offers a fascinating plunge into a subterranean world, while the Middletown & Hummelstown Railroad takes visitors on a scenic ride in vintage coaches along the old Union Canal.

Ideally, this shouldn't really be a daytrip at all. By staying overnight you can more full enjoy the attractions, and perhaps combine it with the previous and following trips to nearby sites.

GETTING THERE:

By car, Hershey lies 30 miles northwest of **Lancaster**. Take PA-283 to its intersection with PA-743, then head north into Hershey. Park at the lot by Chocolate World, from which there is transportation to the other attractions.

From **Philadelphia**, it's a 90-mile drive west to Hershey. Take the Pennsylvania Turnpike (I-76) to Exit 20 and head north on PA-72 for two miles. From there take US-322 west into Hershey and park as above.

PRACTICALITIES:

Hershey is at its best between Memorial Day and Labor Day, although the Chocolate World, Museum, Zoo, and Indian Echo Caverns remain open all year round. Check the individual listings for exceptions. The railroad operates on a complex schedule, mostly between May and October, and should be checked by phone in advance. Bring a jacket or sweater for the caverns.

For further information contact the **Harrisburg-Hershey- Carlisle Tourism and Convention Bureau**, 25 N. Front St., Harrisburg, PA 17101, ☎ 717-231-7788 or 800-995-0969, Internet: www.visithhc.com.

FOOD AND DRINK:

With so many visitors to feed, Hershey abounds in eateries, from food courts and chain outlets to the swankiest dining rooms. Among the restaurant choices are:

Hoss's Steak and Sea House (9009 Bridge Rd. in Hummelstown, 3 miles west of Hershey on US-322) A family restaurant featuring beef, fish, and salads. ☎ 717-566-8799. $$

Pippins (100 West Hersheypark Dr., near Hersheypark) This family restaurant is right in the center of things. ☎ 717-534-3821. $ and $$

Hearth Restaurant (in the Hershey Lodge on W. Chocolate Ave. at University Dr., a mile west of town on US-322 and US-422) Regional country cooking in a casual, Early American setting. ☎ 717-533-3311. $ and $$

LOCAL ATTRACTIONS:

Numbers in parentheses correspond to numbers on the maps.

HERSHEY'S CHOCOLATE WORLD (1), Park Blvd., Hershey, PA 17033, ☎ 717-534-4900. *Open Apr.–Dec. daily 9–5; rest of year Mon.–Sat. 9–5, Sun. 11–5. Closed Christmas. Free. Parking. Tours. Gift shops. Food court, café, restaurant.*

Besides being the official **Visitor Center** for Hershey, where you can get all sorts of information, Chocolate World offers a free 12-minute tour ride through the chocolate-making process, from picking the beans to the final product. You even get to taste the end result, and hopefully buy some at their store.

HERSHEY MUSEUM (2), 170 W. Hersheypark Drive, Hershey, PA 17033, ☎ 717-534-3439. *Open daily Memorial Day weekend to Labor Day, 10–6; 10–5 the rest of the year. Closed Thanksgiving, Christmas, New Year's. Adults $5, seniors $4.50, ages 3–15 $2.50.* ⓑ.

Dedicated to more than just local history, the Hershey Museum has exhibits on Native American life from prehistoric times to the recent past, on the settlement and development of southcentral Pennsylvania, and on Pennsylvania Dutch life and culture. A significant portion of the museum is devoted to the accomplishments of philanthropist Milton S. Hershey, as well as to the industry and town he founded.

*HERSHEYPARK (3), 100 West Hersheypark Drive, Hershey, PA 17033, ☎ 717-534-3090 or 800-HERSHEY, Internet: www.HersheyPA.com. *Open daily*

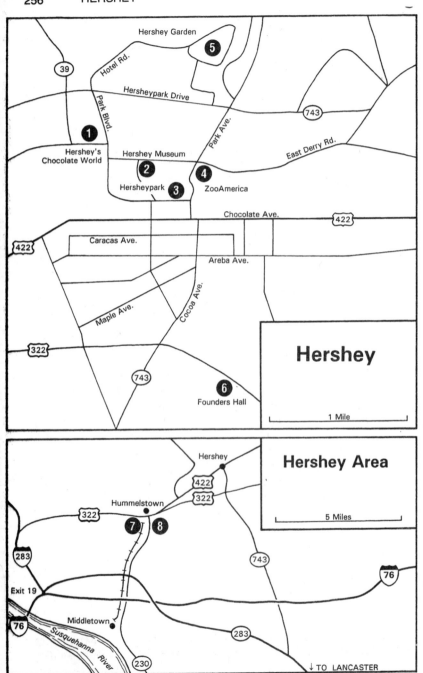

Hershey Garden

5

39

Hotel Rd.

Park Blvd.

Hersheypark Drive

Park Ave.

743

1

Hershey's
Chocolate World

Hershey Museum

2

East Derry Rd.

Park Ave.

4

Hersheypark   **3**

ZooAmerica

Chocolate Ave.

422

422

Caracas Ave.

Areba Ave.

Maple Ave.

Cocoa Ave.

322

743

6

Founders Hall

Hershey

1 Mile

Hershey

Hershey Area

422

322

Hummelstown

322

7 **8**

5 Miles

283

743

76

Exit 19

76

Middletown

Susquehanna River

283

230

↓ TO LANCASTER

from Memorial Day to Labor Day, 10 a.m. to 6, 8, 10, or 11 p.m. according to schedule; also open weekends and selected days from mid-May to Memorial Day and in Sept. Admission including rides and zoo: Ages 9–54 $30.95, seniors (55+) and ages 3–8 $16.95, age 2 and younger free. Special sunset, consecutive day, and preview rates. Additional fee for paddleboats and miniature golf. Shops. Restaurants.

One of America's leading theme parks, Hersheypark features more than 50 rides and attractions. There are seven roller coasters including the ***Wildcat**, a modern version of the wooden coasters of the 1920s that let you really feel the ride, and the new **Great Bear**, whose terrifying loops let you experience weightlessness. The nostalgic **Midway America** celebrates the amusement parks of yesteryear, including a 100-foot-tall **Ferris Wheel** and an old- fashioned Whip ride. There is also daily entertainment with top-name acts, music and dance reviews, and a marine mammal show. On select dates, you can witness a parade of walking candy bars.

ZOOAMERICA (4), Park Ave. Opposite Hersheypark, Hershey, PA 17033, ☎ 717-534-3860. *Open daily 10–5 (extended hours in summer). Closed Thanksgiving, Christmas, New Year's. Admission included with Hersheypark, above, or separately: Adults $5.25, seniors (55+) $4.75, ages 3–12 $4. &.*

Over 200 animals native to the North American continent live here in re-created natural habitats, along with indigenous plants, on an 11-acre site divided into five ecological zones. Among the resident wildlife are bison, deer, bears, alligators, otters, prairie dogs, elk, and eagles. There are also exhibits on the preservation of wildlife and the threat of extinction.

HERSHEY GARDENS (5), 170 Hotel Rd., Hershey, PA 17033, ☎ 717-534-3492. *Open daily mid-May through Oct., 9–6, remaining open until 8 on Fri.–Sat. from Memorial Day to Labor Day. Adults $5, seniors (62+) $4.25, ages 3–15 $2.50.*

Ten theme gardens are spread over some 23 magnificent acres, offering a wide variety of pleasures for gardeners and ordinary folk alike. Among them are an award-winning rose garden, a Japanese garden, an ornamental grass garden, and a rock garden. Come and smell the roses as you meander through acres of sheer beauty!

FOUNDERS HALL (6), US-322 a mile east of PA-743, ☎ 717-520-2000. *Open daily mid-March through Dec., 10–4, rest of year 10–3. Closed school holidays. Free.*

Located on the grounds of the Milton Hershey School, an organization that provides education and housing for over a thousand needy children a year, this striking building is a tribute to the great philanthropist. In it you can see exhibits about the school and its founder, and watch a 22-minute film called "The Vision."

Hershey offers a lot more, including theater and professional sports, but it's time now to head down the road a few miles to:

INDIAN ECHO CAVERNS (7), P.O. Box 745, Hershey, PA 17033, off US- 322, 3 miles west of Hershey in Hummelstown, ☎ 717-566-8131. *Open daily, Memorial Day through Labor Day 9–6, rest of year daily 10–4. Closed Thanksgiving, Christmas, New Year's. Adults $8, seniors $7, ages 3–11 $4. Joint ticket with Middletown & Hummelstown Railroad (below) available. Gift shop. Snack bar.*

Bring a sweater or jacket when you venture underground amid the stalactites and stalagmites in this, one of Pennsylvania's most impressive caves. On the 45-minute tour, you'll hear all about the strange adventures that have happened here over the years before it was opened to the public in 1927. Visitors may also ride in a horse-drawn carriage or pan for gemstones. Nearby is the northern terminus of the:

MIDDLETOWN & HUMMELSTOWN RAILROAD (8), 136 Brown St., Middletown, PA 17057, ☎ 717-944-4435. *Trains run on a complex schedule, mostly from late May into October, but also on special events in fall, winter, and spring. Dinner trains are also offered. Inquire in advance for current schedules and fares. Special event and dinner trains have varying fares and may require prepaid reservations. Trains may be boarded at either end of the line.*

Passengers ride in 1920's vintage coaches on this 11-mile scenic journey along the towpath of the old Union Canal, where they'll see remaining sections of the waterway, a canal lock, and a century-old limekiln. On the southbound trip they are also entertained by an accordionist and invited to join the crew in performing the Chicken Dance—surely the highlight of your day. Bring a camera.

The M & H normally uses vintage diesel traction, although on occasion their 1910 2-6-0 steam engine is fired up as a special treat. Visitors may browse through the Middletown railyards to examine the old rolling stock, including a 1903 trolley freight car, a 19th-century box car, various streetcars, and the like.

Harrisburg

State capitals usually offer their share of outstanding public edifices, parks, and museums. Harrisburg has all that, and a bit more besides. Located on the banks of the wide, wide Susquehanna, it takes full advantage of its delightful riverside setting. Many consider its Capitol building to be nothing less than the finest in America; certainly this is one worth exploring in depth. The town's colorful history has left it with some interesting historic sites, including two 18th-century mansions that may be visited. And, when you tire of official sights, there's always City Island, a mid-river spot for all kinds of outdoor fun.

Way back around 1710, when this was still a wilderness, an Englishman named John Harris established a trading post along the banks of the Susquehanna River, complete with warehouses, barns, residences, slave quarters, and probably a tavern. By 1742, the Harris family was also operating a ferry service, the need for which is instantly apparent when you take one look at the river. The town that developed on their land was originally called Louisburg, after France's King Louis XVI, but this was later changed to honor John Harris. Incidentally, its surrounding county, Dauphin, is still named after the eldest son of that king. Harrisburg has been the state capital of Pennsylvania since 1812.

By staying overnight, this trip could be combined with the ones to Hershey, York, and Gettysburg to form a mini-vacation.

GETTING THERE:

By car, Harrisburg is about 38 miles northwest of **Lancaster** via PA-283, then I-283 to Exit 28, and finally I-83 to Exit 23. Those coming from **Philadelphia** should take the Pennsylvania Turnpike (I-76) west to Exit 19, then I-283 north to Exit 28, and I-83 west to Exit 23, a total distance of 106 miles. There are several parking lots near the Capitol, including a municipal ramp facility at 2nd and Chestnut streets.

By train, Harrisburg is a two-hour ride from Philadelphia's 30th Street Station, or a 45-minute ride from Lancaster, via Amtrak, ☎ 800-USA-RAIL. The station is within easy walking distance of the Capitol.

PRACTICALITIES:

Some of the attractions are closed on Mondays, others on Sundays. The Harris Mansion is also closed on Saturdays from January through March, and the Fort Hunter Mansion shuts down completely from January through April. City Island is most enjoyable on any day from late spring through early fall.

For further information contact the **Harrisburg-Hershey- Carlisle Tourism and Convention Bureau**, 25 N. Front St., Harrisburg, PA 17101, ☎ 717-231-7788 or 800-995-0969, Internet: www.visithhc.com.

FOOD AND DRINK:

For a quick, inexpensive lunch you might try the Food Court in the **Strawberry Square** complex, just south of the Capitol. If the weather is great, why not patronize the various snack stands at City Island's **Riverside Village Park**? Picnic tables are available there, or you can just sit on a park bench by the river.

LOCAL ATTRACTIONS:

Numbers in parentheses correspond to numbers on the map. The most appropriate place to begin is at the:

*PENNSYLVANIA STATE CAPITOL (1), 3rd and State streets, Harrisburg, PA 17120, ☎ 717-787-6810 or 800-868-7672. *Open daily 8:30–4:30; Welcome Center open Mon.–Fri. 8:30–4:30, closed holidays. Guided tours every half-hour Mon.–Fri. 8:30–4, hourly on weekends and holidays 9–11 and 1–3. Free.* ♿.

Many consider this to be the most impressive state capitol in the nation, and one that certainly merits close inspection. Completed in 1906, the massive 633-room structure is topped with a **golden dome** closely resembling the one crowning St. Peter's in Rome. In other ways, the building bears obvious inspiration from the U.S. Capitol in Washington. Inside, the stylistic references are distinctly European, starting with the **Rotunda Staircase**—a near-copy of the famous one in the old Paris Opera House. Some of the outstanding works of art include a huge mural by Edwin Austin Abbey (1852–1911) entitled *The Apotheosis of Pennsylvania*, along with other works by that noted Philadelphia-born painter. There are some wonderful stained-glass windows overhead, and colorful mosaics underfoot, the latter created by the eccentric Henry Chapman Mercer of Doylestown (see page 114). The **Governor's Reception Room** is in the English Baronial style.

Just north of the Capitol stands a large, round, modern structure housing the:

STATE MUSEUM OF PENNSYLVANIA (2), 3rd and North streets, Harrisburg, PA 17108, ☎ 717-787-4978. *Open Tues.–Sat. 9–5, Sun. noon–5; closed Mon. and holidays except Memorial Day, July 4, and Labor Day. General admission is free; possible charge for special shows. Planetarium shows Sat. and Sun. at 1 and 2, plus other times, adults $2, seniors and children $1.50. Museum shop. Snack bar.* ♿.

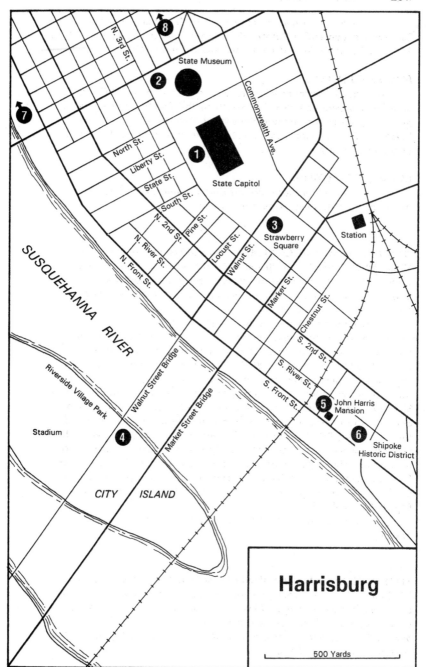

Harrisburg

500 Yards

Pennsylvania's long history, from prehistoric times to the present, is throughly explored in four massive floors of exhibits and activities. Be sure to pick up a free Museum Guide floor plan at the entrance; it can direct you right to the places that interest you most. Take the escalator up past the statue of William Penn and visit the **History Galleries** on the first floor, complete with domestic interiors and a re-created Main Street of a century ago. The second floor features a simulated archaeological dig and a re-created 16th-century **Lenape Indian Village**, along with a **Military History Gallery** that focuses on the Civil War. For many visitors, the most compelling section of the museum is the **Hall of Industry and Technology**, where you can inspect early automobiles, airplanes, railroading and the like—there's even a Conestoga wagon here, plus pioneer radios and TVs. Finally, the third floor covers geology, dinosaurs, a great mastodon, Pennsylvania animal life, natural science, and ecology.

Just south of the Capitol, and connected to it via a footbridge over busy Walnut Street, is the **Strawberry Square** (3) complex of shops, galleries, restaurants, a food court, and the outstanding **Museum of Scientific Discovery**. Located on the third level, the museum offers hands-on learning experiences in science and technology, with activities that are not only fun for children, but for adults as well. Take a "ride" in the 1942 Link Trainer, an early flight simulator used to train pilots, then go visit the dinosaurs or play with electricity. ☎ *717-233-7969. Open Tues.–Fri. 9–5, Sat. 10–5, Sun. noon–5; closed holidays. Adults $5, seniors and children 3–17 $4.*

Whatever else you do in Harrisburg, don't miss a visit to **City Island** (4), a delightful escape from urbanity right in the middle of the Susquehanna River. On foot, it's a short stroll down Walnut Street and across the historic, pedestrians-only Walnut Street Bridge. Completed in 1890, "Old Shakey" is regarded as the oldest metal bridge of its type in the nation. It once carried traffic all the way across the river, but ever since the flood damage of 1972 it has been reserved for pedestrians and bicyclists out for a day of fun on the island. *Those coming by car should use the Market Street Bridge and park in one of the island's lots. A special Handicapped Parking facility is closer to the activities.*

The entire island is operated by the City of Harrisburg Department of Parks and Recreation, so many of its attractions are free. Summer, of course, is the best time to come, but many activities begin in April and continue into early fall, and the park is open all year round—always offering spectacular views and delightful nature walks. It wasn't always this way. Until 1987 City Island was another blighted land mass, unused and unloved, literally a dump in the middle of the river. Today it's a favored destination for residents and visitors alike.

You could literally spend the whole day here, but even a short visit will prove rewarding. Among the attractions is **Riverside Village Park**, a grouping of rustic concession stands offering all sorts of light foods as well as picnic tables; a narrow-gauge steam railroad, horse-drawn carriage rides, a carousel, a games arcade and batting cages, miniature water golf, water taxis, a beach, a nature trail, bicycle rentals, a reproduction of John Harris' 1740 trading post, and much more. There's also **Riverside Stadium** *(☎ 717-231-4444)*, home of the Harrisburg Senators, an AA baseball team affiliated with the Montreal Expos; and the **Pride of the Susquehanna** *(☎ 717-234-6500)*, an authentic paddlewheel riverboat offering hourly public cruises in season along with dinner cruises and special events. *City Island Information Center, just off the Walnut Street Bridge,* ☎ *717-233-8275.*

Back in town, stroll south along Front Street a few blocks to the:

*JOHN HARRIS/SIMON CAMERON MANSION (5), 219 South Front St., *Harrisburg, PA 17104,* ☎ *717-233-3462. Open for 90-minute tours by appointment, Mon.–Sat. 10–4; closed Sun. and some holidays. Adults $7, seniors $6, children 6–15 $4.*

Sometime in the early 1700s, an Englishman named John Harris established a trading post here, expanding it over the years with cabins, barns, storehouses, slave quarters, a ferry service, and very likely a tavern. According to legend, he once refused to sell rum to a group of intoxicated Indians, whereupon they tied him to a tree and were about to burn him. His black slave Hercules is thought to have rescued him, for which Hercules was later freed and eventually buried next to his former master.

After John Harris died in 1748, his son John Jr. took over the business and the estate, which now amounted to some 8,000 acres. He also began to expand the original small stone house of 1740 into a real mansion, and around 1785 set aside a choice bit of property for the Commonwealth of Pennsylvania if they would make Harrisburg their capital. A deal was struck, and the state legislature moved to its new home in 1812.

In 1863 the Harris Mansion was sold to a somewhat shady politician named Simon Cameron, who had secured the Republican presidential nomination for Abraham Lincoln. As a reward, he was made Secretary of War in 1861, but was soon under Congressional investigation for some financial hanky-panky involving army contracts. Lincoln saved his backer by quickly shipping him off to Russia as the U.S. Minister there. Upon his return, he bought the mansion, substantially rebuilding the interior into the luxurious Victorian palace that you see today.

While in the area, take a stroll through the adjacent **Shipoke Historic District** (6), a riverside neighborhood of attractive 18th- and 19th-century rowhouses sensitively interspersed with more modern constructions.

If time permits, you might like to drive north along Second, then Front, streets to a riverside spot about two miles north of the I-81 interchange to visit the:

FORT HUNTER MANSION AND PARK (7), 5300 North Front St., Harrisburg, PA 17110, ☎ 717-599-5751. *Open May–Nov., Tues.–Sat. 10–4:30 and Sun. noon–4:30; also Dec. 1–23, Tues.–Sun. noon–7. Closed Mon., holidays, and Jan.–Apr. Adults $4, seniors $3, children 6–17 $2. Picnic facilities. Special events.*

Visitors can relive sophisticated country living in the 19th century at this elegant mansion and 35-acre estate overlooking the Susquehanna River. There was once a Fort Hunter here, but that is long gone and was replaced in 1787 by a stone house that was considerably enlarged in 1814 and is now decorated with 19th-century furnishings. The grounds feature various outbuildings, nature trails, a Pennsylvania Canal trail, a playground, and picnic pavilions—just the place to relax after a hard day's sightseeing.

Another interesting sight in town is the **Fire Museum of Greater Harrisburg** (8), located in an old, restored firehouse near the Governor's Mansion. Among the hundreds of artifacts on display are some unusual fire engines, a central alarm system, and a huge video wall with presentations every half-hour. *1820 North 4th St., near Maclay St, about 1.5 miles north of the Capitol, ☎ 717-232-8915. Open Tues.–Fri. 10–4, Sat. 10–5, Sun. 1–5. Admission $2.50.*

York

I f you want to get technical about it, the first capital of the United States was not Philadelphia; it was York. For some five months, from September 1777 until June 1778, the wandering Congress, fleeing the British, met here to draft and adopt the Articles of Confederation. As this was the infant nation's first constitution, York was the de facto capital. This was also the scene of a notorious plot to overthrow George Washington as the commander-in-chief wintered at Valley Forge.

Much of York's rich history is preserved in its delightful Historic Center, an eminently walkable neighborhood of Colonial and Victorian buildings, several of which are open as museums. The streets themselves are pleasant, with some brick-paved sidewalks, park benches, trees, and a few cafés.

There's a contemporary side to York, too. "Hawg Heaven," the home of Harley-Davidson, is here, and you're invited to tour the factory and visit their museum of great motorcycles, past and present. Body builders will also want to drop in at the National Weightlifting Hall of Fame, next to the York Barbell Company's plant. The town also has three farmers' markets, and both an agricultural and an industrial museum.

With its good selection of accommodations, York makes an ideal alternative base for touring Gettysburg and much of the Pennsylvania Dutch Country.

GETTING THERE:

By car, York is about 35 miles southwest of **Lancaster** via US-30. Those coming from **Philadelphia** should take the Pennsylvania Turnpike (I-76) west to Exit 21, then US-222 south towards Lancaster, and head west on US-30 to York, a total distance of 110 miles. There is a considerably shorter but much slower route via US-30 all the way.

PRACTICALITIES:

The major historic attractions are open daily, but check the listings for the smaller museums as they vary. The Harley-Davidson plant and museum is closed on weekends, and the Weightlifting Hall of Fame on Sundays.

For further information contact the **York County Convention & Visitors Bureau**, One Market Way East, York PA 17401, ☎ 717-848-4000 or 800-673-2429, Internet: www.yorkpa.org.

FOOD AND DRINK:

Some selections in the downtown Historic Center are:

Commonwealth Room (48 E. Market St., in the Yorktowne Hotel) Open for dinner only, this elegant Victorian restaurant ranks among the best in the region. Continental cuisine. Reservations advised, ☎ 717-848-1111. $$$

Blue Moon Cafe (361 W. Market St., west of the Colonial Courthouse) Classic cuisine in a friendly, casual setting. BYOB. ☎ 717-854-6664. X: Mon. $$

Autographs (48 E. Market St., in the Yorktowne Hotel) An unusually good hotel eatery, right in the heart of the Historic Center. ☎ 717-848-1111. $ and $$

Roosevelt Tavern (400 W. Philadelphia St., 4 blocks northwest of the Colonial Courthouse) A casual place for good American cooking. ☎ 717-854-7725. $ and $$

SUGGESTED TOUR:

Numbers in parentheses correspond to numbers on the map.

Depending on your interests and schedules, you might prefer to begin at the Harley-Davidson plant and museum (11) and/or the Weightlifting Hall of Fame (12), both of which are north of the town, along US-30. The walking tour described below covers the Historic Center, starting with the:

*HISTORICAL SOCIETY OF YORK COUNTY MUSEUM & LIBRARY (1), 250 East Market St., York, PA 17403, ☎ 717-848-1587. *Open Tues.–Sat. 9–5, closed major holidays. Adults $2.50, seniors $2.25, children (6–13) $1.26, Library $4. Combination ticket with Bonham House, Golden Plough Tavern, General Gates House, and Bobb Log House available. Gift shop.*

Even if you don't like local history museums, you'll probably enjoy this one. Considered to be one of the best in the state, it features a re-created York village square of yesteryear, complete with life-size shops stocked with the goods of a bygone era. The Transportation Galley displays a Conestoga wagon along with rare, locally-produced antique automobiles. There are collections of memorabilia from the Revolutionary War and the War of 1812; while costumes, photos, maps, and newspaper accounts tell the history of the town in greater detail. The horologically inclined—who are probably in the neighborhood anyway (see page 224)—will appreciate the elegant "Tall Case" clocks that were made locally.

Across the street stands the old **First Presbyterian Church** (2), erected on land granted in 1785 by the grandsons on William Penn. Step into its

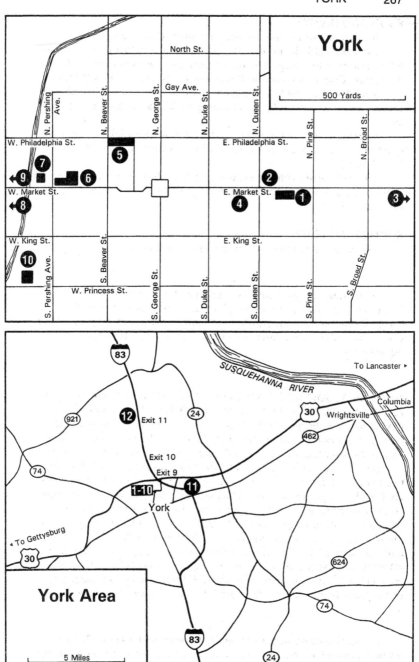

yard to see the grave of one Colonel James Smith (1719–1806), a member of the Continental Congress and a signer of the Declaration of Independence.

At this point you might want to make a short side trip to visit the **Agricultural Museum of York County** (3), which celebrates local farming practices from Indian times to the present. Next to it is a restored **Worker's House** that re-creates the everyday life of a factory worker's family in the 19th century. *480 E. Market St.,* ☎ *717-852-7007. Open Tues., Thurs., & Sat. 10–4, and by appointment. Adults $2, children (4–12) $1.*

Return to the Historical Society Museum and continue west on Market Street to the **Bonham House** (4). The time period between the Civil War and the early 20th century is brought to life in this mostly Victorian town house, once the home of the genre painter Horace Bonham (1815–80), who was locally famous for his depictions of everyday life. The house, typical of the homes of upper-middle-class families around the turn of the century, is beautifully decorated with original family furnishings as well as several of Bonham's paintings. *152 E. Market St.,* ☎ *717-848-1587. Inquire at the Historical Society Museum (above) about visits. Joint ticket with museum available.*

Continue down Market Street past the venerable (and beautifully restored) Yorktowne Hotel, a landmark since 1925. Pass Continental Square and turn right into Cherry Lane, leading through a little park to the **Central Market House** (5) of 1888. This is the most intriguing of York's three colorful farmers' markets, and a "must-see" if you come when it's open. Expect to find everything from antiques to used books, from gourmet foods to freshly made pretzels. ☎ *717-848-2243. Open Tues., Thurs, Sat., 6 a.m. to 3 p.m.*

Return to Market Street and stroll another block to the ***Golden Plough Tavern** (6), York's oldest surviving structure. Built around 1741, this rustic, half-timbered, almost medieval inn reflects the Black Forest birthplace of its owner, one Martin Eichelberger. Adjacent to it is the **General Horatio Gates House**, where a 1778 plot to overthrow George Washington as head of the Continental Army was nipped in the bud by the Marquis de Lafayette, whose toast to Washington signaled in no uncertain terms that France might not support a revolution led by anyone else. Behind these two houses stands the **Barnett Bobb Log House**, a simple log dwelling from around 1812, furnished with period antiques. All three structures are operated by the Historical Society of York County, whose museum is described above. ☎ *717-845-2951. Open Mon.–Sat. 10–4, Sun. 1–4, closed major holidays. Adults $4, seniors $3.50, children (6–13) $2. Joint ticket with the museum available.*

Just across Pershing Avenue is the reconstructed **York County Colonial Courthouse** (7), erected for the Bicentennial of 1976 and filled with authentic period furnishings. It was here, in the original structure, that the

Continental Congress met from September 30, 1777, to June 27, 1778 after fleeing Philadelphia and the British. While here, they learned of General Burgoyne's defeat at Saratoga, declared the first national day of Thanksgiving, received help from the French, and adopted the Articles of Confederation as the new nation's first constitution. ☎ *717-846-1977. Open March–Dec., Mon.–Sat. 10–4, Sun. 1–4. Adults $1, children 50¢.*

York's oldest **Farmers' Market** (8), about two blocks to the west, opened in 1866 and is still operating. ☎ *717-848-1402 for schedules.* Another four blocks west on Market Street brings you to the **Fire Museum of York County** (9), where two centuries of fire-fighting equipment is displayed in an 1911 firehouse. *Tours by appointment,* ☎ *717-843-0464.*

Two blocks to the south is the **Industrial Museum of York County** (10), featuring exhibits of local industries, including pottery, firearms, a locomotive, and a gristmill. *217 W. Princess St.,* ☎ *717-852-7007. Open Tues., Thurs., Sat. 10–4. Adults $2, children $1.*

That's about it for the Historic Center. York offers two more attractions that, depending on your interests, could make this daytrip much more memorable. Because of their schedules, it might be better to see them *first*, before doing the town walking tour. Both are located along highways north of the city. They are the:

HARLEY-DAVIDSON MUSEUM & FACTORY TOUR (11), 1425 Eden Rd., off US-30, a quarter-mile east of the I-83 interchange. ☎ 717-848- 1177, extension 5900. *Plant & museum tours Mon.–Fri. at 9:30, 10:30 a.m. and 12:30, 1:30 p.m. Museum only tours Sat. at 10, 11, 1, and 2. Closed Sun., major holidays, and Sat. prior to a Mon. holiday. Free. Children under 12, cameras, and open-toe shoes prohibited on plant tour. Call ahead to confirm.*

Visitors can watch—and perhaps drool—as the "hawgs" come off the assembly line, one every few minutes. They are then treated to the museum where motorcycles dating back as far as 1903 are displayed in all their glory. Included in the collection are bikes owned by celebrities such as Elvis Presley and Malcolm Forbes, one used at a Super Bowl half-time, and one that President Reagan had his picture taken on. You can pose on one, too, in an area where cameras are permitted.

Follow I-83 north to Exit 11, turn left over the highway, and left onto Board Road to the:

BOB HOFFMAN WEIGHTLIFTING HALL OF FAME (12), 3300 Board Rd., ☎ 717-767-6481. *Open Mon.–Fri. 10–6, Sat. 10–5. Free.*

Located next to the York Barbell Company plant and its huge statue of York's Bob Hoffman, the "Father of World Weightlifting," this facility celebrates the history of Olympic lifting, powerlifting, bodybuilding, and strongman competition. If it inspires you to become another Charles Atlas, you won't have far to go to get the right equipment. Or at least a T-shirt.

*Gettysburg

American history took a profound change during the first three days of July, 1863, when the tragic Battle of Gettysburg made the outcome of the Civil War inevitable. Until then, the Confederacy had high hopes for a negotiated peace and independence; afterwards, those hopes were dashed although the bitter struggle continued for another two years. More men fought, and more men died, at Gettysburg than in any other battle in North American history. Of the 163,000 soldiers involved, at least 50,000 became casualties, including an uncounted number who perished. It is to their memory that the 5,700-acre Gettysburg National Military Park was dedicated in 1895.

Those terrible events were perhaps best burned into the minds of Americans forever by the eloquent words of President Abraham Lincoln, who delivered his short *Gettysburg Address* here just four months after the carnage.

Almost 90 years later, another great American made his home near the sleepy college town of Gettysburg. General Dwight David Eisenhower (1890–1969), affectionately known as "Ike," bought a small dairy farm adjacent to the battlefield as a weekend retreat. Major improvements were made, and during his two terms as President the farm often served as a temporary White House, where leaders from around the world were entertained. Now a National Historic Site, the farm is open to the public.

Today, the battlefield remains much as it was in 1863 except, of course, for the monuments and graves. The natural lay of the land allows you to see the big picture from several vantage points, making the progress of the battle come alive. With just a bit of imagination, you can picture the Blue and Grey forces struggling to decide the fate of a nation.

Easily reached by highway, Gettysburg is a wonderful destination for a daytrip from the Pennsylvania Dutch Country, or perhaps even Philadelphia.

GETTING THERE:

By car, Gettysburg is about 55 miles west of **Lancaster** via Route **US-30.** From **Philadelphia**, it's a long 130-mile drive west taking over two and a half hours via the Pennsylvania Turnpike (I-76), US-222, and US-30.

PRACTICALITIES:

Visits may be made on any day except Thanksgiving, Christmas, or

New Year's. The Eisenhower Farm, however, has a variable schedule that should be checked before making the journey.

Special events include the annual **Civil War Heritage Days** held in late June and early July, when the battle is re-enacted, and the **Anniversary of Lincoln's Gettysburg Address** on November 19th.

For further information, phone the sites directly or contact the **Gettysburg Convention and Visitors Bureau**, 35 Carlisle St., Gettysburg, PA 17325 (in the center of town), ☎ 717-334-6274, Internet: www.gettysburg.com.

FOOD AND DRINK:

Gettysburg has plenty of restaurants in all price ranges, including:

Herr Tavern & Publick House (900 Chambersburg Rd., US-30, a mile west of Gettysburg) An historic 1816 pub with overnight accommodations, near the battlefield. American and Continental cuisine. ☎ 717-334-4332. X: Sun. lunch. $$ and $$$

Dobbin House (89 Steinwehr Ave., a few blocks north of the Visitor Center) Built in 1776, this venerable tavern is the oldest building in Gettysburg, and offers both a casual pub and a gracious dining room, the latter for dinner only. ☎ 717-334-2100. $, $$ and $$$

JD's Grill (Quality Inn, 401 Buford Ave., US-30, west of town) Lunch or dinner in a Civil War setting. ☎ 717- 334-2200. $ and $$

Fast-food outlets abound along Steinwehr Avenue, just west of the Visitor Center. The park has several designated **picnic areas** where you can enjoy an alfresco lunch.

LOCAL ATTRACTIONS:

Park your car at the Visitor Center, from which you can walk to most of the sights. Unless you take the guided bus tour, however, you'll need the car to drive around the battlefield. Visits to the Eisenhower Farm can only be made by bus, leaving from the Visitor Center. *Numbers in parentheses correspond to numbers on the map.*

GETTYSBURG NATIONAL MILITARY PARK—VISITOR CENTER (1), Gettysburg, PA 17325, ☎ 717-334-1124. *Open daily 8–5. Closed Thanksgiving, Christmas, and New Year's. Park and museum free. Electric Map show: Adults $3, seniors (62+) $2.50, children (6–15) $1.50. Guide hire station. Bookshop. &, staff will assist for lower floor; free wheelchair loans.*

NOTE: There are current plans to move the Visitor Center and Cyclorama to a nearby location, making them larger and more accessible; and to use a more appropriate style of architecture. Stay tuned.

Stop here first to pick up a free brochure/map for the self-guided Battlefield Tour, or possibly to hire a licensed guide who can ride along in your car. The fee for the latter is $30 (more for larger vehicles). You can also obtain other information about the official sites, and visit the bookstore.

Just behind the reception area is the superb **Gettysburg Museum of the Civil War**, featuring two floors of artifacts and exhibitions concerning all aspects of the conflict, from weapons to the daily lives of the partici- pants. *Admission is free.*

Beyond this is the **Electric Map**, a 750-square-foot scale model of the battlefield as it was in 1863. The progress of the battle is explained with narration and hundreds of colored lights. This 30-minute show should be seen before touring the actual battlefield, as it helps you to understand the unfolding events. *Showings every 45 minutes from 8:15 until 4:15. Nominal admission, as above.*

A block south of the Visitor Center is the:

CYCLORAMA CENTER (2), ☎ 717-334-1124. *Open daily 9–5, closed Thanksgiving, Christmas, and New Year's. Exhibits, film show, overlook, and walking tour are free. Cyclorama show every 30 minutes 9–4:30, admis- sion: Adults $3, seniors (62+) $2.50, and children (6–15) $2. ♿, steep ramp for Cyclorama show, free wheelchair loans.*

Way back in 1882, a French artist named Paul Phillippoteaux came to America to research and paint a massive 356-foot circular canvas depicting Pickett's Charge, the major offensive of the Battle of Gettysburg. Today, visitors stand in the center of this panoramic view as an exciting 20-minute sound-and-light program re-creates the fighting once again.

Elsewhere in this center, operated by the National Park Service, is an **exhibit** relating to **Lincoln's *Gettysburg Address***. During the summer months, the original draft of the two-minute speech is on display; the rest of the year it returns to the White House and a facsimile is substituted. Contrary to legend, it was not written on the back of an envelope.

While there, you can also see a free 10-minute film about the battle, visit the **overlook point** on the roof, and perhaps take the walking tour described below:

HIGH WATER MARK WALKING TOUR (3), begins at the Cyclorama Center. *Free. Ranger-led twice a day, or ask for a free descriptive brochure/map at the information desk and do it yourself. Most of the one-mile route is ♿.*

This easy walk along Cemetery Ridge is a good orientation to the most critical moments of the battle, and shows you the turning point of the war from the eye-level perspective of the soldiers fighting it. Along the way you'll visit the farmhouse headquarters of the Union commander General George G. Meade, the site of **Pickett's Charge** where 12,000 Confederate soldiers attempted to pierce the Union lines, the stone wall where they lost momentum, and the **High Water Mark** where the tide of battle was reversed after an appalling slaughter.

You're now ready for the:

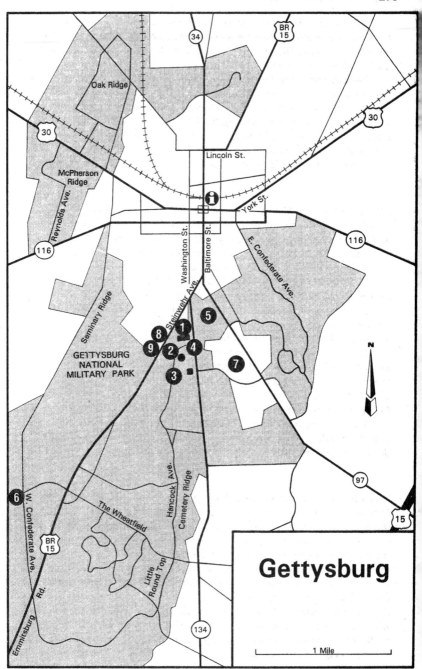

Gettysburg

1 Mile

*BATTLEFIELD AUTO TOUR (4), begins at the Visitor Center. *18-mile circuit by car, bike, or bus. Free park entry. Free explanatory brochure/map for self-guided tours available at the Visitor Center. If desired, licensed guides may be hired at the Visitor Center for $30 (more for larger vehicles). Commercial cassette tape with narration and map available at the Wax Museum (8), for $12.95. Commercial guided bus tours offered by the Gettysburg Tour Center, 778 Baltimore St. ☎ 717-334-6296. ♿, partial access to sites.*

Allow at least two hours to make the suggested tour through the National Military Park, following the "Auto Tour" signs and stopping at the various points of interest. Along the way are several free observation towers where you can get good views, many explanatory signs, hundreds of cannon and monuments, historic structures, restrooms, and picnic sites. For hikers, there are marked trails of various lengths that can be taken from several parking areas.

The Auto Tour route returns you to the Visitor Center, adjacent to which is the:

GETTYSBURG NATIONAL CEMETERY (5). *Open daily. Free. ♿, paved paths, no motorized vehicles allowed.*

It was at the dedication of this cemetery on November 19, 1863, that President Lincoln delivered his famous *Gettysburg Address*, a brief 272-word speech that has become a part of American history. Several thousand Union soldiers, many unknown, are buried here, along with veterans of other conflicts from the Spanish-American War to Vietnam. Confederate soldiers were re-interred in the South after the war.

Return to the Visitor Center for a trip to the:

EISENHOWER NATIONAL HISTORIC SITE (6), Gettysburg, PA 17325, ☎ 717-338-9114. *Accessible only by bus from the Eisenhower Tour office along the north side of the Visitor Center (1). Usually open daily from April through Oct., and Wed.–Sun. from Nov. to early Jan. and early Feb. through March, but schedule may vary; phone ahead. Closed Thanksgiving, Christmas, New Year's, and January. Buses operate 9–4. Bus fees: Adults $5.25, youths (13–16) $3.25, children (6–12) $2.25. Tickets may be ordered in advance, ☎ 877-438-8929. ♿, arrangements can be made to drive there if unable to board the bus; first floor of house is accessible.*

Purchase your bus ticket and, if time permits, watch the short video on the life of the 34th President given in the tour office before departure. Allow at least one hour for the complete trip.

General Eisenhower bought this old dairy farm in 1950 as a weekend retreat, and as his first permanent home. Before that, he and his wife Mamie had lived in temporary housing all around the world ever since their marriage in 1916. Completed in 1955, during his first term as

President, the **main house** incorporates parts of a 200-year-old farmhouse. Your tour begins in the rarely-used form.: living room, then proceeds to the casual enclosed porch, where the Eisenhowers spent most of their time. After seeing the dining room, visitors can climb upstairs to the sitting room, bedrooms, and guest rooms before descending to a typical 1950's kitchen and homey den. The adjacent office, with a desk made from boards from the White House, was used for both farm and presidential business.

From here you can take a short walk around the grounds, stopping at the 1887 **barn** for a peek at Ike's golf carts. A free map is available for a self-guided **farm walking tour** that explores the working parts of the farm, following in the footsteps of the many world leaders who were always taken here by the President.

Return by bus to the Visitor Center.

In addition to official sites operated by the National Park Service, Gettysburg has a number of commercial attractions that might interest you. The most noticeable of these is the **National Tower** (7), just behind the cemetery, which offers bird's-eye views along with a sight-and-sound program describing the battle. Its indoor and outdoor observation levels, some 300 feet above the ground, are reached by elevator. ☎ *717-334-6754. Open daily Apr.–Oct. and Fri.–Sun. in Nov. Adults $5, seniors (62+) $4.50, children (6–12) $3. Gift shop.* ♿.

The **National Civil War Wax Museum** (8) features some 200 life-size figures in 30 tableaux along with a re-creation of Pickett's Charge and an animated figure of President Lincoln delivering his *Gettysburg Address*. Cassette tape tours of the battlefield may be rented or purchased here. *297 Steinwehr Ave.,* ☎ *717-334-6245. Open daily Mar.–Dec., weekends Jan.–Feb. Adults $4.50, ages 13–17 $2.50, ages 6–12 $1.75.* Nearby, the **Lincoln Train Museum** (9) offers a simulated "ride" with the President to Gettysburg, and a large collection of model trains. ☎ *717-334-5678. Open daily, closed Dec.–Feb. Adults $5.75, children (6–11) $3.25.*

Other commercial places to check out include the **Hall of Presidents and First Ladies**, the **Jennie Wade House**, the **Soldier's National Museum**, the **Lincoln Room Museum**, **General Lee's Headquarters**, the **Gettysburg Railroad Steam Train**, the **Magic Town of Gettysburg**, the **Samuel Colt Heritage Museum**, the **Confederate States Armory**, **The Conflict Theater**, and the **Land of Little Horses**. The tourist office in the center of town will happily load you down with brochures describing them all.

Index

Special interest attractions are also listed under their category headings.

Daytrips

• OTHER AMERICAN TITLES •

Daytrips WASHINGTON, D.C.

By Earl Steinbicker. Fifty one-day adventures in the Nation's Capital, and to nearby Virginia, Maryland, Delaware, and Pennsylvania. Both walking and driving tours are featured. 368 pages, 60 maps. Revised 2nd edition. ISBN: 0-8038-9429-5.

Daytrips SAN FRANCISCO & NORTHERN CALIFORNIA

By David Cheever. Fifty enjoyable one-day adventures from the sea to the mountains; from north of the wine country to south of Monterey. Includes 16 self-guided discovery tours of San Francisco itself. 336 pages, 64 maps. ISBN: 0-8038-9441-4.

Daytrips HAWAII

By David Cheever. Thoroughly explores all the major islands—by car, by bus, on foot, and by bicycle, boat, and air. Includes many off-beat discoveries you won't find elsewhere, plus all the big attractions in detail. 288 pages, 55 maps. ISBN: 0-8038-9401-5.

Daytrips NEW ENGLAND

By Earl Steinbicker. Discover the 50 most delightful excursions within a day's drive of Boston or Central New England, from Maine to Connecticut. Includes Boston walking tours. 336 pages, 60 maps, 48 B&W photos. ISBN: 0-8038-9379-5.

Daytrips NEW YORK

Edited by Earl Steinbicker. 107 easy excursions by car throughout southern New York State, New Jersey, eastern Pennsylvania, Connecticut, and southern Massachusetts. 7th edition, 336 pages, 44 maps, 46 B&W photos. ISBN: 0-8038-9371-X.

Daytrips FLORIDA

By Blair Howard. Fifty one-day adventures from bases in Miami, Orlando, St. Petersburg, Jacksonville, and Pensacola. From little-known discoveries to bustling theme parks; from America's oldest city to isolated getaways — this guide covers it all. 320 pages, 47 maps, 28 B&W photos. ISBN: 0-8038-9380-9.

Daytrips

• EUROPEAN TITLES •

Daytrips LONDON

By Earl Steinbicker. Explores the metropolis on 10 one-day walking tours, then describes 45 daytrips to destinations throughout southern England — all by either rail or car. Expanded 6th edition, 352 pages, 62 maps. ISBN: 0-8038-9443-0.

Daytrips GERMANY

By Earl Steinbicker. Sixty of Germany's most enticing destinations can be savored on daytrips from Munich, Frankfurt, Hamburg, and Berlin. Walking tours of the big cities are included. Expanded 5th edition, 352 pages, 67 maps. ISBN: 0-8038-9428-7.

Daytrips SWITZERLAND

By Norman P.T. Renouf. Forty-five one-day adventures in and from convenient bases including Zurich and Geneva, with forays into nearby Germany, Austria, and Italy. 320 pages, 38 maps. ISBN: 0-8038-9417-7.

Daytrips SPAIN & PORTUGAL

By Norman P.T. Renouf. Fifty one-day adventures by rail, bus, or car — including many walking tours, as well as side trips to Gibraltar and Morocco. All the major tourist sights are covered, plus several excursions to little-known, off-the-beaten-track destinations. 368 pages, 18 full-color photos, 28 B&W photos, 51 maps. ISBN: 0-8038-9389-2.

Daytrips IRELAND

By Patricia Tunison Preston. Covers the entire Emerald Isle with 50 one-day self-guided tours both within and from the major tourist areas. 400 pages, 58 maps. ISBN: 0-8038-9385-X.

Daytrips FRANCE

By Earl Steinbicker. Describes 45 daytrips—including 5 walking tours of Paris, 23 excursions from the city, 5 in Provence, and 12 along the Riviera. 4th edition, 336 pages, 55 maps, 89 B&W photos. ISBN: 0-8038-9366-3.

Daytrips ITALY

By Earl Steinbicker. Features 40 one-day adventures in and around Rome, Florence, Milan, Venice, and Naples. 3rd edition, 304 pages, 45 maps, 69 B&W photos. ISBN: 0-8038-9372-8.

Daytrips HOLLAND, BELGIUM & LUXEMBOURG

By Earl Steinbicker. Many unusual places are covered on these 40 daytrips, along with all the favorites plus the 3 major cities. 2nd edition, 288 pages, 45 maps, 69 B&W photos. ISBN: 0-8038- 9368-X.

Daytrips ISRAEL

By Earl Steinbicker. Twenty-five one-day adventures by bus or car to the Holy Land's most interesting sites. Includes Jerusalem walking tours. 2nd edition, 206 pages, 40 maps, 40 B&W photos. ISBN: 0- 8038-9374-4.

HASTINGS HOUSE
Book Publishers

9 Mott St., Norwalk, CT 06850
☎ (203) 838-4083, Fax (203) 838-4084.
☎ orders toll-free (800) 206-7822
Internet: www.daytripsbooks.com

ABOUT THE AUTHOR:

EARL STEINBICKER—a native of Pennsylvania—is a born tourist who believes that travel should be a joy, not an endurance test. For over 35 years he has been refining his carefree style of daytripping while working in New York, London, Paris, and other cities; first as head of a firm specializing in promotional photography and later as a professional writer. Whether by public transportation or private car, he has thoroughly probed the most delightful aspects of countries around the world—while always returning to the comforts of city life at night. A strong desire to share these experiences has led him to develop the "Daytrips" series of guides, which he continues to expand and revise. Recently, he has been assisting other authors in developing additional "Daytrips" books, further expanding the series. He presently lives in the Philadelphia suburbs.